The White Man's Fight

The African American Civil War Memorial,
Washington, D. C.[1]

The White Man's Fight

How African Americans in the Civil War Won the Confidence
of the Nation and the Price They Paid

Michael A. Eggleston

authorHOUSE®

AuthorHouse™
1663 Liberty Drive
Bloomington, IN 47403
. www.authorhouse.com
Phone: 1-800-839-8640

Published by AuthorHouse   03/23/2012

ISBN: 978-1-4685-6683-3 (sc)
ISBN: 978-1-4685-6682-6 (hc)
ISBN: 978-1-4685-6681-9 (e)

Library of Congress Control Number: 2012905049

Any people depicted in stock imagery provided by Thinkstock are models, and such images are being used for illustrative purposes only.
Certain stock imagery © Thinkstock.

This book is printed on acid-free paper.

CONTENTS

ACKNOWLEDGMENTS

This history relies upon the records, letters, diaries, and reminiscences of many of the participants mentioned in this book. In this regard, I am indebted to the staff at the library the U. S. Military Academy who provided me with access to documents within their archives.

I owe a special thanks to David Plum PhD, Winona State University, Jack Harrigan in Arizona, and Frances Rogers in New York, and Emily Smallwood in Virginia. All have provided excellent input in order to help me improve this book.

The Library of Congress has an excellent on-line resource and people can download photographs many of which appear in this book. Documents can also be downloaded. The National Achieves has a few on-line resources that will help a researcher.

Many excellent histories of African American involvement in the Civil War are available, but one stands out as a superior work. James M. McPherson's *The Negro's Civil War*[1] was written nearly fifty years ago and it shattered the myth that African Americans were passive about the war and their freedom. Since then, most scholars and historians have followed McPherson's view of the Civil War.

David R. Logsdon compiled a remarkable book containing hundreds of quotes from soldiers at the Battle of Nashville.[2] I have included some of these within this book.

DEDICATION

To my wife Margaret. For her hard work reviewing this book. Her infinite patience made this book happen. The patience of all of our children also needs to be recognized. They politely listened to my Civil War stories as they quietly went to sleep at family gatherings. As children they knew that I had fought in a war and concluded that it was the Civil War or "Silver Wars" as one young son called it. Unfortunately, I did not fight in either the Civil War or the "Silver Wars".

PREFACE

"The American negroes are the only people in the history of the world . . . . that ever became free without any effort on their own."[1] W. E. Woodward, an avowed racist ("slavery was a good thing."), stated this in his biography of General Ulysses S. Grant. Nothing could be farther from the truth as will be seen in this history which will show that the African Americans fighting in the Civil War may have been one of the deciding factors in determining the outcome.[2]

This book focuses on the records written at the time of the war that were compiled such as *The War of Rebellion: A Compilation of the Official Records of the Union and Confederate Armies.* These provide thousands of first hand reports by commanders engaged in the fighting and other valuable information. A word of caution on these. I have tried to inject some realism into the reports of the time based upon facts. Many losing generals were downplaying their defeats, such as Confederate General John Bell Hood who was declaring victory at the Battle of Franklin (Chapter 6) when a sizable part of his command had been wiped out by the Yankees and his lack of competence had lost the West for the Confederacy. The "coup de grace" for Hood followed at the Battle of Nashville.

Also, I have attempted to simplify flag officer ranks because some were brigadier general and later major general and so forth. These ranks changed over time and mean nothing compared to their position and what they did. I simply refer to these as "general."

Research also concentrated on newspaper articles written at that time. A number of books have been published that provide African American accounts of their participation in the war. I have quoted these as much as I can. These provide insight into what they saw and their reaction to the war.

This book is different since it summarizes and compares the experiences and difficulties of African Americans fighting for the North and the South. No other book has attempted to do this. Additionally, this book focuses on the medical aspects of African American service and the role of women. The difficulty is that a great deal of information on numbers is required in order to present the role of African Americans in the Civil War. Numbers can be tedious for the reader, but they are necessary in order to adequately present the role of African Americans. I have attempted to concentrate the numbers in this Preface and the Introduction so that we can all dispense with that and get on with the amazing story which is the subject of this book.

One publisher asked me if this was a scholarly work (all documented facts) or fiction based upon fact. With dozens of references in the bibliography and over seven hundred notes to support statements in this book, one should conclude that this is a scholarly work. Scholarly books can sometimes be boring so I have tried to capture and maintain the interest of the reader by inserting many statements and the humor of the participants. Soldiers always have had an exquisite way of expressing themselves. This has not changed since Julius Caesar. A good example is a quote from the diary of Private Lord of the 7nd Illinois that I had to read twice before I realized what he was saying. He wrote.

> I went back to get some more water, and about twenty feet above where I got the water (last night) a man shot through the head lay with his head in the little stream. I called George. We didn't say much . . . I can't say that I was really sick but I felt queer, and George said he did. George looked sick, and he said I did. We didn't have any coffee that morning and we didn't drink any water.[3]

I was born and raised in Minnesota. After spending thirty years in the U. S. Army and twenty years in industry, I published a book on a Minnesota regiment during the Civil War (10th Minnesota Volunteers).[4] In writing that book, I was impressed by the valor of African American regiments at the Battle of Nashville where the 10th Minnesota lost many of its people. I found to my amazement that African American regiments, not the white regiments that outnumbered them many times over, may have been the single most important factor in winning this battle for the Union and Nashville was one of the decisive battles of the war as will be seen in this book.

As a U. S. Military Academy graduate of the Class of 1961, I was also interested in how well the members of West Point's "The Long Gray Line" performed in the Civil War. Of course they did well. They were among the few leaders with any military training (at government expense) when this war started. "At government expense" was an important factor during the 19th Century (and perhaps today). It made the difference between a college education or none. Given his family's circumstances when he was growing up, Robert E. Lee could not afford a college education. Had he not received an appointment to West Point, he probably would not have gotten a college degree. In that case he may have spent the Civil War farming a plantation in Virginia rather than fighting a war. I chose to review the records of many of the Civil War West Point graduates. Many on opposing sides were classmates such as Hood and Schofield at Franklin and Nashville.

What is more interesting is how well those with no military background performed. These include, General James Steedman who commanded the U. S. Colored Troops (USCT) at Nashville, and also General Nathan Bedford Forrest, and General John McArthur who served at Nashville, the focus of this book. These were among thousands of leaders, who without military training, stepped up to key responsibilities and made major contributions. There were also tens of thousands of African Americans who fought exceptionally well on both sides. Appendix C provides a record of significant battles fought by African Americans for the Union. As will be explained, the problem was that due to discrimination, the whites were nearly always assigned as the officers of the USCT regiments. There were few African American officers in the Civil War other than the Louisiana regiments. Lincoln attempted to justify this as seen in Chapter 2.

Rosters are important since they allow readers in many cases to connect with their ancestors. Unfortunately rosters of African Americans who served are incomplete, especially for the South. With over 200,000 names of African Americans who fought for the North, space does not permit listing all those who served, but I have incorporated the officer names and summaries of the USCT regiments at Nashville in Appendix A. More important, information about Blacks who won the Medal of Honor and their photos are provided in Appendix B. Other references can be found in the bibliography. The National Park Service web site can be searched for the names of all Blacks who fought in the Civil War and this is perhaps the best resource that one can use to search for ancestors.[5]

What this book does not do is to describe the history of slavery in the United States or describe all of its evils. Many books have done that and that is not my purpose. Instead, I have tried to summarize how especially in the South, slavery motivated African Americans to fight for or against the Union. The conclusion of the reader may be that African Americans were one of the decisive factors in the Civil War which is my point. To provide some grasp of how this was possible, as said earlier, a great deal of tedious numbers are needed to define the contribution of African Americans to the war effort in both the North and the South. This is a difficult task. In the South, the tens of thousands of African Americans who supported the war effort are largely undefined since they were not officially mustered into Confederate units. On the home front, all that can be said is that three million African Americans remained on the plantations or in government service and their very presence supported the Confederate war effort. When describing Black soldiers in the Union army, their accomplishments and hardships, it is relatively easy to define the role of African Americans since the Union army was segregated and there were one hundred seventy regiments of USCT, the records of which are documented.[6] The Confederate army was integrated. There were very few black units (most of these were mustered by individual states). Most of the Confederate African Americans served as body servants (cooks, valets, body guards, etc.) or laborers who fought alongside their Confederate comrades when required to do so. The number of Blacks who bore arms and fought for the Confederacy was large.

The problem with numbers is that it depends on who is counting and when. There are more problems. Confederate numbers are sketchy and very often contradictory: obviously because the South lost the war and many records were destroyed. The Surgeon General's office in Richmond was destroyed when the city was burned in 1865.

Many records were lost.[7] While the South was working to recover from a disastrous defeat, there were many in the North compiling and preserving records. Even so Northern records are not immune to errors. For example, most historians agree that exactly 178,975 African Americans fought for the Union.[8] Another 29,000 served in the Navy.[9] This includes volunteers and those conscripted. The best estimate in this book is that over 200,000 African Americans enlisted to fight in the army for the Union. We see estimates of tens of thousands who served as body servants for white Confederates (as many as 30,000 at the time of Gettysburg) and perhaps hundreds of thousands who worked as laborers. Add to that the millions of African Americans who served the home front harvesting crops and performing other duties as they had done before the war. The conclusion is that the Confederacy survived as long as it did through the loyal service of African Americans in the South. With all of these frailties, I have ventured to provide the reader with what I believe is the best estimate of the number of Black people involved in the war.

At the time of the war and since, in both the North and the South, there was a great deal of prejudice against African Americans indicating that they were an inferior race compared to the whites and could not be trusted to fight. Chapter 4 deals with this. The important point of this book is that the actions of the African Americans in the Civil War speak louder than these detractors. As will be seen, the African Americans fought as well as if not better than the whites. The Battle of Nashville (Chapter 6) is one example.

Some understanding of the number of people involved is necessary in order to measure the impact of African Americans on the Civil War. With this in mind, I have attempted to summarize the numbers. The population of the United States in the 1860 United States Census was 31,364,367. Of this number, 3,953,760 were slaves and 498,070 were free African Americans.[10] All but eighteen of the slaves were located in the slave states that included the border states such as Kentucky.[11] Total population of the Northern states was 18,737,425 including 225,224 free African Americans. Southern state population was 12,127,977 including 3,950,511 slaves and 250,787 free African Americans. 182,000 free Blacks were in the eleven Southern states that would join the Confederacy, nearly 60,000 in Virginia.[12] The remaining free African Americans were in the border states: Maryland, Kentucky, Missouri and Delaware. In terms of percentages, 14.1% of the population of the United States was African American. In the South 34.6 % was African American while in the North the percentage was 1.2%[13]. One of the deciding factors determining the outcome of the war would be how African Americans chose to serve. Would they remain on the plantations or be armed to fight for the South or flee North to join the Union?

The *Montgomery (Alabama) Advertiser* in 1861 predicted that ten percent of the white population of the South would be needed to fight and this could be achieved because the slaves would stay on the plantations while whites unable to fight would be used to oversee the work of the slaves. The *Advertiser* went on to say that in the North, every man enlisted would reduce the manufacturing and farming capability of the North. The conclusion was that the institution of slavery allowed the South to put a greater percentage of its population in the field than the North.[14] The logic was flawed since it assumed that ten percent of the white population would leave their mint juleps on the veranda to march to war and everything would be taken care of in their absence by the happy slaves working in the fields.

The fact was that the majority of men in the Confederate army owned no slaves and their departure from their farms and industry hurt the South as much as the departure of working men in the North who went to war. More important it was assumed that the location and occupation of African Americans was static when nothing was further from the truth. By the end of the war, 500,000 slaves had fled the South and many of these would join the Union army. Added to that number are tens of thousands of laborers and body servants who left the plantation to serve for their masters and the Confederacy. In the end, the Confederacy was no better off than the Union in diminished manpower resources to support the home front. When considering numbers it would probably be better to label people non-white rather than African American since there were thousands of Native Americans and Hispanics that were often counted as African Americans. A good example is the Cherokees who fought at the Battle of Pea Ridge. Furthermore, unsavory practices developed that made accurate counting more difficult. It was said that in some regions an African American soldier killed on patrol or picket duty would be immediately replaced by a new man who was told to answer to the dead man's name at pay call. An order was soon issued to prevent the drawing by collusion of the dead man's pay.[15] As a consequence, the total that entered the Union army may have been 20,000 to 40,000 more than officially counted.

Today, historians are handicapped by the lack of first-hand accounts written by African Americans during the Civil War. This is because the Southern states denied education to African Americans. After all, if a black could read and write, the individual might think beyond his enslavement, might even consider his/her options such as rebellion against the Confederacy that fought for slavery when all other civilized nations had abolished the inhuman practice. Still many records written by African Americans have been incorporated in this book. The African Americans in the North could read and write and they are quoted within. Also, the Union pursued many programs to teach African Americans soldiers who had escaped from slavery how to read and write as seen in Chapter 3. These Black soldiers were probably the best students that the world has ever seen. After escaping from slavery, they realized that the ability to read and write would help them in their future. Dozens of letters and diaries are quoted within. Spelling and grammar errors have not been corrected and quotes are presented as they were written nearly one hundred and fifty years ago.

The battle of Nashville is the focus of this book since it brought together the valor of African American units faced with the hatred of the Confederates and the skepticism of the Union commanders. Still, the USCT won the decisive part of the battle. We are all somewhat confused by the array of units from Tennessee that fought there since many were Confederate and many others fought for the Union. This was because while Tennessee was a Confederate state, many citizens especially in Eastern Tennessee sided with the Union. Nearly all of the Blacks that fought at Nashville were from Tennessee. I have tried to clarify statements from Tennessee soldiers by indicating whether they were from Union of Confederate units.

Michael A. Eggleston

INTRODUCTION

"... the bare sight of 50,000 armed and drilled black soldiers upon the banks of the Mississippi would end the rebellion at once."[1]

Abraham Lincoln

With these words, Lincoln expressed the Nation's enthusiasm for the recruitment of Blacks to fight for the Union. On the same day that Lincoln sent this note to Andrew Johnson of Tennessee, Lorenzo Thomas was sent West to recruit African Americans.

As the presidential election of 1860 approached it was apparent to African Americans that none of the four political parties involved (Republican, Democratic, Constitution Union and Southern Democratic), favored the abolition of slavery. While it would be expected that the Republican party normally an anti-slavery party would take a stand against the institution of slavery, the Republicans only opposed slavery in new territories.[2] The two factions of the Democratic party and the Constitution party were pro-slavery. And so it was, that when the war broke out, it was greeted with enthusiasm by the African Americans. As Frederick Douglass said in a speech in Boston on 3 December 1860 "I am for the dissolution of the Union .... and men can be found ... who would venture into these states [Confederacy] and raise the standard of liberty there."[3]

General Winfield Scott
Courtesy of the Library of Congress

General Winfield Scott the Army General-in-Chief arrived in Washington on 12 December 1860 to meet with Secretary of War Simon Cameron.

His purpose was to argue for the manning of forts in the South. He also had a grand plan should war begin: blockade all southern ports and maintain control of the Mississippi River. Neither the secretary nor President Buchanan endorsed his views.[4] Scott called his plan the "Anaconda Plan" and while rejected at that time, it would eventually be followed as the war progressed. It would have a major impact on recruiting African Americans since it provided an exit for slaves from the South.

When the war started, patriotism swept the North and African Americans were ready to fight. Jacob Dobson wrote to the Secretary of War "Sir: I desire to inform you that I know of some three hundred of reliable colored citizens of this city [Washington], who desire to enter the service for the defense of the City."[5] The problem was the reply they received; this was a white man's war to restore the Union.[6] Other African Americans took a view the opposite of Dobson. Why should they shed their blood for the North when the Union did not oppose, but perpetuated slavery?[7] Another African American from Troy, New York simply stated "We have nothing to gain, and everything to lose by entering the list of combatants."[8]

While the war would become the means of abolishing slavery it did not appear that way at the start. Lincoln and Davis were performing a balancing act. Lincoln maintained that the war was to restore the Union.[9] He did not attack the institution of slavery fearing that if he did so, the Southern states would not return to the Union and border states might also secede. Others grasped the problem. William P. Powell, an African American physician in New York City wrote "Will the government prosecute this war of subjugation, and bring the rebel states,—slavery and all,—back to their allegiance? Ah! sir, if that is the sole aim of the government of President Lincoln and the federal army, they will be surely and shamefully beaten. This war, disguise it as they may, is virtually nothing more nor less than perpetual slavery against universal freedom, and to this end the free states will have to come."[10]

Jefferson Davis, the President of the Confederacy, maintained that the Southern states had seceded to preserve their state's rights. He hoped to win foreign recognition and admitting that the war was to preserve slavery would hardly win foreign recognition. By this time, except for the United States, civilized nations had abolished slavery. Great Britain abolished slavery by the Slavery Abolition Act of 1833.

Two men were instrumental in achieving the right for African Americans to fight; Frederick Douglass, the abolitionist and Lorenzo Thomas, the Adjutant General of the Union army. This book tells their story.

Statistics would determine the outcome of the war and African Americans may have been the deciding factor. In the 1860 Census, the states that would become the Confederacy included nine million people. Of these, 3.5 million were African Americans including 130,000 free and the rest were slaves.[11] In the North, there were over 300,000 free African Americans. Nearly 500,000 slaves escaped to Union lines and many of these fought for the North.[12] A total of over 200,000 African Americans from both the North and the South combined would fight for the Union.[13] Therefore, whichever side could best employ the African Americans had the edge.

Quantifying the extent of African American manpower serving the North and South in the war is difficult but the best estimate of *laboring* manpower in the Union and Confederacy was about ten percent African American.[14] African American soldiers in the Confederacy composed ten percent of the force and for the Union, twelve percent. Chapter 2 provides details. Most African Americans serving for the Confederacy were not officially mustered into Confederate units so it is difficult to substantiate the number who served.[15] African American body servants were not enlisted but followed their owner to war. Literacy among Southern African Americans was low so there are few records that they left behind. African Americans were integrated into Confederate units so they are not highlighted in Confederate battles. Since there were no great battles identified as won by Confederate African Americans or examples of African Americans turning the tide of battle for the Confederacy, their participation for the Confederacy in the war has been largely ignored.[16] This was not true for the Union that segregated African Americans into units called U. S. Colored Troops (USCT). A total of 170 regiments of USCT had been formed by the end of the war.[17] The accomplishments of USCT were visible and can be seen in the chapters that follow. As the war continued and available white manpower diminished on both sides the use of African Americans became crucial.

Throughout the Civil War, African Americans had to prove that they could fight effectively time after time. Eventually they were recognized as valuable soldiers who were needed to win the war. Details of several battles to show the valor and competence of the African American soldiers are in Appendix C.

Over 200,000 enlisted and 7,122 officers served in African American regiments in the Civil War for the Union. Unfortunately, this officer strength included not more than one hundred African Americans excluding chaplains.[18] for reasons defined in Chapter 2. African Americans fought in 449 engagements including thirty-nine major battles for the Union: See Appendix C for details of significant African American battles. Approximately 68,000 African Americans lost their lives while serving for the Union.[19] This represents a mortality rate that far exceeds that of the whites (Appendix D). The Nation's highest award then and now is the Medal of Honor. Seventeen African American soldiers and four sailors received this award.[20] (Appendix B) To the total of African Americans who served in the army must be added 29,000 African Americans in the Union navy.[21] and perhaps as many as 200,000 African Americans who were hired as laborers. The contribution to the Union victory was immense. For the South, thousands enlisted to fight for the South and hundreds of thousands were employed as laborers.

There are always problems with definitions. An example is free men versus freed men. During the Civil War, free men were those who were freed by their masters while freed men were those who escaped slavery and fled North to Union lines where they were freed. Today it makes no difference, but during the Civil War it affected the pay that Union soldiers received as seen in Chapter 2.[22] When one attempts to quantify African American soldiers who served in the Confederate and Union armies, what should be counted? Is a Confederate body servant a soldier? Is an African American laborer contracted by the Union army to build roads a soldier? Webster's dictionary defines the term soldier as "one engaged in military service and especially in the army." By this definition, African Americans bearing arms and serving in military units should be counted as soldiers and others not. In the South, this amounted to about 60,000 soldiers or 10% of the Confederate army that were African Americans.[23] while over 200,000 African American soldiers served in the Union army or about 12% of the force. Numbers are only approximate depending upon when the people are counted and who did the counting. This leaves out hundreds of thousands of laborers and support people that served in both the Confederate and Union armies and occasionally took up a rifle to fight.

African Americans and white troops had a splendid ability to sum up a problem with few words such as "avalanches" to describe the incredibly uncomfortable and sometimes fatal two-wheeled ambulances used during the Civil War. "Worm castles" described the hard bread which was eaten at night so the consumer did not have to look at the maggots. These perceptions are captured within.

The reader may be struck by the incredible ingenuity displayed by the North and the South during the war. In most cases inventive ideas worked such as seeking roots and other plants to replace drugs when the Union blockade prevented delivery of medicine to Southern ports. Other solutions were a disaster such as the Union's attempt to use dried potatoes that when boiled resembled "A dirty brook with all the dead leaves floating around promiscuously."[24] They were strongly loaded with pepper to make them "antiseptic." The result was an inedible mass that could not be consumed unless the soldier was starving.

At one of the decisive battles of the Civil War at Nashville in December of 1864, the African American regiments may have won the Union victory as seen in Chapter 6. The reader may conclude that African Americans decided the outcome of the U. S. Civil War, but this is debatable since there were many forces engaged in different locations and there was no single decisive battle of the Civil War. Read on and decide for yourself. The Union chose to enlist African Americans on a massive scale in 1863 while the Confederacy debated and dithered on enlisting African American soldiers until three weeks before Lee's surrender at Appomattox.

The chronology of key events of African American involvement in the Civil War follows.

1861

12-13 April 1861: The Battle of Fort Sumter; the Civil War begins.

26 May 1861: General Benjamin Butler refuses to return runaway slaves to their Virginia owners claiming that the slaves were contraband of war.[25]

6 August 1861: First Confiscation Act authorizing Union forces to seize property including slaves.

1862

17 July 1862: Second Confiscation Act (Militia Act) authorizes the Union to enlist African Americans for the purpose of constructing trenches and other camp duties.[26]

2 September 1862: The Union's Black Brigade is organized to perform labor in defending Cincinnati, Ohio.

1863

1 January 1863: The Emancipation Proclamation

22 May 1863: U. S. General Order No. 143 authorizing the establishment of the Bureau of Colored Troops to recruit African Americans.[27]

27 May 1863: 1st and 3rd Louisiana Regiments lead the assault on Port Hudson, Louisiana.

7 June 1863: Battle of Milliken's Bend.

4 July 1863: Union victory at Gettysburg. Vicksburg surrenders.

17 July 1863: Battle of Honey Springs.

18 July 1863: Battle of Fort Wagner, 54th Massachusetts loses with heavy casualties.

October 1863: Battle of Baxter Springs

1864

20 February 1864: Battle of Olustree

12 April 1864: The Fort Pillow Massacre.

June 1864: U. S. Congress authorizes all African Americans who were free in April 1861 to be paid the same wages as white soldiers.

15 June 1864: Battle of Petersburg.

30 July 1864: Battle of the Crater.

29 September 1864: Battle of Chaffin's Farm (also called Chapin's Farm and New Market Heights).

30 November 1864: General Cleburne killed at the Battle of Franklin.

3 December 1864: 25th Army Corps of USCT organized,

15-16 December 1864: Battle of Nashville. Two brigades of U. S. Colored Troops break the Confederate line.

1865

11 January 1865: R. E. Lee sanctions the policy of arming the slaves.[28]

March 1865: After much debate, the Confederate Congress authorizes raising 300,000 new troops "irrespective of color" (General Ordnance Number 140). As Howell Cobb of Georgia put it "If slaves make good soldiers our whole theory of slavery is wrong . . . .".[29]

3 March 1865: Enrollment Act authorizes U. S. Army to pay all African American soldiers the same wages as whites retroactive to 1 January 1864.

2 April 1865: Siege of Petersburg ends.

3 April 1865: Richmond falls.

9 April 1865: The Battle of Appomattox Court House: Lee surrenders. Battle of Fort Blakely ends.

15 May 1865: Battle of Palmetto Ranch. The last battle of the Civil War.

CHAPTER 1

Why We Fight[1]

I have no ambition, unless it be to break the chain and exclaim: 'Freedom to all!' I will never be satisfied so long as the meanest slave in the south had a link of chain clinging to his leg. He may be naked, but he shall not be in irons.
Sergeant Charles W. Singer of the 107th USCT[2]

South

Free African Americans in the South could be counted upon to fight for the Confederacy. They were part of the society that had slavery as its foundation and free Blacks were committed to support slavery because they were a part of Southern society. By volunteering for duty in the Confederate army, they could gain acceptance into the white society in which they lived.[3] As an example, of the 3,000 free African Americans in Alabama, nearly all served in the Confederate army in one capacity or another.[4]

Twenty five percent of free African Americans owned slaves and some in large numbers. In 1830, 1,556 free African Americans owned 7,188 slaves.[5] Some amassed considerable wealth. One hundred sixty African Americans in Virginia owned a total of $41,158 in real estate.[6] Many African Americans thought that they would receive expanded privileges and recognition after the war.

Historian Wayne Austerman summarized best. "While every black in the South naturally craved personal freedom, many of them also shared a distinctively-southern attachment to their native soil. Moreover, they dreaded the South's despoliation by any invader, even one who promised 'emancipation.' Although the passage of a Union force nearby always triggered a joyful exodus of slaves from the fields, there were also those who realized that a future raked from the ashes of their homeland was a poor prospect for any man, slave or free."[7]

Perhaps most important was the work on the plantation that African Americans performed. Many were household staff who were close to and attached to their white masters. These people would be inclined to go to war as body servants and fight for the Confederacy. At the other end of the spectrum were the field hands that did the heavy labor and received most of the white brutality. These would be expected to depart for Union lines at the first opportunity.

Nevertheless, some scholars such as William E. B. Du Bois, the founder of the NAACP, have denied that African American Confederate soldiers existed.[8] This is a difficult position to maintain given the abundance of evidence such as thousands of pension applications from African Americans that show that they existed and fought well for the South. One author compiled a listing of all African Americans who applied for pensions to the Southern states. There were thousands in the list compiled by Ricardo J. Rodriguez.[9]

Historian Ervin L. Jordan, Jr. summarized the case against African Americans who served for the South. "Pro-Confederate blacks were riddles; white Southerners did not trust them, Northerners thought them lunatics and the majority of blacks feared them as fools or traitors."[10] This view continues to this day. Many African Americans, descendants of ancestors who fought for the South, view it as their dirty little secret that should be kept in their closet: their ancestors betrayed their race and fought to keep African Americans in bondage. Nothing can be farther from the truth.

There were efforts in the South to get a count of African Americans serving, but there is no record of any such census being reported. Pension applications provide some data, but the laws to provide African American pensions were enacted in the 1920s by which time most of the participants were dead. Nevertheless, thousands of African American pension applications poured into the Southern states. In Tennessee between 1921 and 1936, over 249 verified pension applications were approved. These provide data of interest since they show the relationship between African Americans who served, their job in the army, and their owners. Nearly all were house servants not field hands so they would be expected to have close relationships with the white owners. As a consequence they would be expected to follow their owner in to war and they did.[11]

For the South, the concept of recruiting African Americans to fight was initially unthinkable. First, fears that enlisting African Americans would lead to a Black insurrection was a major factor against recruiting them.[12] Second. it would admit that African Americans were equal in ability to the whites. Third, arming a slave to fight would mean that the armed African Americans could return to destroy the South as Nat Turner, an African American leader of the uprising against the Whites had attempted to do, and finally, slavery was the foundation of the Southern society and if the slaves were sent to war, who would grow the crops and perform the other tasks that were necessary for the Southern society to survive? Nevertheless, on 2 January 1864, General Patrick R. Cleburne, an expatriate from Ireland and a Confederate General in the Army of Tennessee dared to propose the unthinkable: recruit African Americans to fight for the South with a promise of freedom for faithful service.[13]

Patrick R. Cleburne
Courtesy of the Library of Congress

Cleburne summed up his case. "We can see three great causes operating to destroy us. First, the inferiority of our armies to those of the enemy in point of numbers; second, the poverty of our single source of supply [slavery] in comparison with his several sources; third, the fact that slavery, from being one of our chief sources of strength at the commencement of the war, has now become, in a military point of view, one of our chief sources of weakness [slaves were fleeing north to join the Union army]".[14]

Throughout the war, the question of enlisting African Americans to fight was debated. African American bandsmen were legally enlisted and the Confederate Congress passed legislation requiring that African Americans and white bandsmen would receive the same pay.[15] It was a small step between beating the drum while on the march and firing on the enemy when the battles were in progress.

While the Confederate army and Congress hesitated to enlist African Americans and other non-whites, the Confederate navy had no reluctance and enlisted many throughout the war. The navies on both sides are the most neglected in terms of historical coverage of African Americans that served. The Confederate government limited to 5% the number of African Americans allowed to serve in their navy, but some suggest that the actual number may have been as high as 20%. The Confederate navy was an integrated force as was the Union navy.

Jefferson Davis refused to consider Cleburne's recommendation to enlist African Americans and banned any further discussion.[16] Nevertheless, in a letter to John Forsyth in February 1865, President Davis wrote, "It is now becoming daily more evident . . . that we are reduced to choosing whether the negroes shall fight for or against us."[17] As Confederate casualties mounted and manpower requirements became desperate, Robert E. Lee added his prestige to the dispute in January 1865 urging that the slaves be armed in a letter to Jefferson Davis.[18]

> I do not know whether the law authorizing the use of negro troops has received your sanction, but if it has, I respectfully recommend that measures be taken to carry it into effect as soon as practicable. It will probably be impossible to get a large force of this kind in condition to be of service during the present campaign, but I think no time should be lost in

trying to collect all we can. I attach great importance to the result of the first experiment with these troops, and think that if it prove successful, it will greatly lessen the difficulty of putting the law into operation.[19]

By then it was too late. The South would surrender in less than four months. Cleburne would die at the Battle of Franklin before Lee joined the fight to enlist African Americans.

In his last letter to Davis on 2 April 1865, Lee stated "I have been willing to detach officers to recruit negro troops, and have sent the names of many . . . I am glad Your Excellency has made an appeal to the Governors of the States, and hope it will have a good effect."[20] A week later, Lee surrendered at Appomattox.

From the above, the reasons why African Americans served the Confederacy could be summarized as follows:

— Uncertainty about the war's outcome. Most thought the Confederacy would survive and if so, the African Americans wanted to be on the winning side rather than be cast as traitors.
— Free African Americans had a vested interest in the Confederacy and many were slave owners.
— Pressure from the white Confederates. They dare not refuse service.[21]
— If the South won, the African Americans hoped for grateful white recognition of their loyalty.[22]
— Conscription: free African Americans were taken in to labor battalions and had no choice.[23]
— Free African Americans wanted to be accepted into the white society in which they lived. Service in the Confederate army would help.[24]
— Service in the Confederate Army meant that they could remain connected to their families rather than volunteering to fight for the Union and separation. For those who served for the South, their wives and little ones remained safe on the plantation.[25]
— While the myth of the "happy slave" died many years ago, the fact is that a society based upon slavery was the only environment that the slaves had ever known.[26] An African

American in the South had the instinctive feeling that his/her fortunes were connected to the South.[27] Stories of the New York City draft riots in July 1863 featured the murder of many African Americans by the rioters. The fact that the rioters targeted African Americans made the situation more chilling (the African Americans in New York City were in competition for poor white jobs). The New York City riot murders were circulated by a gleeful Southern press throughout the South.[28] The message was not lost on the African Americans in the South as they considered where their loyalties should reside.

North

The main reason why African Americans in the North served was because they were conscripted as were hundreds of thousands of their fellow white citizens. Many others volunteered.

When James Spikes a former slave was interviewed in the 1930's about why he volunteered for the Union army to fight he said "Why did I enlist? I did not know no better. They told us the war was supposed to set the darkies free. My old master did not want me to go—course not."[29] James Henry Hill of the 54th Massachusetts wrote. "We do not covet (sic) your wives nor your daughters, nor the position of political orator. All we ask is the proper enjoyment of the rights of citizenship, and a free title, and acknowledged share in our noble birthplace."[30]

CHAPTER 2

The Campaign to Recruit

In 1861, the African Americans in the North were told when they tried to enlist that this was the white man's fight, with which niggers had nothing to do with.[1]

General Ben Butler
Courtesy of the Library of Congress

Benjamin Butler, the Massachusetts politician in the House of Representatives had become a Union general. He started the campaign to recruit and mustered tens of thousands of African Americans to fight for the Union in spite of prejudice in the North.[2]

In both the North and the South, the African Americans were viewed with suspicion. In the North some considered the African Americans as the cause of the war which would persist if they fought for the Union. Many believed that the war was to save the Union and slaves had nothing to do with that.[3] In the South the cause was state's rights and the specter of armed African Americans terrified the public with memories of Blacks butchering the whites on plantations such as had occurred in the Nat Turner uprising. In a speech on March 21, 1861, Alexander Stephens, Vice-President of the Confederate States of America, stated.

> The new constitution [Confederate] has put at rest all questions relating to African slavery as it exists among us—the proper "status" of the Negro in our form of civilization. The prevailing ideas at the time of the formation of the old constitution were that the enslavement of the African was in violation of the laws of nature; that it was wrong in "principle," socially, morally and politically. Those ideas were fundamentally wrong. They rested upon the assumption of the equality of the races. This was an error . . . . Our new government is founded upon exactly the opposite ideas; its foundations are laid, its corner-stone rests upon the great truth, that the negro is not equal to the white man; that slavery-subordination to the superior race-is his natural and normal condition. This, our new government, is the first, in the history of the world, based on this great physical and moral truth.[4]

In both the South and the North the view expressed by Stephens that African Americans were inferior to the whites led many to believe that they could not be trusted as soldiers. At the start of the war, the United States Army numbered 1108 officers and 15,259 organized into nineteen regiments. Twenty-nine percent of the officers left the army to join the Confederacy, but few enlisted men left.[5] There is no record of any African Americans in the army at the start of the war. The Union raised an army of 714,231 men in the first year of the war. None were African Americans.[6]

There were fundamental differences in the service of African Americans in the Confederate and Union armies. In the North, nearly all African American enlistments were into African American units called USCT. In the Confederate army, African Americans were integrated into white units but while the North authorized creation of African American units, the Confederacy would not allow African American enlistments in the army until very late in the war. As a consequence, African Americans enlisted in state militia or home guard units.[7] The result of all of this was that the North was segregated and the African Americans in the South were integrated into units. More important, the South employed tens of thousands of African Americans with the consent of their owners as laborers to build fortifications, etc. During the course of the war there were dozens of engagements fought by the Union army that featured African American units who behaved with incredible valor and much was written then and now about these African American units. In the South the participation of African Americans in Confederate units was invisible. There is no evidence that African Americans in the South fought as a large group in any engagement.[8] As a result, when writing of successes in battle of African American units in the North it is straight forward to describe the valor of African Americans fighting for the Union at battles such as Fort Wagner (the 54th Massachusetts Infantry), but there is no counterpart to this when writing about African Americans in the Confederate army. Years after the war when many Northern African Americans were receiving pensions for service with their white colleagues, Southern African Americans were receiving very little. Pensions were offered by the Southern states many years after the war. The pension applications of African Americans are one of the few surviving records that provide names of African Americans fighting for the South. Unfortunately, in most cases, the Southern states denied the pension applications of African Americans.

In both the North and the South, it was recognized, as the war progressed and both sides became stressed for manpower, that the use of African Americans could decide the outcome of the war. For the South, early in 1865, General Robert E. Lee continued to press for the enlistment of African Americans in the Confederate army.

Lincoln reported to Judge Mills of Wisconsin "The slightest knowledge of arithmetic will prove to any man that the rebel armies cannot be destroyed with the Democratic [Party] strategy [disband African American units]. It would sacrifice all of the white men of the North to do it. There are now in the service of the United States near two hundred thousand able-bodied colored men, most of them under arms, defending and acquiring Union territory."[9] The problem both sides had was in bringing the public and respective Congresses on board to arm the Blacks to fight.

As Lincoln said, the slightest knowledge of arithmetic proved the case. The South had about 3.5 million African Americans nearly all slaves (except for 130,000 free). Most slaves would serve the Confederacy as body servants or laborers with a few armed to fight except for the Confederate Navy. The Navy had an established practice of enlisting African Americans[10] and this practice continued and expanded as more ships were launched to fight the war. The North had over 300,000 African Americans, nearly all free. On both sides the numbers are deceiving. In the North, African Americans were armed to fight in USCT regiments, but initially their service was mostly that of laborers "to free up white soldiers to fight." As will be seen, this practice was ended later in the war to allow these African American soldiers to train and fight as infantry and the white soldiers would pull their fair share of duty building fortifications and other fatigue duty (labor unrelated to soldiering). For the South, the arithmetic problem was different. Half a million slaves deserted the South to serve the Union. Of the remaining three million slaves, the vast majority kept the war effort going by serving on the plantations and other functions as they had always done. Exact numbers for those serving the Confederate cause in uniform (except for the Navy) are not known. The number of "body servants" who served with their masters is quoted by several sources as 30,000 and many of these were armed and would fight.[11] Dr. Lewis Steiner of the U. S. Sanitary Commission (USSC)[12] recorded in his diary what he observed shortly before the battle of Antietam. Steiner estimated that 5% of the Confederate army was black.

Wednesday, September 10

At 4 o'clock this morning the Rebel army began to move from our town, Jackson's force taking the advance. The movement continued until 8 o'clock P.M., occupying 16 hours. The most liberal calculation could not give them more than 64,000 men. Over 3,000 Negroes must be included in the number . . . They had arms, rifles, muskets, sabers, bowie-knives, dirks, etc. They were supplied, in many instances, with knapsacks, haver-sacks, canteens, etc., and they were manifestly an integral portion of the Southern Confederacy army. They were seen riding on horses and mules, driving wagons, riding on caissons, in ambulances, with the staff of generals and promiscuously mixed up with all the Rebel horde." [13]

Unfortunately, body servants were not mustered into the Confederate army, so the exact number is not known since they were not on rosters, but African American pension applications that were submitted to the Southern states half a century after the war numbered into the thousands.[14] Author Ricardo J. Rodriguez compiled a list of the applications in 2010 and body servants were the most common job.[15] The Union army system in place at the time made matters worse. New recruits were funneled into newly created regiments meaning that regiments composed of new inexperienced people were committed in battle with subsequent heavy losses. The high toll due to disease added to the casualty rates. Only Wisconsin practiced a system that sent new recruits as replacements to existing regiments. This meant that they had experienced soldiers looking after them as they learned the art of war and survival in a camp plagued by lack of sanitation and disease.[16] Appendix D provides additional details.

Arming African Americans in the South was an enduring problem that hampered their use in fighting the North. Southern whites lived in a state of paranoia throughout the war. The fear was that if you arm the slaves to fight against the North, they could use the weapons for a bloody rebellion. On any given plantation, whites felt comfortable with their own slaves who were considered to be loyal, trustworthy, etc., but it was those "other slaves" outside of the plantation who would murder the whites in their beds. The discomfort increased as more and more whites moved North to fight the Yankees. This meant that there were fewer whites on the plantations to defend against an African American uprising. Would this loss of white manpower in the South encourage an insurrection? African Americans remained loyal on the plantations and no African American insurrection occurred during the war.[17] Nevertheless, the fear of this prevented the arming of the slaves until the end of the war. There were other problems. Joseph T. Wilson, a Union soldier summarized best in his history of the Civil War.

> An innate reasoning taught the negro that slaves could not be relied upon to fight for their own enslavement. To get to the breastworks was but to get a chance to run to the Yankees; and thousands of those whose elastic step kept time with the martial strains of the drum and fife, as they marched on through city and town, enroute to the front, were not elated with the hope of Southern success, but were buoyant with the prospects of reaching the North. The confederates found it no easy task to watch the negroes and the Yankees too; their attention could be given to but one at a time; as a slave expressed it, "when marsa watch the Yankee, nigger go; when marsa watch the nigger, Yankee come." But the Yankees did not always receive him kindly during the first year of the war.[18]

While Lincoln hesitated to enlist African Americans at the start of the war, the South acted. While there was no official Confederate policy of enlisting African Americans to fight until 1865, the states took action even before Fort Sumter. In Louisiana three regiments were formed in 1861 with officers of their own race.[19] In Tennessee on 28 June 1861, the legislature authorized the governor "at his discretion, to receive into the military service of the state all male free persons of color between the ages of 15 and 50."[20] The African Americans enlisted would receive $8 a month.[21] They would be used to accomplish manual labor.[22] Everyone in both the North and the South realized that once a slave was equipped with a firearm and trained to use it, he would never be a slave again. Aside from labor battalions and body servants that the African Americans provided, they also provided service to the South on the home front. It was estimated that ten percent of the white population was needed to fight and this heavy commitment could only be achieved because of the slave labor that allowed more whites to fight.[23] Those whites incapacitated and unable to fight could oversee the slave labor.[24] Slavery was the "tower of strength" for the Confederacy. It was the foundation of the society and, once gone, the society would collapse and it did in 1865. To counter the flow of slaves to Union lines, all sorts of lies were invented by the plantation owners, the Southern press and the government. They did little good. Mrs. Taylor recalled. "The whites would tell their colored people not to go to the Yankees, for they would harness them to carts and make them pull carts around in place of horses."[25] Lies were not always necessary. When the New York City draft rioters of July 1863 targeted African Americans to be killed, the Southern press gleefully reported details to their readers. What started as a riot against the draft in New York City turned into a riot against African Americans because they were competing for white jobs. Despite the lies and facts such as the draft riots, many African Americans in the South were eager to join the fight against slavery. Others were not. *The Providence (R. I.) Post* reported that "Negroes as a mass have shown no friendship to the Union . . . . The few thousands who have come into our lines to live at the expense of the whites seek rather a life of laziness than self-dependence . . . . Their sympathies are with the Rebels."[26] Elizabeth Keckley, a companion of Mary Todd Lincoln recalled "Often I heard them [the African Americans] declare that they would rather go back to slavery in the South and be with their old masters than to enjoy freedom of the North."[27]

South

As stated, thousands of African Americans in the South accompanied their masters to war as body servants (cooks, valets, body guards, etc.) but service was frequently far beyond that. Many were armed and fought with their masters in battle.[28] There are hundreds of stories of these African Americans fighting for the Confederacy but the problem is that since they were not mustered into the Confederate army, it is difficult to quantify how many of these people actually fought for the South. Numerous stories told of Confederate African Americans who were wounded or separated from their Confederate unit and eventually found their way back to their organization. They gave no thought of joining the Union forces. To those that did occasionally join Union forces, they were faced with a dilemma. An African American Union soldier refused to fire on a Confederate unit. "My young master is thar (sic); and I played with him all my life and he has saved me from getting a many whippings I would have got, and I can't shoot thar (sic), for I loves my young master still."[29]

In November 1864 Jefferson Davis continued his resistance to allowing African Americans to enlist in the Confederate army to fight "until our white population shall prove insufficient for the armies we require." Apparently, President Davis had not gotten the word: the Confederacy was surrounded, cut into pieces like a pie, and was on the verge of collapse. General Robert E. Lee summed up the situation in a letter to Senator Andrew Hunter. "I think we must decide whether slavery shall be extinguished by our enemies and the slaves be used against us, or use them ourselves at the risk of the effects which may be produced upon our social institutions."[30] In other words, once you arm the slaves and offer them freedom for their enlistment, the society in the South that was based upon slavery would collapse, which it did. Lee, Davis and others may have wanted to end slavery much earlier, but the citizens of the South and their representatives in the Confederate Congress would not allow it. Some say that lack of unity in the Confederacy caused its demise or put another way "States rights killed the Confederacy."

It was not until 13 March 1865, a few weeks before the Confederacy collapsed that the Confederate Congress enacted legislation authorizing the enrollment of African Americans in the Confederate army.[31] "Of course the negro people about the city of Richmond heard of the proposition to arm and emancipate them if they would voluntarily fight for their old masters. They discussed its merits with a sagacity wiser than those who proposed the scheme, and it is safe to say that they concluded in the language of one of them who spoke on the matter 'It too late, de Yankees am coming."[32]

In a measure detached from reality the legislation provided that each Confederate state was ***required*** to furnish 300,000 men for duty.[33] If one does the math, the total requirement would exceed the African American population and the remaining available whites in the South. Several African American units were actually formed before the end of the Confederacy, but none fired a shot.[34]

Fragmentary records of African Americans in the Confederate army have survived. Author Charles Kelly Barrow listed African Americans records from Georgia, Virginia, and North Carolina.[35] Total number listed by Barrow is 120. Most of these African American records list occupation as cooks, musicians, body servants or teamsters. Many of these soldiers also fought as infantry but that does not show in the records. Pension applications from African Americans tell more about their duties and units.

General William T. Sherman recorded in his memoirs sights that he saw during his march to the sea. ". . . the negroes were simply frantic with joy. Whenever they heard my name, they clustered around my horse, shouted and prayed in their particular style."[36] This same general refused to allow African American regiments to join his column in his march to the sea because he did not trust them to fight.

North

Once let the black man get upon his person the brass letters, U. S., let him get an eagle on his button, and a musket on his shoulder and bullets in his pocket, and there is no power on earth which can deny that he has earned the right to citizenship in the United States.[37]

Frederick Douglass

Frederick Douglass
Courtesy of the Library of Congress

With these words, Frederick Douglass pressed the Union to enlist African Americans. In the months that followed Fort Sumter, nothing of note happened in the White House or Congress to enlist African Americans to fight for the Union. While rumors were circulating in both the North and South that the other side was raising African American regiments, in fact nothing was happening. The urging of Frederick Douglass and others went unheeded. "Would to god you would let us do something. We lack nothing but your consent. We are ready and would go, counting ourselves happy in being permitted to serve and suffer for the cause of freedom and free institutions. But you won't let us go."[38]

William Lloyd Garrison suggested that slave insurrections be promoted in the South, but few backed this proposal.[39] The Lincoln administration made it clear that this was not an abolitionist war and servile insurrection had no part in it.[40] The war was to preserve the Union, not free the slaves or so he said at that time.[41]

John C. Fremont
Courtesy of the Library of Congress

On 30 August 1861 General John C. Fremont, commander in the West challenged this policy when he declared martial law in Missouri freeing the slaves of every rebel in the state.[42] Lincoln modified the Fremont order to indicate that only those rebels who had directly aided the Confederate war effort.[43]

In May 1861, General George McClellan on campaign in what is now West Virginia made his sentiments clear. "See that the rights and property of the people are respected, and repress all attempts at Negros insurrection."[44] In July, Frederick Douglass assailed Lincoln and McClellan because they were seen as not respecting the human rights of the African Americans.

> ABRAHAM LINCOLN is no more fit for the place he holds than was JAMES BUCHANAN, and the latter was no more the miserable tool of traitors and rebels than the former is allowing himself to be. As to McClellan he still leaves us in doubt as to whether he is a military imposter, or a deliberate traitor. The country is destined to become sick of both McClellan and Lincoln, and the sooner the better . . . . The signs of the times indicate that the people will have to take this war into their own hands and dispense with the services of all who by their incompetency give aid and comfort to the destroyers of the country.[45]

It was Gideon Wells the Secretary of the Navy that reversed the policy (for the Navy). Contraband (escaped slaves from the South) had been collected by Navy vessels as they cruised the Rappahannock River in Virginia.

The Contraband
Courtesy of the Library of Congress

What to do with these Blacks? Also, the Navy was short of manpower. Wells solved both problems with his order on 15 September 1861.

> The Department finds it necessary to adopt a regulation with respect the large number of persons of color, commonly known as contrabands, now subsisted at the navy yard and on board ships of war . . . You are authorized . . . to enlist them for the naval service, under the same forms and regulations as apply to other enlistments. [46]

Gideon Welles

The Integrated U. S. Navy
Courtesy of the Library of Congress

While they would be enlisted in the Navy, they would receive a lesser wage than whites ($10 versus $13 a month) and would man the guns on warships and perform all other duties accomplished by whites.[47]

The Wells order was not reversed, but when the Secretary of the War, Simon Cameron tried to move in the same direction, he lost his job.[48] It seemed logical and a good idea at the time: in November 1861, General Thomas W. Sherman was given the task to invade the coast of South Carolina. As he invaded he was given authority to ". . . avail yourself of the service of any persons . . . as you may deem most beneficial to the service."[49] This meant that Sherman could use African Americans to fight, but than a clause was added, some say by Lincoln, that no arming of "them" was authorized. With this hodgepodge of instructions, Sherman moved inland, but did not take advantage of his opportunity to enlist African Americans.[50] The end came for Cameron when he joined a speaking tour the theme of which was to arm and equip the slaves of the Rebels. He followed this up with his annual report as Secretary of War that emphasized the same goal. He sealed his fate when he released his report to the press before submitting it to Lincoln. Cameron soon found himself the new ambassador to the Czar.[51]

In May 1861, General Benjamin Butler the Union commander at Fort Monroe refused to return three runaway slaves to their owner.

This had been an issue since the war started. Rev J. Sella Martin pastor of Joy Street Baptist Church in Boston wrote to Frederick Douglass "They [Union officers] refuse to let white men sell the Southerners food, and yet they return slaves to work on plantations to raise all the food that the Southerners want. They arrest traitors, and yet make enemies of the colored people, North and South."[52] Butler viewed the escaped slaves as "contraband of war" and the U. S. Congress endorsed Butler's decision through the First Confiscation Act that was signed by Lincoln on 6 August 1861. This law authorized the federal government to seize property (including slaves) of all those participating directly in the revolution. These African American "contrabands" could be freed at locations occupied by the U. S. Army, but they were prohibited from joining Union forces.[53] Clearly, this was a way to punish Southern slave owners, but did not help the Union war fighting capability. It was not until July 1862 that the U. S. Army was allowed to hire African Americans but as laborers, only. They were not allowed to fight. Wages were one ration a day and $10 a month, $3 of which was to be provided as clothing.[54]

While Lincoln and Congress backed away from allowing African Americans in combat, commanders in the field saw the advantage and started recruiting African Americans to fight. General David Hunter, the successor to General Thomas Sherman recruited a regiment of runaway slaves in South Carolina in April 1862.

David Hunter
Courtesy of the Library of Congress

Hunter was one of the oldest officers in the field at that time. He was an 1822 graduate of West Point and his class standing was 25th in a class of 40. Hunter had a long record of Army service and was nearly 59 years old at the start of the Civil War. Hunter had repeatedly asked the War Department for reinforcements and had received none.[55] In addition to his other problems, rumors were circulating that the African Americans would be collected and shipped to Cuba, Africa and the West Indies.[56] This hindered enlistments. Hunter's approach became at the least heavy-handed. Under Sherman, African Americans "contraband" had been put back on their master's former plantation growing cotton. Hunter had them conscripted from their plantations to be armed and equipped as the 1st Carolina Colored Regiment. ". . . Wives and children embraced the husband and father thus taken away, [to serve in the Union army] they knew not where, and whom, as they said, they should never see again."[57] Lincoln wanted to distance himself from Hunter's order and on 19 May announced.

> I, Abraham Lincoln, President of the United States, proclaim and declare, that the government of the United States, had no knowledge, information, or belief, of an intention on the part of General Hunter to issue such a proclamation; nor has it any authentic information that the document is genuine. And, further, that neither General Hunter, nor any other commander, or person, has been authorized by the Government of the United States, to make proclamations declaring the slaves of any State free; and that the supposed proclamation, now in question, whether genuine or false, is altogether void.[58]
>
> *Abraham Lincoln*

Lincoln and his administration were changing their view. Some of his cabinet supported arming the African Americans, but in July 1862, Lincoln would not go that far.[59] At this point without any backing from Washington, Hunter disbanded the regiment[60] except for one company.[61] There were aftershocks. The Confederacy reacted violently suggesting that Hunter was promoting a slave insurrection throughout the South by arming the African Americans in his region.[62] Jefferson Davis wrote to R. E. Lee.

> The newspapers, received from the enemy country, announce as a fact that Major-General Hunter has armed slaves for the murder of their masters and has done all in his power to inaugurate a servile war which is worse than that of the savage, insomuch as it superintends other horrors to indiscriminate slaughter of all ages, sexes and conditions.[63]
>
>

Jefferson Davis after the War
Courtesy of the Library of Congress

The South's paranoia over the possibility of an African American uprising was always in the background. Further, the Confederacy decided that any Union officer commanding an African American unit would be executed if captured for "inciting negro insurrections."[64]

The result was an uproar in the U. S. Congress with the abolitionists winning. On 17 July 1862, the Second Confiscation Act of 1862 was signed into law. It attempted to broaden the authority of the federal government to seize property of anyone giving aid and comfort to the enemy. All slaves entering Union lines would be "forever free."[65] The Second Confiscation Act also provided a special authority allowing the arming of Negroes.[66] This act passed authority to the President not Hunter, and the President at this point had no intention of arming the African Americans. Lincoln's concern was that if he armed the African Americans, he would lose the border slave states such as Kentucky to the Confederacy. The *Times* reported ". . . that the nation could not afford to lose Kentucky at this crisis, and gave it as his opinion that to arm the Negroes would turn 50,000 bayonets from the loyal Border States against that were now for us."[67] In practice, neither confiscation act had much effect on the war and very little property was seized.[68] In the same month, the Militia Act was passed authorizing the president to receive into the service of the United States "for the purpose of construction entrenchments, or performing camo (sic) duties, or any other labor, or any military or naval . . . . persons of African descent."[69]

The Summer of 1862 found General Benjamin Butler in New Orleans. In April he had moved up the Mississippi River with Admiral Farragut to seize New Orleans. While Butler commanded at New Orleans, one of his subordinates, General John W. Phelps was located nearby at Fort Parapet. Phelps was an abolitionist determined to arm African Americans to fight for the Union. Complaints started to arrive about Phelp's activities. He was enticing the slaves to leave their plantations and cross lines into his camp. He then started organizing five companies of African Americans. On 30 July 1862 he sent a requisition to Butler for arms and equipment for three regiments that he was forming. Phelps presented a very interesting case to Butler:

> Society in the South seems to be on the point of dissolution; and the best way of preventing the African Americans from becoming instrumental in a general state of anarchy, is to enlist him in the cause of the Republic. If we reject his services, any petty military chieftain by offering him freedom, can have them for the purpose of robbery and plunder. It is for the interests of the South, as well of the North, that the African should be permitted to offer his block for the temple of freedom. Sentiments unworthy of the man of the present day-worthy only of another Cain-could alone prevent such an offer from being accepted.[70]

Nevertheless, Butler refused and Phelps submitted his resignation.[71] At this point, Butler, a clever Massachusetts politician before he became a general decided to out-Phelps Phelps. He realized that the Confederate army had raised three regiments of free African Americans to defend New Orleans and the regiments had been disbanded. Why not recall them to fight for the Union? On 22 August he published his General Order Number 63. It called for free colored militia men to volunteer for the Union.[72] Butler was successful in circumventing Washington policy. He raised three regiments of African Americans cleverly stating that he was merely recommissioning Confederate regiments that already existed and had surrendered in New Orleans.[73] He got away with it although his claim was a real stretch: less than 10% were members of the original Confederate regiments.[74] The Confederate government that had condemned Hunter and Phelps "for having organized and armed negro slaves against their masters" did not have a word to say about Butler.[75]

The summer of 1862 found war weariness setting in after a series of Union defeats. The realization that the North needed more manpower to prosecute the war led to acceptance that African Americans should be brought into the Union army. The Militia Act was passed that removed the restrictions of the 1792 law that banned African Americans from serving. This act authorized the employment of free African Americans as soldiers.[76]

West of the Mississippi River arming of African Americans for the Union had started with far less pain than in the South and East. Senator James H. Lane started enlisting African Americans in Kansas.

James H. Lane
Courtesy of the Library of Congress

Lane was a lawyer born in Indiana who moved to Kansas in 1855. He was a Jayhawker (Union guerrilla) who committed more than his fair share of atrocities but was respectable enough to have a university named for him later. Also, Lincoln had enough confidence in him to direct that he be promoted to Brigadier General[77] In August 1862, Lane started recruiting whites and African Americans at Lawrence, Kansas. African Americans would be laborers and would not be armed. Lane sent glowing reports back to Washington. "Recruiting opened beautifully good for four regiments of whites and two of blacks."[78] Secretary of War Stanton cabled Lane on 23 September 1862. "You are not authorized to organize Indians, nor any but loyal white men."[79]

Things seemed to get out of hand. There were complaints of African American troops moving into Missouri and attacking Missouri State Militia. These were followed by a pitched battle between five companies of African Americans and a large guerilla force in Missouri: "The first engagement of the war in which colored troops were engaged [they won]."[80] This was great publicity for the African American troops, but complaints flowed in to Washington. Stanton continued to complain about the arming of African Americans, but was ignored.

Secretary of War Edwin Stanton
Courtesy of the Library of Congress

Policy in Washington was about to change and Lane sensed that. The 1st Kansas Colored Volunteers Regiment was formed and became the fourth African American regiment activated after Ben Butler's three regiments in Louisiana.

When General Hunter failed and left the Sea Islands of South Carolina, General Rufus Saxton took over. Like the phoenix, the disbanded 1st South Carolina Colored Volunteers was about to rise from its ashes.

After nearly eighteen months of war, the manpower pinch in both North and South was starting to drive policy. On 25 August 1862, Secretary of War Stanton directed Saxton to recruit no more than 5,000 African American troops. They would be armed. They were to receive the same pay as their white comrades, but it took two years to get the equal pay part implemented.[81] This was a turning point for the Lincoln administration and while Lincoln had not entirely decided to arm African Americans, Stanton told Saxton to do it. It was not long before the African Americans were fighting and winning against the Confederate army in a series of raids along the coast. With every raid, they brought in more African Americans to fight.[82] White acceptance of African American soldiers was growing. When asked about African American troops one white soldier commented "They've as much right to fight for themselves as I have to fight for them."[83] On 31 January 1863, the 1st Carolina was made a part of the Union army. This was the fifth African American regiment to be mustered.

The Emancipation Proclamation of 1 January 1863 established Lincoln's commitment to the use of African Americans as soldiers: "And I further declare and make known, that such persons of suitable condition, will be received into the armed service of the United States to garrison forts, positions, stations, and other places, and to man vessels of all sorts in said service."[84] Lincoln was concerned about the reaction of the border states and Southern plantation owners who might view the document as encouraging slave insurrections and attacks on whites. For this reason his proclamation stressed the use of African Americans in defensive situations such as garrison forts.[85] Also, it applied only to the Confederate states and not the border states and parts of Virginia and Louisiana were exempted.[86] Make no mistake about this, the genie was out of the bottle. Once enlisted to fight, the African Americans would go and do what was required in all situations. By March authorization had been granted to form eight new regiments of African Americans.[87] Henry M. Turner the pastor of the Israel Bethel Church in Washington recalled the events of 1 January 1863. "I went to the office of the *Evening Star* and got the proclamation . . . Great processions of colored and white men marched to and from the White House and congratulated President Lincoln on his proclamation. . . . Nothing like that will be seen again in this life."[88] It was not until 31 January 1865 that Congress adopted the Thirteenth Amendment to the Constitution that abolished slavery throughout the United States.[89]

Daniel Ullmann
Courtesy of the Library of Congress

Daniel Ullmann a politician from New York had commanded the 78th New York Volunteers during the Peninsular Campaign and visited Lincoln to urge the enlistment of African Americans. Lincoln simply said "Ullmann, would you be willing to command black soldiers?" After recovering from the surprise Ullmann agreed and what followed was a marriage made in Hell. Ullmann would raise white cadre in New York City and enlist African Americans in Louisiana.[90] Since New York society was not enthusiastic about providing officers for an African American brigade, no progress was made on recruiting cadre (by July the New York City draft riots that targeted African Americans for murder were in full swing). Vice President Hamlin came to Ullmann's assistance and was successful in obtaining support from the governor of Maine who agreed to find white officers for Ullmann's new brigade. One of the new regimental commanders would be Cyrus Hamlin the Vice President's son. So with white officers from Maine and the new general Ullmann from New York the entourage cast off on 10 April 1863 for New Orleans to raise an African American brigade.[91] The reason for the odd arrangement was that recruiters had to go where recruits were plentiful and New York was unlikely to enlist enough African Americans to fill the new brigade. On the other hand New Orleans had a large population of African Americans and Ben Butler had already enlisted three regiments.

In January 1863, Governor John Andrew of Massachusetts asked Stanton for permission to form a new African American regiment which was approved. Andrew first planned to raise the regiment from African Americans in North Carolina where many recruits were available. He planned to use Ben Butler to accomplish this but when permission to use Butler was denied, he proceeded to recruit in Massachusetts. This would be difficult since the last census indicated that of a total of 1,973 African Americans only 394 could be counted upon to enlist in Massachusetts (based upon the ratio of whites who enlisted from the white population). This was hardly enough to raise a regiment.[92] This was the first African American regiment raised in the North. In this way, the 54th Massachusetts Infantry Regiment was born. [93] It would become the most famous of the African American regiments and was the subject of the motion picture *Glory* and two books: *One Gallant Rush* and *Lay this Laurel*. Andrew selected Robert Gould Shaw as its commander.

Robert Gould Shaw
Courtesy of the Library of Congress

Shaw was born in Boston in a wealthy family and, in 1863, was a captain in the 2d Massachusetts regiment. With the help of abolitionists, recruits were soon flowing in from other states. By March, four companies had been formed and recruits were following at a rate of one hundred a week. Andrew now moved to form another new Massachusetts African American regiment, the 55th. Soon changes would arrive that would cause the formation of new African American regiments on a massive scale in the captured territories of the South. But while recruiting of African Americans in the South was blossoming, recruiting in the North was drying up. There were three reasons. First, by 1863, free African Americans in the North were enjoying a booming wartime economy that meant better wages. Second, news was spreading throughout the North of Confederate murders of African American soldiers or sending them into slavery.[94] This point is contested among historians today. Some say it strengthened resolve and aided recruitment, others, not. Third, the requirement that all officers of African American regiments be white was a wet blanket on recruitment. Robert Purvis, a disgusted African American in Philadelphia, wrote ". . . it argues a sad misrepresentation of the character, aspirations and self-respect of colored men, to suppose that they would submit to the degrading limitations which the government imposes in regard to the officering of said regiments [whites only]. From that position and error, the government must recede, or else . . . failure to secure the right kind of men will result."[95] Lincoln and Stanton would not budge. From their point of view the public needed to digest the enlistment of African American privates that would be armed before they had to swallow the concept of African American officers.[96] Enlistment was not easy in the North. Washington, D. C., a Southern city was also not a good place to enlist. Recruits were attacked by mobs. A reporter for the Christian Recorder wrote "I saw an excited rabble pursuing a corporal of the 1st Colored Regiment. Such taunts as 'Kill the Black . . . . strip him . . . . we'll stop this negro enlistment' . . . the corporal received some pretty severe bruises."[97] In spite of discouragement, recruiting continued. A Private from the 54th Massachusetts penned the following song.

> **Fremont told them, when it first began,**
> **How to save the Union, and the way it should be done;**
> **But Kentucky swore so hard, and old Abe he had his fears**
> **Till every hope was lost but the colored volunteers.**
>
> **McClellan went to Richmond with two hundred thousand brave;**
> **He said, "keep back the niggers," and the Union he would save.**
> **Little Mac he had his way—still the Union is in tears—**
> ***Now* they call for the help of the colored volunteers.**
>
> **So rally, boys, rally, let us never mind the past;**
> **We had a hard road to travel, but our days are coming fast,—**
> **For God is for the right, and we have no need to fear,—**
> **The Union must be saved by the colored volunteer.**[98]

General Lorenzo Thomas
Courtesy of the Library of Congress

General Lorenzo Thomas graduated with the U. S. Military Academy class of 1823. He spent his career in the army as an administrator and was Adjutant General of the U. S. Army at the start of the war.[99] His life changed when Edwin Stanton tapped him to change the way African Americans were recruited. So far, African American regiments had been organized by generals, governors and other individuals. It was time for the War Department to take over and direct the organization of African American units on a large scale that could have a significant effect on the war.[100] Lorenzo Thomas was charged to do that. Relations between Secretary of War Stanton and Thomas had been less than cordial and some said that this was a way for Stanton to get Thomas out of Washington. Stanton, when he took office, was quoted as saying that he would pick up Thomas with a pair of tongs and drop him in the Potomac.[101] In March 1863, Stanton sent Thomas west to recruit new African American regiments along the Mississippi River. It worked. In April he was warming to the task. He was one of the oldest officers in uniform but his energy and persuasiveness had an effect. By issuing orders to commanders along the Mississippi and talking to the troops, white and African American, the regiments were quickly formed. "I come from Washington clothed with the fullest power in this matter . . . I can act as if the president of the United States were himself present. I am directed to refer nothing to Washington, but to act promptly. What I have to do, to do at once . . . to strike down the unworthy and elevate the deserving."[102]

Lorenzo Thomas Addressing the USCT
Courtesy of the Library of Congress

The methods used to recruit were heavy handed. Robert Cowden who would become the commander of the Fifty-ninth Regiment described recruiting.

> The plan for "persuading" recruits while it could hardly be called the shot-gun policy was equally as convincing, and never failed to get the "recruit." . . . The cavalry of the division was continually employed as scouts and skirmishers, and almost daily brought into camp hundreds of animals and negroes as spoils. The former were used in replenishing the army and increasing its effectiveness for the summer campaign, and the latter were turned over to Colonel Bouton, whose recruiting

agents accompanied all these excursions . . . In this way, in the space of six weeks, the entire command was made up, without the expense of a single dollar to the Government, and on the 27th of June, 1863, was mustered into the United States military service. [103]

The incentives were enormous as Thomas stated. "I am authorized to give commissions, from the highest to the lowest, and I desire those persons who are earnest in the work to take hold of it."[104] Thomas' authority to promote and appoint was impressive. In round numbers he could appoint thirty-five officers and dozens of non-commissioned officers for each African American regiment.[105] The officers were nearly all white, but the non-com ranks were also available to African Americans. This created a talent drain on white regiments in the west. Experienced officers from white regiments departed to join the African American regiments and get a promotion, but it also created vacancies in the white regiments that allowed promotion to back fill vacancies. No doubt Thomas had this all figured out and it worked. By the end of 1863, Thomas had recruited twenty new regiments and a year later the number was up to fifty.[106]

Nathan Banks
Courtesy of the Library of Congress

In December 1862 General Nathan P. Banks replaced Butler and found that the condition of the contraband was deplorable.

They were living in huts on substandard food. Banks encouraged them to return to their old plantations and work there at a wage of ten dollars a month.[107] Frederick Douglass complained "It practically enslaves the negro, and makes the Proclamation of 1863 a mockery and delusion."[108] Bank's approach did, however, improve the living conditions of the African Americans and included one provision supported by all: a school board was set up to educate African Americans.[109] This was perhaps Banks' greatest contribution to the war. His next step was a disaster. He replaced the African American officers of the Louisiana regiments with whites. The African Americans stopped enlisting so Banks was forced to use conscription to fill new regiments.[110]

By the time the Ullmann entourage arrived from New York, Banks had received his orders from Washington to cooperate. On 1 May 1863, Banks launched his own program to recruit African Americans. He planned to form "Corps d'Afrique" composed of eighteen regiments of African American troops.[111] In June, Banks merged the regiments being created by Ullmann into his own "Corps d'Afrique". The French-English African American newspaper sounded the call "To arms! It is our duty. The nation counts on the devotion and the courage of its sons . . . . We are the sons of Louisiana, and when Louisiana calls, we march."[112] In Mid-August, Banks reported to Lincoln that he had raised 10,000 or 12,000 men.[113] Changing from slaves to soldiers was not a pleasant experience. Robert Cowden described the recruits.

> The average plantation negro was a hard-looking specimen, with about as little of the soldier to be seen in him as there was of the angel in Michael Angelo's block of marble before he had applied his chisel. His head covered with a web of knotted cotton strings that had once been white, braided into his long, black, curly wool; his dress a close-fitting wool shirt, and pantaloons of homespun material, butternut brown, worn without suspenders, hanging slouchily (sic) upon him, and generally too short in the legs by several inches . . . . He had a rolling, dragging, moping gait and a

cringing manner, with a downcast thievish glance that dared
not look you in the eye . . . . [114]

The period of hodge-podge formation of units by individuals was
ending. General Orders Number 143, 22 May 1863 centralized control
by the Bureau of Colored Troops under the Adjutant General. The
movement to arm African Americans was now under the control of
Washington.[115] The problem remained that of finding locations where
an abundance of African Americans lived who would volunteer or could
be conscripted, if necessary.[116] This led to the Jacksonville, Florida raid
in March 1863 to seize and hold the town. As Confederate General
Joseph Finegan wrote. "That the entire negro population of East Florida
will be lost and the country ruined there can be no doubt, unless the
means of holding the St. John River are immediately provided."[117] The
two African American regiments held Jacksonville and accomplished
further forays up the St. John River collecting supplies and more free
African Americans. The problem was that they were being worn down
by constant Confederate probes and so two white regiments were sent
to reinforce Jacksonville. This was the first time that white and African
American regiments fought together and it worked well.[118]

In the fall of 1862 reality set in: hardly anyone in North or South
believed that this bloody war was primarily to preserve the Union or
protect the South's states rights. The issue was the abolition of slavery
and with the Emancipation Proclamation effective on 1 January
1863, Northern states were clamoring for permission to raise African
American regiments.[119] Hunter's original regiment was reorganized as
the 1st South Carolina (Colored) Regiment.[120] By the end of 1863, over
50,000 African Americans had been enlisted to fight for the North,
and by the end of the war, the official number stood at 178,975.[121]
Recruitment was spurred by offers of freedom and pay. Enlistment was
voluntary in loyal slave states such as Maryland, Delaware, Missouri
and Kentucky,[122] but in Northern states, African Americans could be
conscripted the same as whites. Kansas, Louisiana and the Carolinas
used conscription and could draw on those African Americans who
were contraband.[123]

Enlisting from a slave state presented challenges. The slave had
to first find his way to Union lines and then find a recruiting place.
John Young a slave recalled his flight. "I run off from home in Drew

County [Arkansas]. Five or six of us run off to Pine Bluff [Arkansas]. We heard that if we could get with the Yankees we'd be freed, so we run off to Pine Bluff and got with some Yankee soldiers . . . then went to Little Rock and I joined."[124] The African Americans were organized into African American regiments and were not integrated into white units,[125] although groups of African Americans joined white regiments. Integration in the U. S. armed forces did not occur until the U. S. National Security Act of 1947.

In 1863 another step forward was taken by the Union on the eve of Gettysburg when the state African American regiments were Federalized and converted into regiments of U. S. Colored Troops (USCT). These were combat units: infantry, cavalry and artillery. There were a few exceptions to this conversion in Massachusetts and Connecticut. General Hunter's original regiment was designated as the 33rd Regiment, USCT.[126] In his third annual message to Congress, President Lincoln stated that "Of those who were slaves at the beginning of the rebellion full 100,000 are now in the United States military service."[127] This was double trouble for the Confederacy. Not only had they lost slave manpower, but it had added to the bayonets of the North. By the end of the war, the total number of African Americans composed about 12% of the Union army's strength.[128]

CHAPTER 3

Equipping, Education and Training

Equipping

Lack of adequate clothing was a problem for both sides during the war. One of Stonewall Jackson's troops had a vivid recollection of the march from Romney to Winchester, Virginia, and back in January, 1862.

> As the men 'marched along," he wrote, "icicles hung from their clothing, guns, and knapsacks; many were badly frost bitten, and I have heard of many freezing to death along the road side. My feet peeled off like a peeled onion on a march, and I have not recovered from its effects to this day . . . The soldiers in the whole army got rebellious-almost mutinous-and would curse and abuse Stonewall Jackson; in fact, they called him 'Fool Tom Jackson.'" This same Confederate chronicler also related that eleven members of the Fourteenth Georgia and Third Arkansas regiments froze to death while on guard duty near Hampshire Crossing during the same campaign. "Some were sitting down," he recalled, "and some were lying down; but each and everyone was as cold and as hard frozen as the icicles that hung from their hands and faces and clothing-dead! They had died at their post of duty. Two of them, a little in advance of the others, were standing with their guns in their hands, as cold and as hard frozen as a monument of marble-standing sentinel with loaded guns in their frozen hands![1]

Many similar stories were related by soldiers in the North. After a long campaign in Missouri pursuing the Confederate General Sterling Price, T. J. Hunt of the 10th Minnesota Volunteers described the end of a 1,000 mile march much of which was accomplished by soldiers marching barefoot in the snow.

Sterling Price
Courtesy of the Library of Congress

T. J. Hunt in Old Age
Courtesy of the Minnesota Historical Society

When near Jefferson City, we forded the Osage River, thirty rods wide (snow having covered the ground in the morning) during a severe rain, lest it should rise so we could not cross at all. With the wet and cold, our sufferings were intense, as we could not start fires with green wood which was all that could be gotten. On Nov. 3rd we faced a northeast snowstorm, the whole day. Minnesota never had so severe a one so early. At first it melted freely, then freezing, it lay more than four inches deep before night, which it ceased snowing but froze hard. We spent night in open fields with little fuel and no shelter from wind. I got some sleep lying on a brush heap from which I had shaken the snow. Others sat or lay on their rubber blankets, but were obliged to get up and stir briskly and keep our little fires going, taking turns in warming one side at a time, as our scanty fires were made against stumps while wood was cut from other stumps to feed them. Axes were too few but were in constant use. Three houses nearby sheltered a few sick, probably saving a few lives. I thought many would die that terrible night, but I believe none did. The next day, the snow melted and the second day, it nearly disappeared. Mud took its place, and we moved on. In a few days we reached St. Louis, a muddy, ragged worn army.[2]

Uniforms were always a problem throughout the war. Fortunately the USCT were organized in 1863 when the army supply system had caught up with demand. Additionally, their late arrival worked in their favor. Some of the African American regiments were equipped with light weight uniforms that were the envy of white regiments who still suffered from heavy uniforms weighing six pounds.[3] The problem was that the uniforms were only a small amount of weight that a soldier had to carry. The cartridge box weighed over four pounds and to that needed to be added the weight of the rifle, canteen and all the other items that a soldier needed to sustain himself in battle. The result was many soldier injuries such as hernia, bad back and other physical problems that result from carrying a large load over long distances. There is nothing new about this and it has been a problem in wars before and since. The major problem is that in a campaign, needed replacement items are generally not immediately available. As an example, the 10th Minnesota Volunteers arrived at Benton Barracks, Missouri after a long campaign defeating General Price. Some were without uniforms except undergarments in December of 1864.[4] They were quickly rearmed and reequipped for the Battle of Nashville. One historian has suggested that Western units fared better because they were composed of "outdoor men" who could survive hardship, but there is no statistical evidence to support this.[5] On the contrary Western units suffered a higher percentage of losses due to battle and disease. Most historians agree with this.[6] They were at the end of the supply chain and suffered from that.[7]

White regiments occasionally received bad rations but for African American regiments, bad rations such as wormy meat and bug infested bread were the order of the day. Both white and African Americans were scheduled to receive the same rations.[8]

The problem was the quality. The commissariats steered the bad rations to the African Americans. They were the newest units and were less likely to complain because of inexperience. African American regiments learned fast, and by the time they were being organized into African American brigades they had ample rank and experience to refuse the bad rations as did the white regiments.[9]

Education and Training
North

Trying to track individual black soldiers after the war was a nightmare. Many enlisted under an alias (to avoid retribution against their kin back home) while many had no surname. As an example a soldier enlisted as "George" or "Jim" and that was it. To make matters worse, most were illiterate because it was against the law in the South to educate an African American. One recruiter asked the soldier his name. "Dick," was the reply. When told he needed a second name the reply was "Don't want none-one name enough for me." After some persuasion, most would select a second name. Since most did not want the name of their slave holder many selected names like Grant, Sherman, Lincoln, Butler, etc.[10]

On the Firing Line
Courtesy of the Library of Congress

Training was difficult because most African Americans were illiterate and few knew how to handle a firearm. Once trained with a firearm, it became clear to all that trained African Americans were too dangerous to keep as slaves.[11]

The illiteracy of the African Americans that enlisted demanded a better educated and versatile officer corps that could improve the new soldiers and educate them beyond drill and rifle practice. Officers in white regiments frequently volunteered for service with the USCT since promotion went with the reassignment. In this way, the USCT received a flow of experienced white officers who knew how to fight and train. Additionally a candidate officer training academy, the Free Military School was established in Philadelphia for new candidate officers that would be assigned to USCT. It was very similar to Officer Candidate School in the U. S. Army today. At the conclusion of training a board examination was administered to the white officers and this arrangement was very successful.[12] Unfortunately, few African Americans served as officers in the USCT.[13]

The search for qualified officers eventually led to the establishment of boards at the division level in the field or post level in the Northern cities to review applicants and select those who would be officers in the African American regiments.[14] Boards were inclined to select white applicants although a few African Americans were selected.[15]

In spite of Jefferson Davis's threat that white officers of African American regiments would be executed if captured by the Confederate army, the surge of applications to serve in African American regiments increased. The Confederates apparently never realized that their murders of prisoners of war had created a crusade in the North and molded a fighting force that would fight to the death. By 26 December 1863, 1051 applications had been received and 560 were approved.[16] The failure rate would be vastly reduced by the Free Military School.

As George R. Sherman an officer in the 7th USCT pointed out, "These slaves came to us ignorant of anything outside of their plantation. They were kept that way on the plantation since an ignorant African American was less likely to hold disruptive ideas."[17]

Daniel Ullmann outlined the task ahead for officers of the African American regiments in his General Order, Number. 7, 10 June 1863.

> [They] were selected for qualities which . . . . eminently qualify them for this duty, namely: accurate knowledge of drill, long experience in the field, patience, diligence, and patriotism the constant exercise of all these qualities necessary. You are brought into contact with a race, who, having lived in abnormal condition all of the days of their lives, are now suddenly elevated into being soldiers of the United States fighting against their oppressors, as well for their own liberties as for the integrity of the republic. They are to be molded by you into drilled and disciplined troops. You cannot display too much wisdom in your conduct, both as regards yourselves and them. Let the law of kindness be your guide.[18]

The African Americans worked hard at training and were highly motivated. For slaves the opportunity for freedom was important. For Northern free African Americans, the motivation was to gain acceptance and equality through their service.[19] Training meant drill and a great deal of it. The regiments were divided into lettered companies of one hundred men each. Many African Americans were promoted to corporal and sergeant based upon literacy, appearance and leadership skills, but literacy was not a prerequisite especially for those who enlisted from the South. Enlisted slaves quickly learned to read and write since they saw this as important to their future.[20] Education was important for their performance in their regiment as well. By August 1865, more than 200,000 free African Americans had received instructions in reading and writing.[21] As the Annual Cyclopedia stated. ". . . When deprived of their commanders [they] would not in general fight independently as well as those who have had more education."[22] Frances Beecher the wife of Colonel James Beecher commander of the Thirty-fifth Infantry recalled "My mornings were spent in teaching the men of our regiment to read and write, and it became my pleasing duty and habit whenever our moving tents were pitched there to set up school . . . . the result was when the men came to be mustered out, each one of them could proudly sign his name to pay-roll in a good legible hand. When enlisted, all but two or three of them were obliged to put a mark to their names."[23] James T. Wilson of the Fifty-fourth Regiment recalled that every company had someone to instruct reading if nothing more. [24]

CHAPTER 4

What the White Soldiers Thought and Did

In both the North and the South the whites viewed the African Americans as an inferior race: lazy, shiftless, slovenly, childlike and dull-witted.[1] The logic that followed was that they were unfit to be free and could not be trusted to be soldiers. The concept of racial inferiority therefore became one of the main justifications for slavery. As Frederick Douglass put it "In truth, this question is at the bottom of the whole controversy."[2] In 1861 an Anglo-African took the argument a step further.

> If we are ignorant, it is you that have shut the light of knowledge from our souls and brutalized our instancts. If we are degraded, yours is the disgrace, for you have closed up every avenue whereby we might energe from degradation and robbed us of all incentive to elevation. The enormity of your guilt, the immensity of the wrong does not appear in contemplating what you have made us, but what you have prevented us from being. [3]

After the Fort Pillow massacre (See Appendix C), Nathan Bedford Forrest reported "These facts [Union losses] will demonstrate to the Northern people that negro soldiers cannot cope with Southerners."[4]

Nathan Bedford Forrest
Courtesy of the Library of Congress

Two main reasons have been advanced to explain the opposition to African Americans in the Union army. Racial prejudice: the thought that the white race was too superior to fight alongside the African Americans. Second and related to the first: African Americans were too servile and cowardly to be effective soldiers. [5]

The notion that African Americans were inferior to whites dominated thought in the Union army. Of course there was no basis in fact and proponents of this notion were often contradictory in what they said. As one answer to a USSC survey said "Certainly not. Taken in a body, they [African Americans] are at present, too much animal to have moral courage or endurance."[6] It is difficult to reconcile this statement with a field hand who has spent his life laboring in the fields or an escaped slave who may have had to travel many miles through enemy territory in order to reach Union lines and enlist. Certainly among the poorer classes of white society such as the immigrant Irish, this sort of thought process was an effort to keep African Americans in their place. Surprisingly many who were proponents of this sort of racism were educated officers. Joseph Smith the medical director for Union troops in Arkansas observed. "They however have not the intelligence of white troops and must be made to take proper steps for the police of their persons and their camp."[7] Not all shared this racist view. A physician in Troy, New York noted. "The colored man (sic), as far as my observation goes, make excellent soldiers. They are a race, remarkable free of hernia, are muscular, and capable of great endurance."[8]

Bell Wiley in *The Life of Billy Yank* noted "One who reads letters and diaries of Union soldiers encounters an enormous amount of antipathy toward negroes. Expressions of unfriendliness range from blunt statements bespeaking intense hatred to belittling remarks concerning dress and demeanor".[9]

In 1863 a young soldier from Boston wrote "As I was going along this afternoon a little black baby that could just walk got under my feet and it looked so much like a big worm that I wanted to step on it and crush it, the nasty, greasy little vermin was the best that could be said of it."[10]

Many white soldiers viewed African Americans as the cause of the war and there was no love lost for them. This changed over time, especially after the Emancipation Proclamation. Among white soldiers, the African Americans were viewed as bullet stoppers. The following poem by Miles O'Reilly of the Irish Brigade.[11] was in a way a tribute by a white soldier to the fact that the African Americans were good soldiers and capable of fighting well.

> Some tell us 'tis a burning shame
> To make the naygers fight;
> An' that the thrade of bein' kilt
> Belongs but to the white;
> But as for me, upon my soul!
> So liberal are we here,
> I'll let Sambo be murthered instead of myself
> On every day of the year.
> On every day in the year, boys,
> And in every hour of the day;
> The right to be kilt I'll divide wd' him,
> n' divil a word I'll say.[12]

Inequality was the hallmark of how African Americans were treated in both North and South, and it led to much higher casualty rates among the African Americans.

In 1862, one Southern newspaper reported. ". . . One of the most awful and revolting specimens of these creatures [Southern overseers] was related yesterday, where a free negro on fortifications had his back actually cut into a mangle of bleeding flesh, the driver having given him as we were told by a policeman, five hundred and sixty-one lashes with the whip . . . In the name of God, is there no justice to be found in the courts of human justice for iniquities like this?"[13]

The negative attitude toward African Americans would change as the USCT won battles and these troops demonstrated their courage.

Thousands of African American Union troops and their white officers were murdered by the Confederate army. The prevailing view of Confederate generals such as Forrest, Pickett and Confederate troops was that African American Union soldiers were insurgent armed murderers who wanted to kill all Southern whites. The specter of Nat Turner and his slave uprising years earlier never left their minds. Armed African Americans should be executed immediately when captured or returned to slavery. Obviously, it was easier for a Confederate soldier to just shoot them than to try to figure out how to return them. The Confederate policy was that their Union white officers were promoting an African American uprising and should be put to death or otherwise punished at the discretion of a military tribunal.[14]

The point is that publically promoting murder by Davis or exercising it does not make good copy in the press. There followed public statements and Confederate policy which fell short of advocating murder but encouraged it and this led to countless murders by the Confederates.

The murders of African Americans and their white officers were conducted secretly and exact numbers are not known. Retaliation by executing Confederate soldiers was conducted without fanfare and no count was kept. Eventually Lincoln yielded to public pressure over the murders of African Americans by establishing a policy that for every African American murdered, a Confederate soldier would be executed. A typical reaction to the Confederate murders follows. This occurred near Baxter Springs in what is now Oklahoma.

While encamped here, on the 18th of May [1863], a foraging party, consisting of twenty-five men from the Phalanx [African American] regiment and twenty men of the 2nd Kansas Battery, Major R. G. Ward commanding, was sent into Jasper County, Missouri. This party was surprised and attacked by a force of three hundred confederates commanded by Major Livingston and defeated, with a loss of sixteen killed and five prisoners, three of whom belonged to the 2nd Kansas Battery and two of the Black regiment. The men of the 2nd Kansas Battery were afterwards exchanged under a flag of truce for a like number of prisoners captured by the negro regiment. Livingston refused to exchange the black prisoners in his possession, and gave as his excuse that he should hold them subject to the orders of the Confederate War Department. Shortly after this Colonel Williams received information that one of the prisoners held by Livingston had been murdered by the enemy. He immediately sent a flag of truce to Livingston demanding the body of the person who had committed the barbarous act. Receiving an evasive and unsatisfactory reply, Colonel Williams determined to convince the Major that this was a game at which two could play, and directed that one of the Confederate prisoners in his possession be shot, and within thirty minutes the order was executed. He immediately informed Major Livingston of his action, sending the information by the same party that brought the dispatch to him. Suffice it to say that this ended the barbarous practice of murdering prisoners of war, so far as Livingston's command was concerned.[15]

It was obvious to those on both sides that the South could not afford to lose soldiers as a result of Union retaliation. As the number of white executed Confederate prisoners started to mount, it occurred to some in the Confederacy that it might be a good idea to establish a policy that made sense and had teeth to prevent the loss of Confederate soldiers executed by the North in retaliation. Unfortunately, that was not the course chosen by Davis. Initially Jefferson Davis and the Confederate government followed a very clever policy designed to avoid suborning murder but at the same time leaving it up to the states and the army to continue murder without the blessing of the Confederate government. Confederate policy was vague and permissive. On 1 May 1862, the Confederate Congress authorized Jefferson Davis to direct that white officers of African American regiments should be executed and armed African Americans should be turned over to the state where captured.[16] Confederate General Order, Number 60 of 21 August 1862 established that Union officers who recruited African Americans were to be treated as "outlaws" not prisoners of war. The punishment was that these should be held as prisoners of war for execution as felons at such time as the president shall order.[17] Jefferson Davis received a blunt response from Union General David Hunter who was recruiting African Americans at that time.

> Mr. Davis, we have been acquainted intimately in the past. We have campaigned together, and our social relations have been such as to make each understand the other thoroughly. That you mean, if it be ever in your power, to execute the full rigor of your threats, I am well assured; and you will believe my assertion, that I thank you for having raised in connection with me and my acts, this sharp and decisive issue. I shall proudly accept, if such be the chance of war, the martyrdom you menace; and hereby give you notice that unless your General Order against me and my officers be formally revoked, within thirty days from the date of the transmission of this letter, sent under a flag of truce, I shall take your action in the matter as finale; and will reciprocate it by hanging every rebel officer who now is, or may hereafter be taken, prisoner by the troops of the command to which I am about returning.[18]

With Lincoln's Emancipation Proclamation on 1 January 1863 which freed the slaves in all states at war with the Union came the realization in the South that a large pool of African American labor was being encouraged to fight for the North and their freedom. Jefferson Davis responded by stating that all white officers of African American regiments should be handed over to the state where captured for action by that state. African Americans were to be returned to slavery.[19] There were some honest officers in the Confederate army. General Beauregard commanding at Charleston had men of the 54th Massachusetts captured at Fort Wagner. He had qualms about treating them like slaves and he queried the Governor of South Carolina proposing that he turn over his prisoners to the governor.[20] Ultimately these troops were imprisoned until the end of the war.

Grant and other Union generals adopted a very pragmatic policy. For every African American murdered by the Confederate army, a white Confederate prisoner would be executed.[21] As the scale of the murders increased and rumors of 54th Massachusetts soldiers who had been murdered, Frederick Douglass protested to Lincoln over the murder of African Americans. He would stop recruiting for the Union unless Lincoln took action against the Confederacy. Lincoln responded by quoting General Order 100, the Lieber Code which established a code of conduct for those engaged in war. Lincoln ordered that "for every soldier of the United States killed in violation of the laws of war a rebel soldier shall be executed and for every one enslaved by the enemy or sold into slavery by the enemy a rebel soldier shall be placed at hard labor on the public works."[22] This only drove the Confederate murders of prisoners underground. African Americans and the white officers were secretly murdered by the Confederates. Henry Freeman of the 12th Regiment USCT reported three cases of murder by the Confederate army. "Lieutenant W. L. Clark, captured on a train, was made to kneel down and shot in cold blood, because he belonged to this colored regiment. Three other officers captured after the battle of Nashville, "were led off, under pretense of being sent to General Forrest's headquarters and in a secluded ravine, without warning, were shot down like so many dogs. Two were killed instantly; a third . . . left for dead, subsequently recovered to tell the story."[23] The total murdered during the war and left in unmarked graves will never be known.[24]

Among the outcomes of the Emancipation Proclamation was that it ruined any hope of foreign recognition of the Confederacy. The barbarous treatment of prisoners by the South also ended any hope of foreign recognition. Because of the Confederate Congress 1 May declaration, prisoner exchanges stalled. Rather than discouraging recruitment of African American soldiers, the Confederate policy turned the war into a crusade for the African Americans. More important, the African Americans would fight more stubbornly than before to defeat the Confederacy.[25]

Mob violence against African Americans in the North continued during the war. The underlying cause of the brutality was the fear by working class whites that the African Americans would take their jobs especially if they were conscripted. The most famous of these was the

New York City draft riot in July 1863 that targeted African Americans to be killed. There were similar riots in other towns in the North. It has been alleged that these were caused by Confederate agents who incited the riots but this has not been proven.

CHAPTER 5

Duties

South

We are a band of brothers
And native to the soil
Fighting for our liberties
With treasure, blood and toil

The Confederate Battle Hymn commonly played by
African American Bands[1]

Many Blacks were body servants (cooks, valets and personal attendants) who were armed and would on occasion fight against the Union troops to protect their master or replace him if he was wounded. There are numerous accounts of the bravery of African American body servants defending their masters and many were killed doing that. One estimate was 30,000 body servants serving in the Army of Northern Virginia in 1862.[2]

A Cook at Work
Courtesy of the Library of Congress

This number seems exorbitant but other historians confirm the number of body servants in the range of 30,000.[3] One Confederate officer recalled that at Brandy Station "My negro servant Edmund, formed the officers' servants and colored cooks in line immediately in the rear of the regiment and flourishing an old saber over his head, took command of them."[4]

A body servant Jack and his master Lieutenant Shelton were both wounded at the battle of Belmont. Before he fell, Jack fired at the enemy twenty-seven times and after he was down, his son helped him load and fire three more rounds. Jack did not survive his wounds.[5]

Other Blacks dug fortifications, acted as guards, washed clothing, acted as teamsters, helped maintain the railroad, and performed a variety of other manual labor tasks.[6] Finally they joined and fought as individuals or in a few cases African American units. Nearly one half of the 3rd Alabama Infantry was made up of African Americans in 1861.[7] This was in spite of the fact that it was against Confederate law for African Americans to serve in combat units. In June 1863 one estimate is that 5% of Confederate combat troops before Gettysburg were African Americans.

African American spies for the South were common and very effective since Northerners could not believe that African Americans could be spies, especially women. One, "Confederate Mary" was very successful crossing the lines to deliver messages for Southern agents and returning with medicine.[8]

Many were employed in food preparation. In 1862, four African American cooks per company were authorized.[9] Teamsters were hired by the Quartermaster's Department in large numbers because of their experience on the plantations.[10] Hospital workers, railroad workers and ambulance drivers were recruited in large numbers.[11] The greatest number were employed in construction such as digging defenses.[12]

For those African Americans on the plantation, a different situation existed. At first, they were voluntarily released by their masters to serve, but as the war went on, the plantation owners became reluctant to release their slaves so the Confederate government impressed them to perform labor.[13] In most cases the African Americans served willingly.

The amount of labor that African Americans provided to the Confederacy was enormous. In Virginia, alone, 180,000 worked as laborers suffering poor rations and health care. R. E. Lee realized the need and suggested that the African Americans should be organized into Confederate Negro Labor Battalions, regiments, etc.[14] Most of these laborers were slaves, but some free African Americans volunteered as carpenters and craftsmen. In 1924, the State of Virginia established state pensions of $25 for African Americans who had served.[15] Most Southern states did the same. The African American pension applications included the duties performed during the war. The listing of jobs follows.[16]

Navy: Pilot, Sailor, Powder Boy, Servant, Landsman, and Cabin Boy. The most common jobs were Pilot and Sailor.

Army: Body Servant, Drummer, Fifer, Musician, Cook, Teamster, and Private. Most of the jobs were Cooks and Body Servants except for Louisiana where hundreds were soldiers listed as Privates.

African American "Show Units" (unofficial state militia regiments) were organized to demonstrate to visiting foreign dignitaries that African Americans were fighting for the South. These paraded in front of Europeans but had no official duties.

North

> From the commencement of the war, I had found the negroes of invaluable assistance, and I never hesitated to employ them when after investigation, I found them to be intelligent and trustworthy.[17]
>
> ### *Alan Pinkerton*

Over 200,000 free African Americans served as laborers, teamsters, cooks, carpenters, scouts, etc. for the Union forces.[18] They loaded and unloaded ships and performed a variety of other tasks outside of the duties of a soldier.

The Dock Workers
Courtesy of the National Archives

These non-military duties were not without danger. On 12 March 1863, a party of soldiers with twelve African Americans left Elizabeth City, North Carolina to collect wood. A group of forty guerillas attacked killing one African American and wounding two others.[19]

African Americans in the South provided an excellent source of military intelligence to the North. Since they worked as laborers on fortifications and many other jobs, they could relate Confederate strengths and positions. Allan Pinkerton, the chief of the United States Secret Service during the first two years of the war, would interview African Americans coming in to Union lines and he extracted a great deal of information during these interviews. Beyond that, he also hired African Americans as spies and they were well suited for this task since they were not suspected by the Confederates and could cross lines and disappear into Confederate labor groups. Pinkerton recalled one African American spy, John Scobell that he recruited ". . . the manner in which his duties were performed, was always a source of satisfaction to me and apparently of gratification for himself. From the commencement of the war, I had found the negroes of invaluable assistance, and I never hesitated to employ them when after investigation, I found them to be intelligent and trustworthy."[20]

African American regiments got the worst assigned duties such as burial details, digging latrines and other heavy labor work.

Reburying the Dead
Courtesy of the Library of Congress

African Americans were doing dirty details when they should have been drilling and practicing with their rifles. The result was that heavy labor details hurt readiness and the health of the command which drove up the number of people who died. A part of the problem was a hangover of the earlier policy to use African Americans only as laborers and garrison troops in order to free up white units to fight.[21] When Sherman prepared to march on Atlanta, he set the African American regiments to work building fortifications at Chattanooga. He kept them busy on that because he did not trust their fighting ability.[22] As a consequence, the march on Atlanta was an all white affair. What it came down to was how the department and divisional commanders to which the African American regiments were assigned chose to employ the regiments. In some cases they fought shoulder to shoulder with white regiments. Elsewhere they did endless work building fortifications and other manual labor.[23] In part the use of African Americans soldiers as laborers was caused by the notion that they were more acclimated than whites working in the heat. Surveys at that time seemed to support this since ".... the Black will do a greater amount of work than the white soldier, because he labors more consistent."[24] Something was needed to break this mold if the African Americans were to serve as soldiers. Victories by the African American regiments gradually brought the army around to the point of view that they should serve as soldiers fighting side by side with the white regiments. The victory of the 2nd Kansas Colored over Quantrill's raiders at Baxter Springs in October of 1863 was one of many battles that earned the African Americans the right to fight.[25] See Appendix C for Summary of Battles.

African American regiments usually got the least desirable duties when they had signed up to fight. Occupation duty and guarding supply trains and prisoners were standard duties assigned to African American units. Confederate prisoners complained to no avail that they wanted white guards stating that the African Americans would shoot to kill for any minor prisoner infraction. The Black response was "The bottom rail is now on the top."[26] The African American regiments were also assigned to hunt down guerillas. These sorts of duties could be intensely boring but also at times could become very dangerous. When Southern guerillas were cornered by African Americans, they could expect a stiff fight and instant justice if they were captured. Lieutenant Anson Hemingway of the 70th USCT wrote home. "There has been a party of Guerillas prowling about here, stealing horses and mules . . . A scouting party of African Americans was sent out . . . and came upon the party of whom they were in pursuit. There were seventeen prisoners captured and shot by the colored soldiers."[27] This was in accordance with the rules of war established by the Lieber Code.[28]

In some cases, the African American soldiers were required to perform menial labor for the whites. At Morris Island, S. C. the following General Order 77 was issued on 17 September 1863. "It has come to the knowledge of the Brig. Gen. Commanding that detachments of colored troops, detailed for fatigue duty, have been employed in one instance at least, to prepare camps and perform menial duty for the white troops. Such use of these details is unauthorized and improper, and is here after expressly prohibited."[29]

Picket (guard) duty was never-ending for the African Americans. They got more than their fair share, but it was not without some entertainment. Thomas Morgan of the 14th USCT wrote. "Colored soldiers acted as pickets, and no citizen was allowed to pass our lines, either to enter the village or out, without a proper permit. Thus many proud southern slaveholders found themselves marched through streets guarded by those who three months earlier had been slaves. These negroes often laughed over these changed relationships as they sat around their camp fires, or chatted together while off duty, but it was rare that any southerner had reason to complain of any unkind or uncivil treatment from a colored soldier."[30]

The War Department finally issued a directive dated 14 June 1864 that required white units to do their fair share of this labor "This is necessary to prepare them [African Americans] for the higher duties of conflict with the enemy."[31]

Compensation

By the time African Americans were enlisting in great numbers, the Union had ample supplies of uniforms and firearms so the African Americans received the same equipment as whites. Although promised equal pay African Americans did not receive it until after Congress took eighteen months to approve it. White privates received $13 a month and sergeants got $21. African American privates received $10 a month $3 of which was in clothing. For higher ranks, the difference was even greater. It took two years to rectify this situation. A part of the problem was an interpretation of the Militia Act of 1862 that held that African Americans should be paid as laborers and not as soldiers.[32] This was the same pay as laborers.[33] White soldiers could expect a bounty (a bonus for enlisting) but African Americans received very little or none.[34] Congress authorized a $100 bounty in July 1861 for white men enlisting for three years. With the passage of the Enrollment Act (March 3, 1863), three-year white enlistees received $300 and five-year recruits got $400, but these sums were divided up and paid in monthly installments with the soldiers' regular compensation. African American soldiers could make considerably more money by enlisting as a paid substitute than by enlisting without a bounty.

There were efforts to rectify the inequality. In August of 1864, General Butler established a bounty of one hundred dollars to be paid to the African American recruits.[35] Furthermore, the bounty laws of 1865 and 1873 finally restored equality in bounties.[36] This had a profound effect on their lives. One observer who returned to South Carolina and Florida in late 1870s noted. "I rarely met an ex-soldier [African American] who did not own his house and ground, the enclosures varying from five to two hundred acres."[37] This helped make up for the inequalities of the war when the problems of pay and bounties caused near-mutinies among the troops and hardship for the families of African Americans some of whom ended up in the poor house. Captain Charles P. Bowditch of the Fifty-fifth Regiment recalled that an anonymous letter promised that half the regiment would stack arms and do no duty if pay was not received.[38] The Army Appropriation Bill of 1864 helped fix the inequality of pay but problems of back pay due and inequality in bounties still presented a morale problem for the African Americans.[39] The devil was in the details of this act. The bill was retroactive only to 1 January 1864. It applied to persons of color who were free on the 19th day of April 1861, and who had enlisted between December 1862 and 16 June 1864. This left many out. As veteran Joseph T. Wilson put it "In other words, if one half of a company escaped from slavery on 18 April 1861, they are to be paid thirteen dollars per month and allowed three and one half dollars per month for clothing. If the other half delayed two days, they receive seven dollars a month and are allowed three dollars per month for precisely the same articles of clothing."[40]

CHAPTER 6

The Battle of Nashville

Thursday-Friday, 15-16 December 1864

My feet are torn and bloody,
My heart is full of woe,
I'm going back to Georgia
To find my uncle Joe [Johnston].
You may talk about your Beauregard,
You may sing of Bobby Lee,
But the gallant Hood of Texas
Played hell in Tennessee. [1]

Anon

Courtesy of the Library of Congress

General John Bell Hood was born in Kentucky. He enlisted to fight for the Confederacy from his adopted state of Texas. He was a graduate of the United States Military Academy, West Point in the Class of 1853 graduating 44th in a class of 52. He was not brilliant as a cadet or soldier as evidenced by his nickname, "Sam Woodenhead."[2] By 1864 he was still a fairly young man thirty-three years of age, but he had lost the use of an arm due to a wound at Gettysburg and his leg was amputated after he was wounded at the Battle of Chickamauga. There were serious concerns about his ability to command due to these injuries, but he had been an excellent brigade and division commander. Most important, he was a fighter. The problem was that by the end of 1864 he found himself commanding the Army of Tennessee and had risen in rank to a level beyond his competence. His carelessness, lack of attention to logistics, lack of reconnaissance (although he had arguably the best cavalry in the world under Forrest) and lack of preparation would doom any adventure that he planned for his army. He was ill-suited to lead an independent command and the fact that he did may have sealed the fate of the Confederacy.[3]

Grant's plan to end the war in 1864 was simple. He would attack the two main Confederate armies: one in Georgia under Johnston and the other under Lee in Virginia. Grant would attack Lee and Sherman would attack in Georgia.

U. S. Grant
Courtesy of the Library of Congress

W. T. Sherman
Courtesy of the Library of Congress

The key to victory was in Virginia with the seat of the Confederate government in Richmond. In the West, General George Thomas in Nashville was to contain the Confederate army and General Nathan Banks was sent on an expedition up the Red River Valley in Texas.[4] In this way, the Confederacy would be strangled by assaults on all sides. While Grant was stalemated by Lee in Virginia and Sherman split the confederacy in Georgia, the unknown outcome would be in Tennessee.

In the South, earlier in April 1864, Davis had defined his objectives for Tennessee.

First.   To take the enemy at disadvantage while weakened, it is believed, by sending troops to Virginia, and having others absent still on furlough.

Second. To break up his plans by anticipating and frustrating his combinations.

Third.   So to press him here [in Tennessee] as to prevent his heavier massing in Virginia.

Fourth. To beat him, it is hoped, and greatly gain strength in supplies, men, and productive territory.

Fifth.   To prevent the waste of the army incident to inactivity.

Sixth.   To inspire it and the country, and to depress the enemy, involving the greatest results.

Seventh. To obviate the necessity of falling back likely to occur if the enemy be allowed to consummate his own plans.[5]

The fall of Atlanta on 1 September 1864 signaled that the end of the war was near. The South had lost, but President Jefferson Davis and many of his people would fight on. Jefferson Davis on a speaking tour in September told his citizens that he would send Hood and his army West, but he was not clear on exactly what Hood was supposed to do. After much discussion, he ordered Hood to interdict Sherman's supply line. If Sherman attacked, Hood could fall back on Gadsden, Alabama and fight Sherman there.[6] With Hood heading West as advertised by Davis, Grant and Sherman could now consider their options and they had many. Sherman decided to march to the coast and seize Savannah. This would also force Hood to follow since sitting on the Chattanooga to Atlanta railroad would have lost purpose. While Hood was moving at last into Tennessee, Sherman began his march to the sea that would end at Savannah. Sherman and his 60,000 troops marched out of Atlanta on 14 November 1864. They would live off of the land and the supplies that they carried with them. With Hood in the West, there was very little opposition to Sherman's column. The South had surrendered the initiative to Grant and Sherman.[7] On the other hand, a strong Confederate army in Tennessee had endless opportunities to do mischief. Hood preferred to take action without consulting his superiors which was probably prudent given the caliber of his superiors (Davis and Beauregard). The problem with this was that they were not knowledgeable of his plans and could not support his army although Beauregard tried to keep up with Hood's plans.[8]

On 19 November 1864, Nathan Bedford Forrest's cavalry led Hood's army into Tennessee. Hood had about 30,000 infantry and 8,000 cavalry (some say 6,000).[9] They were headed for Nashville and would find themselves hopelessly outnumbered by the Union army in Tennessee.

By November, the weather in Tennessee was bitter and taking a heavy toll on both sides. The Southerners found that they could make an effective shelter by digging a hole in the ground with twigs at the bottom covered by blankets above and below the sleeping soldiers. It reminded one soldier of a grave.[10] Many of the Confederates were without shoes, leaving bloody tracks in the snow. Corporal Jones of the 18th Alabama wrote. "Men were detailed to make shoes whenever leather could be found."[11] The Union had considerable forces available to meet the Hood threat including

General George Thomas
Courtesy of the Library of Congress

General John Schofield
Courtesy of the Library of Congress

General John Schofield and his commander, General George H. Thomas. Schofield was a West Point graduate with the Class of 1853. He ranked 7th in his class of fifty-two that included Hood. At the time of the battle of Nashville, Schofield was thirty-three years of age and had won the Medal of Honor for bravery at the Battle of Wilson's Creek in 1861. Thomas was a Virginian who remained loyal to the Union at the start of the war. He was born in 1816 and at age forty-eight, was one of the oldest generals in the field, but younger than a few generals at Nashville such as A. J. Smith.

General A. J. Smith
Courtesy of the Library of Congress

Thomas was a West Point graduate with the Class of 1840. His classmate was William Tecumseh Sherman who graduated 6th in the class.[12] Thomas ranked 12th in the class of forty-two.[13] His previous successes on the battlefield were at Chickamauga where he held the Union line and his breakthrough at Missionary Ridge. He was slow and deliberate, the opposite of the impulsive Hood. He never had a good relationship with Grant and this hurt him especially in the post-war years when Grant was President. Thomas would have 55,000 troops to oppose Hood and this number was constantly growing.

General Thomas ordered General Schofield South to slow Hood's advance toward Nashville while defenses were improved and Union reinforcements were pouring in.[14] Thomas did not intend that Schofield engage and defeat Hood, but things were moving in that direction.

While Hood was moving to Franklin, two brigades of African American troops were taking up positions to defend Nashville, twenty miles to the North. The two brigades of USCT would serve under General James B. Steedman (also called Steadman).

General James Steedman
Courtesy of the Library of Congress

Steedman was forty-seven years old at this time. He was orphaned at an early age and was a self-made man. He became an Ohio printer, editor and politician who supported Stephen Douglas for the presidency. Although he had no military training, he rose to the rank of general after service as commander of the Fourteenth Ohio Infantry. A big strong man, his troops called him "Old Steady." He, like his commander General Thomas, was a hero of the Battle of Chickamauga. When the Federal line started to disintegrate, he yelled "Go back, boys, go back; but the flag can't go with you!" He then picked up rocks and threw them at the retreating Federals roaring that they must stand and fight. They did! The Confederates were so surprised by his ferocity that they fell back.[15]

Steedman had a dark side and carried baggage to Nashville as did many others on both sides. While he commanded the military post at Chattanooga in 1864 he became in love with a beautiful local lady. Confederate General David S. Stanley believed that he was "so taken up with making love . . . and drinking champagne, that it was difficult to see the great potentate of Chattanooga."[16] As always, good times must end and Steedman would move to Nashville. There is no record of what happened to the beautiful young lady that he left behind or her name. We do not know if she was a Yankee or a Confederate.

At Nashville Steedman was faced with new challenges. By 1864, USCT had proven their valor in a series of earlier battles as seen in Appendix C, but at Nashville the same question remained: would USCT fight? Earlier, Sherman thought not and refused to take USCT in his march to the sea. At Nashville, Steedman had 7,500 troops most of which were black. His problem was that he had a hybrid of one white brigade and two brigades of USCT. It was known as the Provisional Detachment (District of Etowah), not an awe-inspiring name. Francis McKinney, a biographer of George Thomas described the command.

> . . . a hybrid . . . made up of fragments from . . . ill-provided regiments. A large portion were unfit for duty . . . . Some of these troops were not armed until the evening of the fourteenth [December 1864]. Some of the recruits were untrained. Many were unable to speak or understand English. Whatever their shortcomings, Steedman's brigades would not be lacking in numbers, for each brigade was about the size of a Confederate division.[17]

Union General George H. Thomas also carried baggage to Nashville. As a Southerner from Virginia, he was certain that African Americans were well suited to do labor and defend fixed installations, but they could never advance in the open to attack Confederate positions.[18] Colonel Thomas Jefferson Morgan, one of Steedman's commanders, disagreed and told Thomas that they would attack against Confederate guns.[19]

The First Colored Brigade under Colonel Thomas Morgan was composed of the 14th, 16th, 17th and 18th Regiments, USCT. The Second Colored Brigade was commanded by Colonel Charles R. Thompson. He had the 12th, 13th, 100th and some artillery.[20] The 12th, 13th, 17th, and 100th regiments suffered the highest losses of all USCT regiments in the Civil War.[21] The white 3rd Brigade was commanded by Colonel Charles H. Grosvenor. He had the Sixty-eighth

Indiana Regiment as well as Eighteen and Twenty-eighth Ohio with the Second Battalion of the Fourteenth Army Corps.[22]

In the meantime, while General Thomas was preparing for the defense of Nashville, on the 30 November 1864, Schofield stopped near Franklin to repair bridges so that he could move his artillery and wagons across to reach Nashville. Hood was in hot pursuit and without waiting for all of his forces to arrive, he attacked. Schofield dug in South of Franklin with 22,000 troops.[23] A fierce battle ensued, described as one of the bloodiest battles of the Civil War.[24]

The Battle of Franklin
Courtesy of the Library of Congress

Hood's decisive mistake according to Union General James H. Wilson was that he diverted Forrest to a side operation which left the infantry without cavalry support.[25] Like Pickett at Gettysburg, Hood would lose thousands of troops. It may have been the last grand Confederate attack of the war; certainly the last grand hurrah for the Confederate army in the West. One of Schofield's soldiers described what he saw. "It was worth a year of one's lifetime to witness the marshalling and advance of the rebel line of battle at Franklin. Emerging from the woods in the most perfect order, two corps in front and one in reserve, nothing could be more suggestive of strength and discipline, and resistless power than was this long line of gray advancing over the plain."[26]

Hood's attack from the South used the only practical approach since Franklin was surrounded on three sides by the Harpeth River. Forrest, of course, suggested a cavalry strike, but this would not work because Schofield had cavalry on his flanks. Captain John W. Lavender of the 4th Arkansas had a different opinion.

> This Great and Destructive Battle (of Franklin) was the least called for and the most useless sacrifice of men of any that was Fought in . . . Tennessee. As Every Priveet Soldier Saw afterwards, a slight Flank Movement would have Forced the Enemy out of their works without loosing a man. Our Ranks was So Badly Reduced and seing it Brought on by such useless Reckless Generalship Caused Grate Dissatisfaction in our Ranks . . . . (The) men Could see the serious mistakes . . . cost our army such serious loss and no material to recruit from. They could all see that the time was near that our Strength would be exhausted.[27]

Hood was convinced that if he could defeat or get by Franklin, he had an open path to the Ohio River and the north. He, like Lee at Gettysburg, was also convinced that he could break the Union line. The attack was carried out with all of the flair of the Confederate army complete with the band playing "Dixie" and "Bonnie Blue Flag" and the rebel yell in the final assault as the soldiers were mowed down by Schofield's entrenched troops. In this very bloody battle, Hood lost about a third of his infantry because he employed frontal attacks against an entrenched enemy. He would later report losses far less than these, but whichever count one wishes to believe, the losses were staggering. The actual count 1,750 dead or mortally wounded; 5,000 wounded and 300 taken prisoner. Thirteen of his generals and 50 of his colonels were killed. The fact that he had lost many of his subordinate commanders made a casualty count more difficult at that time. His losses included one of his best generals General Patrick R. Cleburne, the Irish immigrant.[28] Schofield lost 500 killed, 1,300 wounded and

1,200 taken prisoner.[29] General Thomas Jordan who served under Forrest described the Confederate attack.

> The ground of approach to the main position was open, with very slight shelter; but on pressed the Confederates, with little halt, after their first success, though now fully aware of the appalling gravity of the work in hand. They were presently met by a broad, desolating tide of musketry, while shot and canister, both from the entrenchments in front and the redoubts on Figuer's Hill, smote down their gallant ranks from flank to flank. The slaughter, indeed, was now deplorable. The enemy, ensconced behind stout breastworks, with almost a single salvo of their numerous artillery swept away entire Confederate regiments, and thinned all the others to a heartrending degree. But with characteristic, unconquerable resolution the survivors-staggered for a moment-still moved forward, and many reached the entrenchments, and in attempting to surmount them were slain. In this fearful onset the first line of the Confederates had been almost annihilated. A second and indeed a third line were, nevertheless, brought up, and thrown forward with kindred hardihood to meet, as might be expected, the same sanguinary reception, the same repulse with gaping ranks ravaged of their best officers and men.[30]

An Alabaman had seen the Confederate losses and reported: "I have seen many battlefields, but none equal to this. The ground in front of the works . . . is covered with dead bodies and the ditch in front is filled with them." He added that his regiment could muster but thirty men.[31] The Union also suffered losses. Confederate Corporal Edward W. Jones inspected the Union trenches after the battle and later wrote.

> I went round and inspected the line of works, and looked at the dead Yankees as they lay in heaps upon heaps in the ditches. I never witnessed such destruction of life anywhere else, not even in the open. Here in splendid works lay the dead as many as five piled on each other and this, too, for long distances . . . . Our men looking upon this dreadful carnage in good breastworks were more or less demoralized by it. We had concluded that we were almost invulnerable to bullets

when we were in breastworks. We had been charged so often and especially during the Dalton-Atlanta campaign, without much loss to ourselves that we had concluded that men in good breastworks could not be hurt much. This slaughter of men behind works at Franklin was an eye-opener to us and I noticed that our men were not near so confident after looking upon this awful destruction of human life.[32]

Hood had limited choices. If he fell back he would be trapped between Thomas and Sherman in Georgia who was completing his march to the sea and could easily double back. Perhaps if he moved to Nashville he could break Thomas's line and push north.

As the winter sun rose on 1 December 1864 Hood looked at the destruction in front of Franklin and technically could claim victory since Schofield had abandoned the field, but Hood knew it was a disaster and now needed to plan his next move. He finally decided to move on Nashville and dig in before the well-fortified position of Thomas. He would then see what Thomas would do. If attacked, Hood could defend himself. Hood had apparently not read the maxim attributed to Napoleon: "a passive defense is deferred suicide." It would also be suicide to attack Thomas who had plenty of time to turn Nashville into a greater fortress than it already was. Also, Thomas was gaining forces daily and would soon outnumber Hood by two to one. Hood had high hopes of reinforcements but would receive none. Hood would later state that he had over 23,000 troops available after the Franklin disaster. Thomas had the IV Army Corps under General Wood, Schofield's XXIII Corps, and A. J. Smith's XVI Corps. Additionally, he had the usual assortment of cooks and bottle washers who could stop what they were doing and man the line if needed. Most important, he had General Wilson's Cavalry Corps that could screen and go Forrest-hunting, as required.[33] Wilson started with a few nags as his supply of horses and built that up with the help of Thomas to a respectable cavalry force of thousands before the Battle of Nashville. Lieutenant Colonel Rusling, Chief Assistant Quartermaster of the Department of the Cumberland described how this happened.

> Thomas . . . had plenty of cavalrymen, . . . but only about half enough horses . . . and others were not to be had . . .

in the regular way, within the required time. To get them from the North, by purchase and requisition, might take a month or longer . . . . So he issued an order to seize and impress all serviceable horses within our lines, in Tennessee and Kentucky, . . . and within a week he had his dismounted cavalrymen remounted . . . . I think this 'seizure' resulted in over 7,000 horses.[34]

Union supply was the decisive factor. Hood had no such luxury. He had what he left with before crossing the Tennessee River. For Hood it was a "come as you are" campaign with no hope of gaining anything later. There were no great supply trains following him to resupply and reequip his army. In the trenches before Nashville, Lieutenant Stewart of the 49th Ohio summarized. "Rebs rep. Coming, . . . Our end of the lines naturally pretty strong and making it stronger. If they wait a little we will mow them like everything." [35]

The Confederacy was on its knees and falling apart. Hood took the only action that he could in this situation and started digging in just south of Nashville. He was hoping that Thomas would make a mistake as he attacked and provide Hood with an opportunity to destroy Thomas's army. Hood would later justify his decision. "Thus, unless strengthened by these long looked for reinforcements, the only remaining chance of success in the campaign at this juncture was to take position, entrench around Nashville and await Thomas's attack which, if handsomely repulsed, might afford us an opportunity to follow up our advantage on the spot and enter the city on the heels of the enemy."[36]

Hood moved out on the morning of 1 December in pursuit of Schofield. For both sides, it was a bitter cold march to Nashville. Private John Lord of the 72nd Illinois recalled. "An officer got off his horse and told me to get on, saying that I was a tired-looking boy. I didn't ride far until I went to sleep and fell off the horse and rolled twenty feet down an embankment. I crawled back up the bank and got on the horse again and I didn't fall off again. It isn't any wonder that I went to sleep. I had lain down for only two hours in three days and nights.[37]

Union Captain Pressnall later wrote. "As our company . . . was passing through the town of Franklin, a woman came running from a house into the street at the rear of our company, screaming at the top of her voice—'The Yanks are retreating'—over and over—'The Yanks are retreating.' At once amidst her wild screaming, one of my company . . . stepped quickly to her and with the muzzle of his gun within two or three feet of her body, shot her through the heart, returning instantly to his place in the ranks."[38]

Schofield arrived in Nashville and took up positions selected by Thomas just before noon. Mary M. Claiborne, a young resident south of Nashville recalled.

> The Federal army poured into Nashville. The rumble of wagons and artillery was unceasing. Two Yankee guards, who had been detailed from the Federal headquarters for the protection of the family, from stragglers, were at the house. One of them was induced, by Miss (Annie Armstrong) Maxwell (Mrs. Overton's sister), . . . to put upon his cap the insignia of . . . captain of the United States Army. When Captain Claiborne resigned his commission in the U.S. Army to fight for the South, Mrs. Claiborne had stored these relics in her trunk . . . . (The guard) was thus decorated and stood at the smokehouse door. Stragglers and looters recognized his rank and would exclaim from time to time, 'A captain, by G—, guarding these d-Rebels.'[39]

The Confederate prisoners were paraded through town. Copley of the 49th Tennessee recalled.

> We arrived . . . before noon . . . hungry and tired. Many of the prisoners were barefooted and could have been easily tracked by the marks of blood behind them. We were ragged, dirty and blood-bespattered . . . . We were paraded on the capitol grounds. We were kept on public exhibition for five or six hours, and near five thousand people came out to view us. Amongst the number "'was the noted Andrew Johnson, afterwards President of the United States, who greeted this little handful of half-starved, unarmed and defenseless men with a volume of abuse and vituperation; of course, he could afford to do this and be in no danger while we were enclosed by a wall of . . . bayonets . . . . A majority of the citizens who came to look at us were ladies. They were not allowed to approach nearer than the bayonet's point of the double

chain-guard of Federal troops who were between us and them, nor permitted to exchange any words with us. But we saw their looks of tenderness and affection . . . . We were . . . ordered away, ... to the enclosure of the outer dismal walls of the State penitentiary.[40]

On 2 December, Hood's army deployed on the hills south of Nashville and started to dig in. It was drizzling rain. As Thomas was preparing to attack, Hood committed a colossal blunder: he dispatched most of Forrest's cavalry and a division of infantry to besiege a Union force dug-in at Murfreesboro thirty miles South of Nashville. This made no sense at all and some say that Hood was suffering from the use of laudanum [the pain-killer of the day] to treat his old wounds when he made this decision. Hood set up positions on hills several miles South of Nashville. Without Forrest and the infantry that went with him, Hood was left with 23,000 men in his lines South of Nashville and no effective force of cavalry. Forrest took some prisoners at Murfreesboro and seized some supplies but did no serious damage. He then went off raiding and tearing up track as the Battle of Nashville was being fought. Margaret L. Lindsley wrote.

> The Forrest panic . . . was unfounded it seems, but still the soldiers are here, and still destruction at least goes bravely on! Barns, stables, fences all gone now, and the sound of cutting and falling of our glorious forest trees heard from morning till night! Beautiful Edgefield no longer! Her beauty and her pride laid low in these her superb trees. For from the river to Springside there is not a grove left! The bareness and the bleakness are simply intolerable, and make me sick. Whenever I go out on the balcony from my room, I just break down at seeing all those ugly stumps where were our beautiful 'woods.' [41]

Forrest would return to Hood several days after the battle but on 15 December, Hood was outnumbered by about three to one.[42] Hood did his best to improve his defensive position while Thomas planned and prepared for his attack on Hood. Confederate Lieutenant R. M. Collins remembered. "The line on which our brigade was placed was a high, open field. From it we could see the spires, domes, parapets and minarets of the capital city of Tennessee . . . . Around about the high points of the city on the south were many forts and . . . big, black-mouthed cannon pointing our way." [43]

Both armies settled in digging and skirmishing that would last for two weeks while Grant fumed and poked Thomas to attack. Confederate Chaplain McNeilly wrote. "We were scantily clothed; many of us were practically barefooted . . . . My own footgear consisted of a pair of socks almost footless, and the uppers and soles of my shoes were tied together with strings."[44]

Sergeant Broughton of the 21st Illinois recalled. "Soon the Rebels began to come in sight on the top of a hill about half mile from us. As each regiment gained the top of the hill they had a good view of the city. They would halt for a moment and cheer, then file to the right or left and go into position."[45]

Union Private W. A. Keesy of the 64th Ohio recalled. "Our line of works "were run right through (the grounds of) a princely mansion (Belmont) on our company front. The fine lace curtains on gilded windows, with costly upholstery, rich furniture, and Brussels carpets, all spoke of great wealth. But the certain indications of an engagement by the two great armies now confronting each other again, made it too perilous for the occupants and they moved out. Our officers occupied the principal rooms for offices." [46]

Private Huntzinger of the 79th Indiana wrote. "I & 7 men of our comp was detailed for Picket & went out at 5 A.M. before daylight. The rebels was near & we skirmished all day with them & they shot near us & our artillery put the shells & some sollad shot into some of their skirmish Pits & tore their works . . . . I saw a rebel getting in his gofer hole & I shot in a hurry & my gun kicked me in the mouth & split my lip." [47]

Sergeant Dunham of the 12th Iowa wrote. "To us it is nothing new but still it looks beautiful. Every hill and vale is lighted up by the camp fires, On one hill can be seen our signal lights and occasionally (you) can see the flash from the gunboats as they discharge their contents into the enemies camp."[48]

Hood's army did its best to stop Union supplies to Nashville on the Cumberland River while at the same time replenishing Confederate supplies. Confederate Private A. C. McLeary of the 12th Tennessee wrote.

> When we got in sight of the river we saw a transport boat coming down from Nashville. We at once left our horses and ran for the river to stop that boat . . . . We were now very hungry and ready for the good things to eat that those boats carried; but in running over those rocks and vines I sprained my ankle so badly I did not see how I could live much longer. After the boat ran by, Col. D C. Kelley came back to me, sent for my horse, and they put me on him. I rode to a house nearby, got my ankle fixed up, and while I was there another boat ran by; but we had two cannons ready, for the third one, and it surrendered. I rode to where it landed.[49]

Boredom settled in on both sides but this was about to change. Union Private Huntzinger wrote. "We was awaked at 4 A.M. & told that there was a rumor afloat that a spie had said Hood's army was coming in to atak us at daylight. We was relieved & returned to camp at 5 A.M." [50]

On 8 December the weather turned colder. Lieutenant Fike of the 117th Illinois wrote. "Last evening the weather changed, very suddenly, from a pleasant temperature to real wintry weather; but I slept good and warm in my bed of hay. John McGowan and I are bedfellows—he has, among things, a good soft Mackinaw blanket, which we put next to us; and then come my old 'comfort' which is a real comfort, with other blankets in abundance."[51]

Nearby, Captain Hempstead of the 2nd Michigan Cavalry had a similar reaction.

> I sit down in my tent to write shivering with cold although bundled up in hat and overcoat . . . . We have been having a very acceptable rest since we came here. I was on duty for two consecutive days as officer of the day at the bridge crossing to Nashville, and as all passes had to be closely scrutinized to prevent any spies or other informers getting in on forged passes, and my guard being Ken. And Tenn. hardly a man of them could read a word and I had to be in

constant attendance night and day. Worse than that, as 1 only expected to stay one day I took no rations and . . . (was) not able to get away to get a meal.[52]

On the other side of the line, the Confederates wrote of their discomfort. Private William J. Worsham of the 19th Tennessee wrote. "The driving wind rendered it the more uncomfortable. We were out in the open fields on an elevation, without protection from the wintry blasts, and were thinly clad—many of us without shoes—with nothing whatever to keep our sore and bleeding feet from the cold and frozen ground." [56]

Cold weather continued. Corporal Edgar W. Jones of the 18th Alabama wrote. "The weather was bitter cold. We were scarce of food and clothing. Many men were still bare-footed, and more becoming so every day. There were no blankets except the ones we carried all the summer . . . . I had but one, and that had eighteen bullet holes in it." [57]

In the meantime, on 13 December, Sherman seized Savannah and Grant was becoming more impatient with Thomas asking for his removal because he had not attacked Hood. Added to Thomas's problem was the fact that Schofield was a disloyal schemer who was sending cables to Halleck (the Union's General-in-Chief) and Grant distorting information in the hope that Thomas would be fired and Schofield would take over command.[55] Grant continually pushed Thomas to move faster and Thomas, in his slow methodical manner, went at his own pace. He was also hampered by bad weather that delayed everything. Most important, Thomas was building up a superior cavalry force under General James H. Wilson. Wilson was 6th in his 1860 class of forty-one at West Point. He would later serve in the Spanish-American War in 1898. Wilson's cavalry was being equipped with the seven-shot Spencer repeating cartridge carbines that were far superior to the muzzle loading single shot rifles used by both the North and the South.[56] By mid-December Wilson had over 12,000 men and they would be used differently from other cavalry as will be seen in the battle that followed.[57] Finally, Thomas notified Grant that he planned to start his attack on Hood the next day and so he was allowed to remain in command. It was Wednesday, 14 December 1864 and while the generals worried about attack plans, the soldiers were focused on the weather. Union Lieutenant

Thoburn of the 50th Ohio remarked. "Rain set in during the night and the ice is gone. We now have mud in abundance."[58]

On the other side, J. P. Cannon of the 27th Alabama wrote. "The weather has moderated, and we enjoy lying around in the sun, but the Yanks won't let us enjoy it long at a time, for when they see a squad of us they drop over a few shells and we dart into our holes like prairie dogs." [59]

The word was out. The attack would be tomorrow. Private Smith of the 51st Illinois wrote.

> The die is cast, ready or not. Thomas must strike on the morrow. Orders are out that everything must be ready to attack in the morning; orders of instruction for each division and brigade are being sent, and the rank and file are notified. Many of the men set themselves down to write to their homes in the north, some to their families, some to their sweet hearts; . . . no one knows who shall be taken, or who shall be left.[60]

This would be very much like trench warfare during World War I.

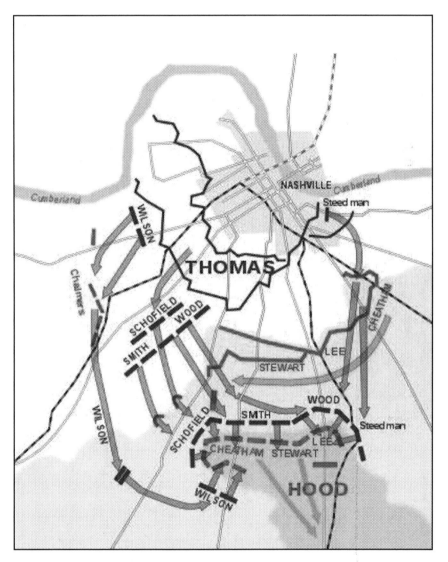

The Battle of Nashville

Courtesy of Jacob Dolson Cox

The Battle of Nashville—The First Day

Thursday, 15 December 1864

The Battle of Nashville opened on the morning of 15 December 1864 after the fog burned off. It was a two day affair. Thomas planned to make a secondary attack on Hood's right flank while the main attack would strike Hood's left flank that was exposed because Forrest had departed. T. J. Hunt of the 10th Minnesota offered the best tribute to Thomas. "Thomas still delayed. He was threatened by Grant and others, but would not sacrifice his men . . . . "Pap" Thomas, the men called him. He had spared them; he had earned their confidence and they his, as well. Hood was better protected as was Lee's army in the wilderness and the fighting was equally severe."[61]

Thomas had the superior forces to make this work. General Steedman commanded against Hood's right and his command included the two brigades of African American troops under Colonel Morgan and Colonel Charles R. Thompson.[62]

The Union troops did not know what they were up against. The night before, Colonel Morgan had slipped up to the Confederate defenses and observed what he thought was a curtain of logs that could be easily overrun. Actually, it was a heavily dug in position with a protective ditch (a deep railroad cut) in the front.[63] Morgan had hoped to surprise the Rebels, but they were well aware of the Union army's advance. Private Charles Martin of the 1st Georgia Volunteers watched the advance of the African American regiments.

> A body of troops was observed on our right moving in the direction of the rear of our position, . . . Half an hour later it was known to be a division of negro troops. Every man was on the alert, as this was the first time our corps was to come in contact with negro soldiers. Seeing that their route of march would bring them across the railroad below the end of the cut, it was decided to make a trap for them, and they were allowed to come on unmolested. After crossing the railroad the darkies formed a line of battle, and . . . prepared to surprise the men in our works by an attack in the rear . . . When they had moved forward far enough to enable our

brigade to form in their rear, one of the divisions in the works about-faced, and the other did likewise and wheeled to the left. We had the negroes in our trap; and when we commenced firing on them, complete demoralization followed . . . . Many jumped into the cut, and were either killed or crippled.[64]

The Confederates were enraged to see African Americans advancing against them. The Confederates were prepared to fall upon and destroy the USCT. Confederate Charles Martin remembered "Everyman was on the alert. This was the first time that our corps had come in contact with negro soldiers."[65]

The United States Colored Troops led the assault on Hood's right flank. To make sure that they advanced a line of white Yankees with bayonets fixed followed behind the USCT to make sure that they "kept to their work."[66] This was quite unnecessary since it would be the whites not the Blacks that fled. "The troops were full of enthusiasm and the splendid array in which the advance was made gave hopeful promise of success. Near the foot of the ascent the assaulting force dashed forward for the last great effort . . . . When near, however, the enemy works, his reserves on the slope of the hill rose and poured in a fire before which no troops could live."[67] It was a perfect slaughter pen. The Confederates rose up and delivered a devastating wall of fire when the USCT were a hundred feet from the Confederate position. The deep railroad cut limited maneuver and made the situation worse. Samuel Cook wrote in his diary "We did not give them any quarter."[68]

The Federals attacking Hood's right flank were driven back in disorder. Union Sergeant Haworth described what he saw.

We got the word that General Steedman's division of colored troops were going to charge on the rebel works. Just about noon the big guns in Fort Negley commenced shelling the rebel works in front of Steadman's troops then all of our artillery to our left joined us. We all got out where we could see. That lasted for about one hour then they all quit and then we could see Steedman's division in two lines of battle with fixed bayonets charge across the little valley. They got up close to the rebel fort but finally had to come back. Twice that day they went under a flag of truce and brought off their dead and wounded.[69]

On the first day, the Union plan to deceive Hood into thinking that the main attack was on his right was not working. On Hood's left, the advancing Union infantry swarmed up the hills and Hood's line started to collapse. Thomas had concentrated overwhelming combat power on Hood's left. As the Union troops overwhelmed Hood's left, Sergeant James R. Maxwell, a Confederate gunner described the chaos.

> When the charging Federals passed my gun on the left of the redoubt, Lieutenant Hargrove ordered us to leave it. I ran towards Captain Lumsden's section, where Sergeant Jim Jones had turned No.2 to fire canister at the Federals who were near gun NO.4. He called to me 'Look out, Jim!'. I dropped on hands and knees whilst he fired that canister right over my head . . . . I went down past Mr. Castleman's house, in front of which Captain Lumsden was reporting to General Stewart, who was congratulating Captain Lumsden for detaining the advance of the Federals so long . . . . Hilen L. Rosser, one of our gunners had had part of his head shot away. That night as I was pouring some water for Lumsden to wash, he was picking something out of his beard and said: 'Maxwell, that is part of Rosser's brains.'[70]

Wilson with 12,000 cavalry swung around Hood's left flank, and positioned his cavalry to Hood's left rear to prepare for the next day's action.[71] Darkness saved Hood's army from destruction and he backed away from Thomas to establish a new line on the Harpeth Hills a few miles to their rear. The first day of the Battle of Nashville was clearly a Union victory. That night everyone became a fan of George Thomas as he sent out his report of the day's action.

> I attacked the enemy's left this morning and drove it from the river, below the city, very nearly to the Franklin pike, a distance about eight miles. Have captured General Chalmers' headquarters and train, and a second train of about 20 wagons, with between 800 and 1,000 prisoners and 16 pieces of artillery. The troops behaved splendidly, all taking their

share in assaulting and carrying the enemy's breast-works. I shall attack the enemy again tomorrow, if he stands to fight, and, if he retreats during the night, will pursue him, throwing a heavy cavalry force in his rear, to destroy his trains, if possible. And, ever the dutiful family man, he telegraphed to his wife in New York: "We have whipped the enemy, taken many prisoners and considerable artillery."[72]

Stanton, the Secretary of War, as soon as he received the news, graciously telegraphed Thomas: "I rejoice in tendering to you and the gallant officers and soldiers of your command the thanks of this Department for the brilliant achievements of this day, and hope that it is the harbinger of a decisive victory, that will crown you and your army with honor and do much toward closing the war. We shall give you a hundred guns [a salute, not a firing squad] in the morning."[73] Grant also sent a telegram of congratulations, saying that "I was just on my way to Nashville" when he received the news, but "I shall go no farther." He went on: "Push the enemy now, and give him no rest until he is entirely destroyed. Your army will cheerfully suffer many privations to break up Hood's army and render it useless for further operations. Do not stop for trains or supplies, but take them from the country as the enemy have done. Much is now expected." The next morning President Lincoln telegraphed "the nation's thanks"; and, having seen too many battles start splendidly and then fizzle added: "You made a magnificent beginning. A grand consummation is within your easy reach. Do not let it slip."[74]

The day was a disaster for Hood. Private Lord of the 72nd Illinois wrote. "We captured some (Confederates) . . . who wanted to quit and why shouldn't they want to quit? No one of them had enough clothes to wad a single-barreled shotgun and many of them had nothing on their feet but any old rags that they could get hold of . . . . Some had old worn out shoes that let their feet on to the snow and ice and many of them left blood in their tracks."[75]

On the other side, Captain Lavener of the 4th Arkansas wrote. "Just about the time we had things all scattered out on the Ground to Do some cooking and cleaning up Fireing Commenced about 400 yards west of us."[76]

Lieutenant Colonel C. Irvine Walker commanding the 10th South Carolina stated the hopelessness of the situation.

> We got into some rough hilly country and were formed in line. Field Officers were not allowed to go into actual battle mounted, so . . . I dismounted. We were moved forward on a double quick for about a mile and debouched from the woods into an open country. The whole face of creation seemed to be covered with bluecoats. I counted flags to estimate their strength until I was tired . . . . One little Brigade attacking a force many times as large! We butt against the stone wall of living, shooting bluecoats and were easily driven back and followed. Lieut. Col. Butler, 28th Ala., . . . was wounded in the attack, which threw the command of the Brigade to me. I was completely exhausted and when Deas' Brigade came up, the relief was so great that I fell as if wounded—numbers of my men rushed to help me . . . . I could not rise, so sent word to Gen. Deas as to what I knew and begged him not to go on. He did not heed my message. So I got up, staggered to him and suggested that he place his Brigade on a nearby hill, and that I would place Manigault's Brigade in his rear and rest my men and support him on either flank as the attack developed. "I told him if he would just wait there for a short time he would get all the fighting he wanted without going to seek it. He accepted my advice. The Adjutant General of the Brigade then rode up on Butler's horse, and I made him dismount and give me the horse . . . A Maj. Mitchell, I believe Chief of Artillery of Gen. Stewart's Corps, brought up a section of Artillery and placed them on the hill. He had a long red beard and behaved with so much coolness and gallantry that he impressed me.[77]

There was much bitterness about the performance of the Confederate infantry on the first day of the battle. Sergeant Eggleston of Cowan's Mississippi wrote.

> We . . . lost our guns & horses. The infantry ran like cowards and the miserable wretches who were to have supported us refused to fight and ran like a herd of stampeded cattle. I blush for my countrymen and despair of the independence of the Confederacy if her reliance is placed in the army of Tennessee to accomplish it.

There are ten men from the batty missing supposed to be killed or captured . . . . All of the Co. papers and records were lost, and all of my blankets, and rations. Expect to freeze this winter.[78]

Hood had an enormous task on the night of 15-16 December. Thomas thought that Hood would retreat, but that thought apparently never entered Hood's mind. Hood was right: it was probably better to fight it out now, hope for a break, and invade the North than be crushed later by an overwhelming Union force. He decided to reestablish his army on a new line of defense factoring into this the significant losses of the day's battle and the absence of Forrest to screen his flanks. His new line had to be shortened and this was probably his downfall as will be seen.

Confederate Captain Gale of Stewart's Corps summarized what many were thinking. "As our men fell back before the advancing Yankees, Mary Bradford . . . under heavy fire . . . did all she could to induce the men to stop and fight, appealing to them and begging them, but in vain." [79]

As night fell, Private Lord of the 72nd Illinois later wrote. "George, my Bunkie, made a fire and I went back into the field to look for water. We remembered a little drain of surface water in the field. I took our canteens and coffee pot and found a pool and filled everything. The weather was moderating and the snow and ice were melting. The water was good and cold to drink and made good coffee." [80]

On the Union side that night Major General Cox of Schofield's Corps summarized. "Hood now realized the mistake . . . (of allowing) Forrest to become so far detached that he could not be recalled in time for the battle . . . . The *cavalry* was too far away to join him in twenty-four hours, but orders were dispatched recalling Forrest, and preparations were made to hold the new line another day."[81]

The Battle of Nashville—The Second Day

Friday, 16 December 1864

For God's sake, drive the Yankee cavalry
from our left and rear or all is lost. [82]

John B Hood

It was afternoon on 16 December 1864 before Thomas's attack against the Confederate line could begin. Thomas had to carefully plan (as he always did) and then move forward on Hood's new position. The Union troops had waited in freezing cold since early morning. Private Lord of the 7nd Illinois wrote.

> I went back to get some more water, and about twenty feet above where I got the water (last night) a man shot through the head lay with his head in the little stream. I called George. We didn't say much . . . . I can't say that I was really sick but I felt queer, and George said he did. George looked sick, and he said I did. We didn't have any coffee that morning and we didn't drink any water. [83]

General A. J. Smith was becoming impatient with the lack of action by Thomas on the 16th and one of his division commanders, General McArthur decided on his own to attack. His units were positioned against the left center of the Confederate position. On Hood's right flank, USCT were preparing to attack.

General John McArthur—The Immigrant from
Scotland wearing his Tam

Courtesy of the Library of Congress

Private Cannon of the 27th Alabama recalled. "It is seldom the case that an army is in worse condition for meeting its enemy . . . than ours is at this time . . . . As soon as the sun had dispelled the morning mists we could see two lines of blue drawn up before us, while the artillery from its commanding position was dealing death and destruction in our thinned ranks." [84]

On the other side, Private Underwood of the 9th Indiana wrote. "We . . . commenced shelling their works with our battery, the 3rd Indiana, and the 2nd Illinois . . . . We run our battery right up on the Reble skirmish line and . . . fired . . . . The enemy had their batteries behind good fortifications. We kept up such a heavy fire on them that they could not use their guns at times, but lay close behind their works." [85]

The second day of the Battle of Nashville was in many respects a rerun of the previous day. Sam Woodenhead was not a fast learner.

Again, Wilson's cavalry moved around Hood's left flank, dismounted and delivered a withering fire on the Confederates in Hood's rear. Wilson intercepted a message from Hood to his rear guard commander and reported.

> In the midst of the heaviest fighting, one of our detachments captured a courier from Hood, carrying a dispatch to Chalmers, directing him 'for God's sake to drive the Yankee cavalry from our left and rear or all is lost'. Regarding this dispatch as of the first importance, I sent it at once to Thomas without even making a copy of it . . . . I rode around the enemy's left flank to Thomas's headquarters, which I found on the turnpike about two miles from my own. This was between three and four o'clock, and as it was a cloudy, rainy day, it was already growing dark . . . . I urged Thomas, with ill-concealed impatience, to order the infantry forward without further delay. Pausing only to ask me if I was sure that the men entering the left of the enemy's works above us were mine, and receiving the assurance that I was dead certain of it, he turned to Schofield and as calmly as if on parade directed him to move to the attack with his entire corps.[86]

As one Confederate soldier said "The Yankee bullets were coming from all directions passing one another in flight."[87] Colonel Henry Stone on Thomas's staff described the Union attack on Hood's left and its result.

> It was more like a scene in a spectacular drama than a real incident in war. The hillside in front, still green, dotted with the boys in blue swarming up the slope; the dark background of high hills beyond; the lowering clouds; the waving flags; the smoke slowly rising through the leafless tree-tops and drifting across the valleys; the wonderful outburst of musketry; the ecstatic cheers; the multitude racing for life down into the valley below-so exciting was it all that the lookers-on instinctively clapped their hands as at a brilliant and successful transformation scene, as indeed it was. For in those few minutes an army was changed into a mob, and the

whole structure of the rebellion in the southwest, with all its possibilities, was utterly overthrown.[88]

Steedman's brigades of USCT again attacked Hood's right flank while Steedman's white regiments were driven back. The flight of the white regiments under Steedman enabled the Confederates to concentrate their fire on the two African American Brigades with divesting results. Corporal Jones of the 18th Alabama described the advance of the USCT. "Just before the negroes entered the open we turned loose a volley. They fell like wheat before a mowing machine. They wavered, staggered and in confusion they fled . . . . The ground was literally blue with dead and wounded . . . . In no time we heard the confusion and noise and cursing and urging forward again, and we discovered they were coming for a second dose of lead pills and blue whistlers. Again we held our fire until they approached the open." [89] The USCT had lost 552 casualties in two days, but this time their charge seized the objective.[90] Private Henry Campbell, bugler of the 18th Indiana described the scene on Hood's left flank.

> I got permission from the Col. to go out & see the battle field . . . during the fight. "'I rode up on this conical hill (Shy's Hill) immediately after the charge. Thirteen of our men lay dead on a spot not 20 ft. square—just as they came over the hill—which was so steep I could not ride up horseback. Behind the earth works—dead rebels lay thick with their haggard, powder begrimed faces turned up to the sky.'" On top of the hill where I stood the rebel battery was placed and an old 'virginia wagon' filled with ammunition—which had just come up to replenish the battery. The mules were standing quietly in the midst of so much noise. The gunners escaped on their horses as soon as they seen all was up with their line.[91]

On Hood's right flank, Adjutant Cope of the 15th Ohio moved forward after the attack he described the scene. "We passed over the same ground and saw the dead black men lying side by side with their white comrades. It was the first time the soldiers of our command had seen colored troops in action, and it was said, 'they fought just like white soldiers, with this difference,—that when a black man was wounded and went to the rear he held on to his gun, while the white soldier dropped or threw his aside."[92]

The USCT attack persuaded Hood to reinforce his right flank since he thought that this was the main attack.[93] This was a decisive error. By reinforcing his right from his troops on the left, he allowed the Yankee main attack to pour through the left and attack his rear while the USCT broke through on the right, defeating the Confederate army. The valor of USCT was a key factor in winning the battle and perhaps the war.

The USCT Breakthrough
Courtesy of the Library of Congress

As Thomas rode across the battlefield after Hood had been beaten, he saw Union soldiers black and white where they had fallen in battle. To his staff he said "Gentlemen, the issue has been settled! Negroes will fight!" As the U. S. Colored Regiments marched past him in pursuit of Hood, Thomas turned his horse, removed his hat in a mark of respect and watched as they filed past.[94] Later that night, Wilson was overtaken by Thomas who pulled abreast of him in the dark and said "Dang it to hell, Wilson, didn't I tell you we could lick 'em."[95]

The battle was a disaster for the Confederacy. Five thousand Confederate troops surrendered in one hour. They had had enough. Hood's army was destroyed and Nashville was the last offensive action of the Confederacy in the West. Private Martin of the 1st Georgia Volunteers described the desperate retreat. "We saw demoralization in the extreme. Riding down the pike about a mile, we saw General Hood, with other commanding officers, trying to rally the men, but in vain. I saw one man who had been stopped by General Cheatham dodge beneath the General's horse and continue on his way while the General was trying to rally others."[96]

As Hood's army fled South, bad weather and the arrival of Forrest's cavalry covered their retreat. Both sides were exhausted by nightfall on 16 December. Union Sergeant Haworth of the 3rd Tennessee wrote.

> We tore out the rails and logs of the rifle pits and made fires and I was getting something to eat. I saw a rebel soldier boy crawling up to my fire. He had been shot through the leg. His leg was broken when I got to him he looked up and saw on the front of my cap the letters 3rd Tenn. Volentier Inft. He threw up his hand and said 'for God's Sake don't kill me.' I told him there was no occasion to kill him for the war would be over before he would be able to fight any more. He said their officers told them that us Tennessee soldiers killed all the prisoners that we captured. I got him up close to the fire, divided coffee and grub with him. Got a gum blanket; spread it over him to keep the rain off. I rolled up my blanket and slept all night. Was worn out never slept any last night.[97]

Both armies struggled through the bad weather and headed South as the year 1864 came to a close. Hood's army was now a disorganized rabble unlikely to fight, if cornered. On Christmas Day, the lead elements of Hood's army reached the Tennessee River and crossed in to Mississippi on pontoon bridges. Thomas ended his pursuit on 27 December.[98] This ended Hood's army. It had disintegrated. Hood resigned his command and would never command troops again. Tennessee was secured for the Union. The heroes of the battle were Thomas, and his African American brigades. Thomas had the advantage of superior numbers and a supply system that could not be matched, but Hood led his troops in a desperate attempt to save the Confederacy that failed. It was now a little more than three months before the surrender of Lee at Appomattox.

Today, urban sprawl has engulfed the Nashville battle field and there are few monuments to the battle that may have been the most significant of the Civil War. The battle monument dedicated in 1927 was destroyed by a tornado and construction of the interstate obstructed public view of the site. Union general Joshua Chamberlain, the hero of Gettysburg who was present at the surrender of General R. E. Lee visited Appomattox years after the surrender and found it in ruins. He was quoted as saying that "You could hardly expect the South to build monuments to their defeat." So it was for Nashville.

EPILOGUE

This epilogue provides the history of the lives of the key participants in this book after 1865.

Alexander T. Augusta taught at Howard University after the war. At his death in 1890, he was the first African American officer to be buried at Arlington National Cemetery in a plot separate from the white officers.

Nathan Banks the "*Bobbin Boy*" from Massachusetts was so named because he had gone to work at an early age in a cotton mill superintended by his father. He was born in Waltham, Massachusetts on 30 January 1816. He was elected to the Massachusetts legislature and he was later elected governor of the state. Lincoln appointed him general in the Union army in 1861. A series of military failures by Banks followed his appointment as general but he contributed greatly to recruiting, morale, money and propaganda to the Union cause. After the war, he was elected to the House of Representatives where he served successive terms. He retired and died in Waltham on 1 September 1894. He was buried in Grove Hill Cemetery.[1]

Clara Barton was born on Christmas Day, 1821 in North Oxford, Massachusetts. She founded the American Red Cross. Barton started as a teacher and then moved to Washington, D. C. where she was employed as a clerk in the Patent Office. She was the first woman to receive a substantial government position and the first to receive a salary equal to men. The men complained and her job was reduced to copyist and then eliminated under the Buchanan administration. She started nursing shortly after the start of the Civil War and rose to the "Lady in Charge" of hospitals in the Union Army on the James. After the war she traveled in Europe returning to found the American Red Cross and serve at its first president in 1881. She died on 12 April 1912 in Glen Echo, Maryland and is buried in North Cemetery in Oxford, Massachusetts.

Nick Biddle
Courtesy of the Library of Congress

Nick Biddle, the first casualty of the Civil War, was an African American soldier wounded by the Confederate mob attack on Union soldiers in Baltimore on 18 April 1861. The soldiers were marching to the train that would take them to Washington, D. C. Before the attack, one of Biddle's fellow soldiers joked with him and asked if he was afraid that the mob would capture him and sell him into slavery in Georgia. Biddle was not amused and replied that he was going to Washington trusting in the Lord and that he did not fear the devil himself or a bunch of thugs in Baltimore. As he marched through Baltimore, Private Biddle of the Washington Artillery was singled out by the mob because he was an African American. The mob shouted "Nigger in Uniform." A rain of bricks showered down on the Pennsylvania unit and Biddle took a hit in the head, but he and his comrades made it to the railroad station and then to Washington. When they arrived in Washington, Lincoln greeted the Pennsylvanians and allegedly shook hands with Biddle. Biddle survived the war but died in poverty in 1876. His white comrades made sure that he was properly honored and buried.

Benjamin Butler was born on 5 November 1818 in Deerfield, New Hampshire and was well known as a Massachusetts politician who gained flag rank during the Civil War. He did great service for Blacks as seen in this book, but he is best remembered for his general order that stated that any females in New Orleans that disrespected Union soldiers would be treated as prostitutes. From that he got the nickname "Beast Butler." He was fired by Grant in January 1865 after his defeat at Fort Fisher. After the war he served in Congress as a Radical Republican and participated in the Impeachment of President Andrew Johnson. He wrote the initial draft of the Civil Rights Act of 1871 which later passed after a less sweeping bill was written and this was signed into law by President Grant. Butler died in Washington, D. C. on 11 January 1893 and was buried in the family plot in Lowell, Massachusetts.[2]

John Julian Chisolm (*also known as Julian John Chisolm*) was born in Charleston, South Carolina on 16 April 1830. He received his degree from the Medical College of the State of South Carolina in 1850. Shortly after the start of the war he published *A Manual of Military Surgery for use by Surgeons in the Confederate States*. He was appointed to the rank of surgeon in the Confederate States Army and worked to collect plants that could be used to replace medicine in short supply due to the Union blockade. After the war he moved to Baltimore, Maryland and founded the Baltimore Eye and Ear Hospital and the Presbyterian Eye, Ear and Throat Hospital. He is considered one of the fathers of American Ophthalmology. Chisolm died on 1 November 1903 in Petersburg, Virginia.

Patrick Ronayne Cleburne "*Stonewall of the West*" was born on 16 (or 17) March 1828 in County Cork, Ireland. He enlisted in the British army after he failed to gain entrance to Trinity College in Dublin in 1846 and he emigrated to the United States three years later. By 1860 he was a naturalized citizen and a practicing lawyer. He sided with the South and quickly rose through the ranks to general. Robert E. Lee called him "a meteor shining from a clouded sky." Cleburne was killed at the Battle of Franklin, Tennessee on 30 November 1864.

Jefferson Davis was born on 3 June 1808 in Christian County, Kentucky. Davis graduated from the U. S. Military Academy in 1828 and served in the Mexican War. He was wounded at Buena Vista and later served as Senator from Mississippi and Secretary of War in the Pierce administration. He served as the President of the Confederacy throughout the war and in the last days of the Confederacy, Davis fled south intending to maintain a government in exile (in Cuba). Davis and other members of his government stopped at Danville, Virginia which has since been called the last Capitol of the Confederacy. Davis was captured in Georgia and imprisoned for two years charged with treason. The case was dropped in 1869. He was the first president of Texas A & M. In his final days he wrote extensively and completed *A Short History of the Confederate States of America*. Davis died on 6 December 1889 in New Orleans, Louisiana. He is buried in Hollywood Cemetery, Richmond, Virginia.[3]

Dorthea Dix was born on 4 April 1802 at Hampden, Maine. She was an activist on behalf of the insane and indigent. She taught and established mental asylums and a school. By the start of the Civil War she had a national reputation and was selected to be Superintendent of Union Army Nurses. She assured equal treatment for soldiers of both the North and the South. After the war she continued her work to provide care for prisoners, the insane and the disabled. Dix died on 17 July 1887 at Trenton, New Jersey and was buried in Mount Auburn Cemetery in Cambridge, Massachusetts.

Frederick Douglass was born into slavery c. February 1818 in Talbot County, Maryland. After he escaped from slavery he became an orator, writer and statesman. He was a leader of the abolitionist movement and a champion for civil rights and women's suffrage. By the start of the Civil War he was perhaps the most famous African American in the United States and used his influence to recruit Blacks for the Union army. After the war he continued his work to achieve civil rights for African Americans and supported Grant's run for the presidency. In 1872, Douglass was the first African American to be nominated as Vice President of the United States on the Equal Rights Party ticket but was not elected. Douglass died in Washington, D. C. on 20 February 1895. He was buried in Mount Hope Cemetery, Rochester, New York.

Nathan Bedford Forrest, *"The Wizard of the Saddle"* was born on 13 July 1821 at Chapel Hill, Tennessee. He was the Memphis merchant who became a general and is remembered as one of the greatest cavalry leaders of the South. After the war, both Jefferson Davis and R. E. Lee agreed that the South had not fully utilized Forrest's talents. He was also accused of being a war criminal who was never prosecuted for the murder of African American Union soldiers after their surrender at Fort Pillow. This episode has been disputed by historians ever since. After the war he served as the first Grand Wizard of the Ku Klux Klan. Forrest died in Memphis, Tennessee on 29 October 1877. He was buried in Forrest Park in Memphis.

John Charles Fremont was born in Savannah, Georgia on 21 January 1813. He was the son of a French emigre dancing master and a Virginia housewife. He was described as precocious, handsome, and daring. He led expeditions in the West and played a key role in the conquest of California before the Civil War. He was elected as the Presidential candidate for the Republican party in 1856, but lost to Buchanan. Lincoln appointed him general at the start of the war, but he generally failed at all of his military assignments and resigned in 1864. After the war, he served as territorial governor of Arizona and died in New York City on 13 July 1890. He was buried in Rockland Cemetery, Piedmont-on-Hudson, New York.[4]

Ulysses S. Grant *"Sam"* was born on 27 April 1822 in Point Pleasant, Ohio. He was appointed to the U. S. Military Academy and graduated in the Class of 1843 with class standing of twenty-first out of thirty-nine. He served with success during the Civil War leading the Union Army by the end of the war. He was elected U. S. President after the war. He served as the 18th President of the United States from 1869-1877.

Grant was an honest man victimized by others less honest during his presidency. After his presidency, he lived in poverty but with the help of Mark Twain, got his memoirs published which were immensely successful. He died of throat cancer in Wilton, New York on 23 July 1885. His book about his reminiscences served to provide for his wife after he died. His remains are in a mausoleum on Riverside Drive in New York City.[5]

John Bell Hood "Sam Woodenhead" was born in Owingsville, Kentucky on 1 June (or 29 June) 1831. He graduated from the U. S. Military Academy with the class of 1853. His class standing was forty-four out of fifty-two. Bell did well as a brigade and division commander but failed when he was promoted to larger independent commands. The decisive defeats that he suffered at Atlanta and in the Franklin-Nashville campaigns destroyed his reputation. His attack at Franklin was called "Pickett's Charge of the West." After the war he retired to New Orleans where he worked as a cotton broker and in the insurance industry. Hood died on 30 August 1879 in the Yellow Fever epidemic in New Orleans with his wife and oldest son. He was buried in Metairies Cemetery in New Orleans. His ten orphans were farmed out to other families in Louisiana, Mississippi, Georgia, Kentucky, and New York. A very sad ending for a hero. If his children ever had a family reunion it must have been a very grand affair with much to discuss. His son, Duncan Norbert Hood graduated from West Point with the class of 1896. Apparently he inherited some of his father's leadership ability. He was a colonel of U. S. Volunteers during the Spanish-American War in 1898.[6]

Thomas Jefferson Hunt of B Company, Tenth Minnesota Regiment was born in Vermont in 1831. His reminiscences were extensive and comprehensive providing the reader with information not found elsewhere. Hunt's reminiscences were never published, but were transcribed to a typed copy that is maintained at the Minnesota Historical Society. His description of one of the last major battles of the Civil War at Spanish Fort provides a level of detail not found elsewhere.[7] He was the last surviving officer of the Tenth. During his career after the war he served in the Minnesota legislature and was elected a probate judge. His jaw wound sustained at the Battle of Nashville handicapped him for the rest of his life. He was a prohibitionist and author of the first dry laws. He died at age ninety-three in Minnesota in 1924.

David Hunter was born in Washington on 21 July 1802. He was the grandson of a signer of the Declaration of Independence, Richard Stockton. Hunter graduated from the U. S. Military Academy in 1822 (a year ahead of Lorenzo Thomas). Lincoln appointed him general in 1861. Hunter abolished slavery in the Department of the South in 1862 which was repudiated by Lincoln. He retired in 1866 and died on 2 February 1886. He was buried in Princeton, New Jersey.[8]

Benito Juarez was born on 21 March 1806 in San Pablo Guelatao, Oaxaca, Mexico. He was a lawyer and politician who served five terms as President of Mexico. His greatest challenge was to overthrow the empire of France established in Mexico which ended when Juarez executed the French emperor Maximilian, in 1867. The Confederate soldiers who had left the United States after the Civil War to fight for Maximilian departed Mexico before they would share Maximilian's fate. Juarez was reelected for two terms as President of Mexico (1867 and 1871) after the U. S. Civil War. Perhaps his greatest quote that appears on monuments in Mexico was "Among individuals as among nations, respect for the rights of others is peace." Juarez died in Mexico City on 18 July 1872 while reading a newspaper in his office.

James H. Lane was born on 22 June 1814 at Lawrenceburg, Indiana. Lane was a Kansas politician and Union general during the Civil War. He was accused of atrocities inflicted on Confederate sympathizers, but these did not hamper his career. He recruited one of the first African American regiments to fight in the war, the 1st Regiment Kansas Volunteers (Colored) which was successful in fighting Southern guerillas and sympathizers. In their first action, thirty members of the 1st Regiment defeated 130 mounted Confederate guerillas. After the war he served in the U. S. Senate but became depressed. Lane shot himself on 1 July 1866 and died on 11 July 1866 in Leavenworth, Kansas.

Robert E. Lee was born on 19 January 1807 in Stratford Hall, Virginia. His father served in the Revolutionary War, General Henry, "Light Horse Harry" Lee III. Light Horse Harry lost the family fortune which put him in debtor's prison leaving the family destitute. Lee received an appointment to the U. S. Military Academy and graduated second in the class of 1829. After many military assignments including Superintendent of the U. S. Military Academy, Lee joined the Confederate army and led it for most of the war. After the war, he accepted the position as president of Washington College in Lexington Virginia. By all accounts, he was well liked by the student body and his prestige insured the continued flow of funds to the college. Lee died at Washington and Lee University (then known as Washington College), Lexington, Virginia on 12 October 1870. He was buried in Lee Chapel on the university campus.[9]

Jonathan Letterman *"Father of Battlefield Medicine"* was born on 11 December 1824 in Canonsburg, Pennsylvania. He graduated from Jefferson Medical College in Philadelphia in 1849. At the start of the war, Letterman was given a charter by his commander, Union General McClellan, to do whatever was necessary to improve the medical treatment system. Letterman established an ambulance corps to speed treatment of the casualties, a system of hospitals to treat the wounded and a system of triage to sort patients after a battle. After the war, Letterman moved to California and served as coroner in San Francisco (1867-1872). Letterman died in San Francisco, California on 15 March 1872. He was buried in Arlington National Cemetery.

Maximilian, the Emperor of Mexico was installed by Napoleon III of France in 1864 since the French believed that the U. S., distracted by the Civil War, would not react to this violation of the Monroe Doctrine. In spite of the French effort to lure ex-Confederates such as Sterling Price into Mexico to join their cause, it was doomed. Many citizens of Mexico joined Maximilian in his war against Benito Juarez, the nationalist and patriot of Mexico but it was not enough when Napoleon III withdrew French troops in 1866. The stay of USCT regiments in Texas to protect the border against Maximilian was unnecessary. Maximilian was captured and executed by the forces of Juarez in spite of the pleas by monarchists such as Pope Pius IX in Europe. The U.S. had been aiding Juarez in his war and Juarez wanted to send a message to foreign nations that their intrusion in Mexican affairs would not be tolerated. The U. S. lodged no objection to the execution of Maximilian as he faced his firing squad in 1867. His wife Carlota never returned to Mexico and went insane shortly thereafter. Many African Americans died from disease in Texas because of this French adventure. Maximilian paid gold to the execution squad to avoid shooting him in the face. He wanted his mother to be able to recognize his corpse (apparently he had no concern about his wife). It did not work. They shot him in the face. The gold might have been better spent on engineering his escape, but apparently he never thought of that. There is no cure for stupid. Most historians agree that Maximilian was a rather "dim fellow."

John McArthur was born on 17 November 1826 on the Clyde River in Renfrewshire, Scotland. At the age of twenty-three he emigrated to the United States and settled in Chicago where he was the successful proprietor of the Excelsior Iron Works. He enlisted in a militia company and at the start of the war was appointed colonel of the 12th Illinois Infantry. He was promoted to general and was cited for gallantry at the Battle of Nashville. After the war he was plagued by misfortune. The iron works failed and he was the commissioner of public works when the great fire of 1871 occurred in Chicago. A bank failure occurred for which he was held personally responsible. McArthur died in Chicago, Illinois on 15 May 1906 and is buried in Rosehill Cemetery.[10]

Samuel Preston Moore was born on 16 September 1813 in Charleston, South Carolina. He graduated from the South Carolina Medical College in 1834 and served as a surgeon during the Mexican War. During the Civil War he was appointed as Surgeon General of the Confederate Army Medical Department. He raised recruiting standards for surgeons and designed the barracks-hospital layout that is still in use today. After the war he returned to medical practice. Moore died in Richmond, Virginia on 31 May 1889 and is buried there in Hollywood Cemetery.

Florence Nightingale *"The Lady with a Lamp"* was born on 12 May 1820 in Florence, Italy. She is famous for her work during the Crimean War. She and her nurses improved patient care, vastly reducing the mortality rate among the wounded by improving hygiene. Lessons learned by Nightingale would be applied during the U. S. Civil War. Nightingale died on 13 August 1910 in London, United Kingdom. She was buried in St. Margaret Church graveyard in East Wellow, Hampshire, United Kingdom. Henry Wadsworth Longfellow's 1857 poem "Santa Filomena" was a tribute to Nightingale.

> Lo! in that house of misery
> A lady with a lamp I see
> Pass through the glimmering gloom
> and flit from room to room

Frederick Law Olmstead was born on 26 April 1822 in Hartford Connecticut. He was a journalist, social critic, public administrator, and landscape designer. During the Civil War, his ideas sparked the creation of the U. S. Sanitary Commission. Olmstead died in Belmont, Massachusetts on 28 August 1903.

John Wolcott Phelps was born on 13 November 1813 at Guilford, Vermont. He graduated from the U. S. Military Academy with the Class of 1836. He took part in the Florida war against the Seminoles, 1836-1839. He also fought in the Mexican War. He was an abolitionist who resigned from the army in 1859 and spent the next two years inveighing in print against the institution of slavery. At the start of the Civil War he became Colonel of the 1st Vermont and was later promoted to general. After his attempt to arm African American troops was repudiated by the government, he resigned in disgust. He moved to Brattleboro, Vermont. He died at Guilford on 2 February 1885 and is buried there.[11]

Sterling Price *"Old Pap"* was born in Prince Edward County, Virginia on 20 September 1809. He was a Missouri politician and Southern general who lost at the Battles of Pea Ridge and Westport. Rather than surrender at the end of the war he took some of his troops to Mexico hoping to enlist in the service of Maximilian. When this failed, he returned to St. Louis, Missouri where he died in poverty on 29 September 1867. He was buried in St. Louis in Bellefontaine Cemetery.

Rufus Saxton was born in Greenfield, Massachusetts on 19 October 1824. He graduated from the U. S. Military Academy in the Class of 1849. He was appointed a general of volunteers in 1862 and commanded the defense of Harper's Ferry. Later he served in various roles in the Union army the most important of which was recruiting African Americans into the Union army. After the war, he worked in the Freedman's Bureau. After his retirement in 1888 he moved to Washington where he died on 23 February 1908. He was buried in Arlington National Cemetery.[12]

John McAllister Schofield was born on 29 September 1831 in Gerry, Pennsylvania. He graduated from the U. S. Military Academy with the class of 1853. He inflicted a disastrous defeat on the Confederate army under John Bell Hood at the Battle of Franklin and commanded the XXIII Corps at the Battle of Nashville in December 1864. After the war, he served as Secretary of War in 1868 but resigned after Grant became president. Schofield was the Superintendent of the U. S. Military Academy (1876-1881) and commanded the U. S. Army after the death General Sheridan in 1888. Schofield died in Saint Augustine, Florida on 4 March 1906 and is buried in Arlington National Cemetery.[13]

Winfield Scott *"Old Fuss and Feathers"* was a Virginian born in 1786. He served longer than any other person as a general in U. S. history with a career of forty-seven years. He commanded forces from the War of 1812 through the start of the Civil War. By then he was too old and sick to sit a horse, but had the knowledge and experience to chart a course for the Union army. He developed the "Anaconda Plan." This provided a plan to strangle the Confederacy through a naval blockade of the South and cutting it in two by controlling the Mississippi River. Scott's plan was not accepted, but became the template for Union success later in the war. The Anaconda Plan was never a top priority strategy, but warfare in the West along the Mississippi continued at a slow pace and finally started to succeed in the way originally planned by Scott. To African Americans, the blockaded ports on the Atlantic coast provided an escape route to the Union.[14] Scott was replaced early in the war and he died in 1866.

Robert Gould Shaw was born on 10 October 1837 in Boston, Massachusetts of a wealthy family. He attended Harvard University but did not graduate. He was a Second Lieutenant in the 2nd Massachusetts Infantry before his appointment as colonel of the all Black 54th Massachusetts Infantry in 1862. Shaw was killed in action leading the 54th Massachusetts Infantry at Battery Wagner, Morris Island, South Carolina on 18 July 1863. He was buried there in a mass grave with his troops. His wife moved to Europe and did not remarry.

William Tecumseh Sherman *"Cump"* was born on 8 February 1820 in Lancaster, Ohio. His father, a justice of the Ohio supreme court died suddenly in 1829 which left the family in poverty. Sherman received an appointment to the U. S. Military Academy graduating sixth in his class of 1840. His classmates included George Henry Thomas the Union commander at the Battle of Nashville and General Richard Ewell a senior commander in the Confederate army. His promotions continued and he is best known for his march to the sea in Georgia which divided the Confederacy and hastened its defeat. After the war he commanded the U. S. Army in 1869 and retired in 1884. Sherman died in New York City on 14 February 1891 and was buried in Calvary Cemetery, St. Louis, Missouri.[15]

Robert Smalls the African American hero returned to South Carolina after the war and entered politics. He was a state representative from 1868-70 and state senator from 1870-74. In 1874 he was elected to the U.S. House of Representatives and served intermittently until 1886. In 1889 President Benjamin Harrison appointed Smalls the U.S. Collector of Customs for the port in Beaufort, an office he held until 1913. Smalls died on Feb. 22, 1915.

Andrew Jackson Smith *"Whiskey"* was born in Bucks County, Pennsylvania on 28 April 1815. He attended the U. S. Military Academy at West Point graduating with the Class of 1838. He ranked thirty-six in a class of forty-five. Smith served in the Mexican War. He rose in rank to command a corps during the Civil War and is best remembered for his defeat of the Confederate army at Tupelo, Mississippi which included one of the few defeats of Nathan Bedford Forest. A. J. Smith was admired by his troops because he shared their hardships. They called themselves "A. J.'s Guerillas" Smith resigned his volunteer commission in 1866 and became colonel of the U.S. 7th Cavalry Regiment. He retired from the military service in April 1869 to become postmaster at St. Louis, Missouri. A. J. died there on 30 January 1897 and is buried in St. Louis.

Edwin McMasters Stanton was born on 19 December 1814 in Steubenville, Ohio. Throughout his life he suffered from asthma which may have contributed to his death. He was the 25th United States Attorney General serving in the Buchanan administration. Soon after the start of the war he was appointed Secretary of War after Lincoln fired Stanton's predecessor, Simon Cameron. Stanton's policies did not always agree with Lincoln's in which case Lincoln in his words "plowed around him." Stanton was too valuable to fire. With the death of Lincoln, Stanton, as a Radical Republican, did not support the lenient polices toward the South of Andrew Johnson, the new president, who tried to fire Stanton. This led to a confrontation between the Radical Republicans in Congress and Johnson leading to his impeachment. When impeachment failed, Stanton was removed from his position as Secretary of War soon after President Johnson's impeachment hearing. Stanton died in Washington, D. C. on 24 December 1869.

James Steedman "*Old Steady*" was born on 29 July 1817 in Northumberland County, Pennsylvania. Steedman was a self-made man who inspired confidence among his troops. He had very little formal education but learned the trade of a printer and advanced to public printer of the U. S. government in 1857. At the start of the war he was selected as colonel of the 14th Ohio and was promoted to general in 1862. He led his troops to several victories; perhaps the best known was his successful attack on Hood's right flank at the Battle of Nashville in 1864. After the war he became a collector of internal revenue in New Orleans. Later, he served in the Ohio state senate and became Chief of Police in Toledo, Ohio in 1883. Steedman died on 18 October 1883 in Toledo, Ohio and was buried in Woodlawn Cemetery.[16]

George Henry Thomas, *"The Rock of Chickamauga"* was born on 31 July 1816 in Southampton County, Virginia and was one of the few Virginians to fight for the North as a general officer. He was born in the area that was the center of Nat Turner's slave rebellion in 1831 from which the family was forced to flee. The sisters of Thomas would disavow him to the end of their days because he fought for the Union. Thomas graduated from the U. S. Military Academy with the class of 1840 that include William T. Sherman. His victory at Nashville destroyed the army of John Bell Hood and is considered to be one of the most decisive battles of the war. There was always antipathy between Thomas and Grant. He never reconciled with Grant. Perhaps Grant did not trust him because he was a Southerner. After the war he commanded the Division of the Pacific where he died in San Francisco on 28 March 1870. He was buried in Troy, New York.

Lorenzo Thomas was born in New Castle, Delaware on 26 October 1804. He graduated from West Point in 1823. In those days, college students were often younger than they are today, and he entered the Academy from Delaware at age fourteen. He came from a military family; one of his uncles had served with General Washington. He graduated seventeenth out of thirty five that graduated that year.[17] He was older than nearly all other generals that served in the Civil War. He survived the war and his journey after that is more remarkable than his service during the Civil War. His old adversary Secretary of War Stanton came to the front. After Lincoln was killed, Thomas was selected by the new president, Andrew Johnson, to replace Stanton. An ugly controversy followed which led to the impeachment proceedings against Johnson not seen before or after until President Clinton's affair. In the impeachment proceedings both Thomas and General Butler were major players in the testimony about Johnson. Johnson was much hated by the Radical Republicans in Congress who objected to his lenient treatment of the South. The radicals found an excuse to impeach based upon Johnson's dismissal of Stanton that violated the Tenure of Office Act passed by Congress to protect Stanton. The impeachment of Johnson failed in part due to the testimony of Lorenzo Thomas. General Thomas died on 2 March 1875 in Washington, D. C. He was buried in Oak Hill Cemetery in Georgetown, Washington, D. C.[18]

Charles Stuart Tripler was born in the Bowery in New York City on 19 January 1806. He graduated from the College of Physicians and Surgeons in New York in 1827. In 1830, he was commissioned as an Assistant Surgeon in the U. S. Army Medical Service. Many years of service followed including the Mexican War. After the start of the Civil War, he was assigned as the Army of the Potomac's first Medical Director. His greatest contribution may have been his *Manual of the Medical Officer of the Army of the United States.* This identified recruiting, requirements, and physical examinations. Tripler died on 20 October 1866 and is buried in Elmwood Cemetery, Detroit, Michigan.

Sojourner Truth was born c. 1797 in Swatekill, New York. She escaped from slavery with her daughter in 1826. She was an author, abolitionist and women's civil rights activist. After the war she moved to Michigan where she pursued women's rights, prison reform and spoke against capital punishment. Truth died on 26 November 1883 in Battle Creek, Michigan and was buried in Oak Hill Cemetery.

Daniel Ullmann was born on 28 April 1810 in Wilmington, Delaware. He graduated from Yale in 1829 and moved to New York City where he practiced law. At the start of the war, he helped recruit the 78th New York Regiment and was commissioned as a colonel of this regiment. In 1863 he was promoted to general and sent to New Orleans to raise five regiments of African Americans. After the war he retired to Nyack, New York. He spent his time in scientific and literary studies. He died in Nyack on 20 September 1892 and is buried there.[19]

James Harrison Wilson was born near Shawneetown, Illinois on 2 September 1837. He graduated from the U. S. Military Academy, sixth in the class of 1860. He was the Union cavalry leader at the Battle of Nashville who was instrumental in destroying the army of John Bell

Hood. He survived the war and resigned as a major general in 1870. He returned to the Army in 1898 to fight in the Spanish-American War as a major general of volunteers. Wilson died in Wilmington, Delaware on 23 February 1925 and was buried in Old Swedes Churchyard. He was the last surviving member of the West Point class of 1860.[20]

APPENDIX A

African American Regiments at Nashville

Listed below are the regimental histories, officers, and losses at the Battle of Nashville. Most of the soldiers were recruited in Tennessee. Nearly all officers were white. Officer assignments to companies changed over time so some officers show more than one company assignment. Space in this book does not allow the listing of enlisted soldiers in these regiments that amounted to 5,000-10,000 troops. The National Park Service provides an on-line listing of all Civil War regiments that can be searched by those wishing to track their ancestors.[1] USCT units at Nashville include the First Colored Brigade under Colonel Thomas Morgan which was composed of the 14th, 16th, 17th and 18th Regiments, USCT. The Second Colored Brigade was commanded by Colonel Charles R. Thompson. He had the 12th, 13th, 100th and the Kansas Light Artillery, 1st Battery.[2] The casualties listed are for the entire war, but nearly all occurred at Nashville. Frederick H. Dyer compiled a history of the Civil War units over one hundred years ago.[3] This appendix is based upon his research.

12th REGIMENT INFANTRY

Organized in Tennessee at large July 24 to August 14, 1863. Attached to Defenses of Nashville & Northwestern Railroad, Dept. of the Cumberland, to October, 1864. 2nd Colored Brigade, District of the Etowah, Dept. of the Cumberland, to January, 1865. Defenses of Nashville & Northwestern Railroad, District of Middle Tennessee, to May, 1865. 3rd Sub-District, District Middle Tennessee, Dept. of the Cumberland, to January, 1866. SERVICE.-Railroad guard duty at various points in Tennessee and Alabama on line of the Nashville & Northwestern Railroad till December, 1864. Repulse of Hood's attack on Johnsonville November 2, 4 and 5. Action at Buford's Station, Section 37, Nashville & Northwestern Railroad, November 24. March to Clarksville, Tenn., and skirmish near that place December 2. Battle of Nashville December 15-16. Pursuit of Hood to the Tennessee River December 17-28. Action at Decatur, Ala., December 27-28. Railroad guard and garrison duty in the Dept. of the Cumberland till January, 1866. Regiment lost during service 4 Officers and 38 Enlisted men killed and mortally wounded and 242 Enlisted men by disease. Total 284.

Name	Company	Rank
Ambrose, Geoman	K	Second Lieutenant
Anderson, David M.	FE	Assistant Surgeon
Barber, Richard F.	CG	Second Lieutenant
Barr, Theophilus H.	A	Captain
Bartholomew, William A.	C	Captain
Bechtel, Alfred B.	FC	Second Lieutenant
Bowdle, Ancel M.	I	Captain
Bullen, Alphonzo A.	F	Second Lieutenant
Butler, George A.	G	Second Lieutenant
Cain, William S.	HC	First Lieutenant
Caughlan, John	B	Second Lieutenant
Cavalier, Louis	H	Second Lieutenant
Clark, William L.	GH	Second Lieutenant
Collier, John H.	GF	Second Lieutenant
Cook, Benjamin F.	KE	Second Lieutenant
Cooke, David G.	EH	Second Lieutenant
Coughlan, John	B	Second Lieutenant
Danner, Samuel T.	A	First Lieutenant
Deal, Wm. G.	F&S	Assistant Surgeon

Dease, Dennis	H	Second Lieutenant
DeMuth, Jesse A.	DA	Second Lieutenant
Douglass, Wm. R.	FE	First Lieutenant
Eaton, Wm. Wentworth	F&S	Chaplain
Everett, George M.	H	Captain
Finch, Amasa J.	F&S	Major
Fitch, George W.	EC	First Lieutenant
Freeman, Henry V.	D	Captain
Frost, Silas E	G	Captain
Headon, Robert	E	Captain
Hegner, Henry	B	Captain
Jagger, Joseph	K	First Lieutenant
Kurle, David J.	H	First Lieutenant
Lane, James H.	K	First Lieutenant
Payne, William G.	G	First Lieutenant
Ream, Wm. C.	I	Second Lieutenant
Richardson, James W.	AID	Second Lieutenant
Riggs, Frank H.	DA	First Lieutenant
Russell, Ezra R.	F&S	Assistant Surgeon
Sellon, William R.	F&S	Lieutenant Colonel
Sexton, Thomas L.	I	First Lieutenant
Strong, James C	F	Second Lieutenant
Sylvester, Roscoe G.	BD	Second Lieutenant
Thompson, Charles R.	F&S	Colonel
Thornton, J.B.H.	K	Captain
Torrence, Lewis G.	BG	Second Lieutenant
Wildey, William H.	CH	First Lieutenant
Woolsey, R. Dickson	B	First Lieutenant

13th REGIMENT INFANTRY

Organized at Nashville, Tenn., November 19, 1863. Attached to Defenses Nashville & Northwestern Railroad, Dept. of the Cumberland, to November, 1864. 2nd Colored Brigade, District of the Etowah, Dept. of the Cumberland, to January, 1865. Defenses Nashville & North western Railroad, District Middle Tennessee, Dept. of the Cumberland, to May, 1865. 3rd Sub district, District Middle Tennessee, Dept. of the Cumberland, to January, 1866. SERVICE. Railroad guard duty in Tennessee and Alabama on line of Nashville & Northwestern Railroad till December, 1864. Repulse of Hood's attack on Johnsonville, Tenn., September 25, and November 4 and 5. Eddyville, Ky., October 17 (Detachment). Battle of Nashville December 15-16. Pursuit of Hood to the Tennessee River December 17-18. Railroad guard and garrison duty in the Dept. of the Cumberland till January, 1866. Mustered out January 10, 1866. Regiment lost during service 4 Officers and 86 Enlisted men killed and mortally wounded and 265 Enlisted men by disease. Total 355.

Officer Roster

Name	Company	Rank
Babbitt, James C.	KI	First Lieutenant
Bacon, Charles H.	F&S	Surgeon
Bennett, Charles W.	F	Captain
Bensinger, William	C	Captain
Brierson, Julius	A	First Lieutenant
Brunner, Emory W.	E	Second Lieutenant
Campbell, Chas. H.	B	Second Lieutenant
Chamberlain, E. Kirby	B	Captain
Clark, Jefferson M.	CI	Second Lieutenant
Creth, John E.	A	Captain
Dickerson, Perley B.	H	First Lieutenant
Dougall, William	I	Captain
Dowd, John B.	H	Captain
Duncan, William	D	Captain

Ekstrand, John H.	H	Second Lieutenant
Ernest, George W.	E	First Lieutenant
Frederick, Eugene P	D	Second Lieutenant
Friedrick, Eugene P	D	Second Lieutenant
Grosskoff, Edward	F&S	Major
Hart, Lucus L.	G	First Lieutenant
Hollinger, William H.	AD	Second Lieutenant
Hottenstein, John A.		Colonel
Inness, William	F&S	Major
Isom, James A.	B	Second Lieutenant
Jacoby, Andrew	G	Captain
LeCaron, Henri	EB	Second Lieutenant
Marble, Horace	AC	Second Lieutenant
Musgrave, Philip D.	F&S	Assistant Surgeon
Nelson, George F.	FD	First Lieutenant/ Regimental Quartermaster
Park, Ervin K.	IK	First Lieutenant
Parks, Luther L.	FA	Second Lieutenant
Reilly, John D.	HGL	First Lieutenant/ Adjutant
Ricketts, Barnabas	HEB	Second Lieutenant
Rodabaugh, Daniel	A	First Lieutenant
Russell, James W.	F&S	Chaplain
Scudder, A.M.	G	Second Lieutenant
Sherman, William B.	DB	First Lieutenant
Snell, Charles B.	AEF	Second Lieutenant
Snider, Samuel P.	A	Captain
Tambling, Villeroy A.	GK	Second Lieutenant
Taylor, George	FB	Second Lieutenant
Thomas, Lancaster	F&S	Assistant Surgeon
Tracy, Jno M.	C	Second Lieutenant
Trauernicht, Theodore	F&S	Lieutenant Colonel

Trine, Samuel G.	B	First Lieutenant
Wallace, Richard M.	FKE	Second Lieutenant
Wilson, William	I	Second Lieutenant
Woodruff, J. V.	C	First Lieutenant

14th REGIMENT INFANTRY

Organized at Gallatin, Tenn., November 16, 1863, to January 8, 1864. Attached to Post of Gallatin, Tenn., to January, 1864. Post of Chattanooga, Tenn., Dept. of the Cumberland, to November, 1864. Unattached, District of the Etowah, Dept. of the Cumberland, to December, 1864. 1st Colored Brigade, District of the Etowah, to May, 1865. District of East Tennessee, to August, 1865. Dept. of the Tennessee and Dept. of Georgia till March, 1866. SERVICE.-Garrison duty at Chattanooga, Tenn., till November, 1864. March to relief of Dalton, Ga., August 14. Action at Dalton August 14-15. Siege of Decatur, Ala., October 27-30. Battle of Nashville, Tenn., December 15-16. Overton's Hill December 16. Pursuit of Hood to the Tennessee River December 17-28. Duty at Chattanooga and in District of East Tennessee till July, 1865. At Greenville and in the Dept. of the Tennessee till March, 1866. Mustered out March 26, 1866. Springfield, District of Nashville, Dept. of the Cumberland, to March, 1865. 5th Sub-District, District of Middle Tennessee, Dept. of the Cumberland, to April, 1866. SERVICE.-Garrison and guard duty at Nashville, Columbia and Pulaski, Tenn., till June, 1864. Post duty at Springfield, Tenn., and in District of Middle Tennessee till April, 1866. Mustered out April 7, 1866.

Officer Roster

Name	Company	Rank
Ames, Fisher W.	F&S	Surgeon
Apthorpe, George H.	EK	Second Lieutenant
Austin, Henry R.	B	Second Lieutenant
Avery, William H.H.	F&S	First Lieutenant/ Adjutant
Baker, Clarence W.	A	Captain

Bateman, Christopher H.	E	First Lieutenant
Billingsley, Lorenzo W.	K	Second Lieutenant
Block, Marx	F&S	Assistant Surgeon
Boutwell, George W.	C	Second Lieutenant
Cone, Ela	H	Second Lieutenant
Corbin, Henry C.	F	Major
Cressy, Frederick J.	G	Captain
Cunningham, David A.	BKI	Second Lieutenant
Curtis, Samuel F.	H	Captain
DeLancy, John	D	Second Lieutenant
Elgin, William	F&S	Chaplain
Foos, Henry E.	F	Second Lieutenant
Garrett, Richard	H	Second Lieutenant
Gibson, Alexander	A	Second Lieutenant
Gillet, Frank	G	Second Lieutenant
Graydon, Andrew	G	Second Lieutenant
Green, Willard H.	F&S	First Lieutenant/ Assistant Surgeon
Guernsey, Henry H.	D	Second Lieutenant
Hassler, Dan'l K.	E	First Lieutenant
Jackson, Sylvester S.	CH	Second Lieutenant
Jones, Orson	F	Second Lieutenant
Keinbort, Daniel	AF	First Lieutenant
Kienbort, Daniel	AF	First Lieutenant
Kimbart, Daniel	AF	First Lieutenant
Loomis, Orville A.	FK	Second Lieutenant
McMillan, Eli	C	First Lieutenant
McNeill, Francis	HC	Second Lieutenant
Meteer, J. H.	K	Captain
Miller, James	E	Second Lieutenant
Mitchell, John A.	G	Second Lieutenant
Morgan, Thomas J.	F&S	Lieutenant Colonel
Munk, Edward	C	Captain

Ong, Jacob B.	F&S	Assistant Surgeon
Persons, Elvero	AID	Second Lieutenant
Recker, Alexander	C	Second Lieutenant
Reichman, Charles	D	First Lieutenant
Ricker, Alexander	C	Second Lieutenant
Riechman, Charles	D	First Lieutenant
Rolph, Albert H.	E	Captain
Romyen, Henry	B	Captain
Safford, Edward P.	F	Captain
Salisbury, Ambrose C.	G	First Lieutenant
Sladen, Joseph A.	AG	Second Lieutenant
Smock, Samuel J	A	Second Lieutenant
Snyder, Andrew C.	BI	First Lieutenant
Tear, Wallace	H	First Lieutenant
Thornton, Gardner P.	BI	Second Lieutenant
Vance, Wilson J.	A	Second Lieutenant
Wheeler, Henry C.	D	Second Lieutenant
Wright, Daniel K.	F&S	Regimental Quartermaster
Wyrill, William	FK	First Lieutenant

16th REGIMENT INFANTRY

Organized at Nashville, Tenn., December 4, 1863, to February 13, 1864. Attached to Post of Chattanooga, Dept. of the Cumberland, to November, 1864. Unattached, District of the Etowah, Dept. of the Cumberland, to December, 1864. 1st Colored Brigade, District of the Etowah, Dept. of the Cumberland, to January, 1865. Unattached, District of the Etowah, to March, 1865. 1st Colored Brigade, Dept. of the Cumberland, to April, 1865. 5th Sub-District, District of Middle Tennessee, to July, 1865. 2nd Brigade, 4th Division, District of East Tennessee and Dept. of the Cumberland. SERVICE.-Duty at Chattanooga, Tenn., till November, 1864. Battle of Nashville, Tenn., December 15-16. Overton Hill December 16. Pursuit of Hood to the

Tennessee River December 17-28. Duty at Chattanooga and in Middle and East Tennessee till April, 1866. Mustered out April 30, 1866.

Officer Roster

Name	Company	Rank
Abdill, William J.	A	Captain
Achenbach, Archibald H.		Assistant Surgeon
Acker, Edward S.	G	Second Lieutenant
Albee, Thomas J.	H	First Lieutenant
Barbour, Joseph H.	K	First Lieutenant
Beach, Clayton		First Lieutenant/ Regimental Quartermaster
Brunt, William	D	Captain
Buzzell, Marcus	KA	Second Lieutenant
Chauncy, Jeremiah	FE	First Lieutenant
Clark, Thomas C.	F&S	Chaplain
Clark, William H.	I	Captain
Collins, William	CF	Second Lieutenant
Courtney, Michael L.	F&S	Lieutenant Colonel
Crider, Martin H.	BG	Second Lieutenant
Curtis, Artemas	B	Captain
Dickinson, David H.	F	Second Lieutenant
French, Russel B.	HE	Second Lieutenant
Galloway, Samuel	F	Captain
Gaw, William B.	F&S	Colonel
Giffe, Thomas	H	Captain
Gilman, Oliver L.	F&S	Assistant Surgeon
Gordon, John A.	E	Captain
Gordon, Peter	K	Second Lieutenant
Hayslit, James R.	E	Second Lieutenant
Hewett, Orville B.	E	Second Lieutenant
Hislop, Thomas	A	First Lieutenant
Hoyslit, James R.	E	Second Lieutenant

Huett, Orville B.	E	Second Lieutenant
Irvine, Chas. D.	AI	Second Lieutenant
Jefferson, Wm. H.	F&S	Major
Jones, Wm.	KD	Second Lieutenant
Ketcham, Frank T.D.	C	Captain
Montgomery, John H.	F&S	Chaplain
Passel, James L.	K	Captain
Perkins, Bishop W.	CFI	First Lieutenant
Pierce, Hannibal	D	First Lieutenant
Rivenburg, Lovett S.	IA	Second Lieutenant
Rowland, Bent D. C.	G	Second Lieutenant
Scott, John T.	C	First Lieutenant
Seidel, Charles W.	G	First Lieutenant
Sibbald, James	F	Second Lieutenant
Wadsworth, Elihu H.	BD	First Lieutenant
Warfield, Charles		Second Lieutenant
Waterbury, Fordyce H.	E	First Lieutenant
Welch, John	F&S	Surgeon
Woods, Alexander W.	I	Second Lieutenant

17th REGIMENT INFANTRY

Organized at Nashville, Tenn., December 12 to 21, 1863. Attached to Post of Murfreesboro, Tenn., Dept. of the Cumberland, to April, 1864. Post and District of Nashville, Tenn., Dept. of the Cumberland, to December, 1864. 1st Colored Brigade, District of the Etowah, Dept. of the Cumberland, to January, 1865. Post and District of Nashville, Tenn., Dept. of the Cumberland, to April, 1866. SERVICE.-Duty at McMinnville and Murfreesboro, Tenn., till November, 1864. battle of Nashville, Tenn., December 15-16. Overton Hill December 16. Pursuit of Hood to the Tennessee River December 17-27. Decatur December 28-30. Duty at Post of Nashville, Tenn., and in the Dept. of Tennessee till April, 1866. Mustered out April 25, 1866.

Officer Roster

Name	Company	Rank
Aldrich, Job H.	G	First Lieutenant/ Adjutant
Ayers, Gideon H.	AE	First Lieutenant
Baker, Loyd W.		Assistant Surgeon
Bateman, Christopher F.	KC	Captain
Bell, George W.	I	Captain
Bleakney, Franklin	BD	Second Lieutenant
Bleakney, Lewis	AH	Second Lieutenant
Bowers, Lawrence M.	B	Second Lieutenant
Canfield, Henry A.	CGK	First Lieutenant
Clark, George L.	F	First Lieutenant
Clemons, Phineas H.	F&S	Surgeon
Cline, William	G	First Lieutenant
Davie, Lyman E.	B	First Lieutenant
Earnshaw, Charles W.	CK	Second Lieutenant
Ferris, Benjamin H.	F	First Lieutenant
Freeland, Joseph H.	AF	First Lieutenant
Fulton, Christopher C.	C	Second Lieutenant
Gardner, Samuel J.	E	Second Lieutenant
Gettenger, David F.	D	Second Lieutenant
Goodwin, Terence	G	Second Lieutenant
Hayward, George A.	C	First Lieutenant/ Regimental Quartermaster
Heimbach, Thomas	F	First Lieutenant
Hendryx, Corydon D.	FG	Second Lieutenant
Jones, Tilden	F	Second Lieutenant
Kelly, James	KI	Second Lieutenant
Kliese, Augustus F.	BE	Second Lieutenant
Longmire, Joseph M.	I	Captain

March, Fletcher E.	GD	Captain
Marsh, Fletcher E.	GD	Captain
McKee, John	A	Second Lieutenant
McKenzie, Sumner	HK	Second Lieutenant
Murphy, Marcena M.	A	Second Lieutenant
Nixon, John B.	AF	Captain
O'Neill, John	EH	Captain
Patten, Harrison H.	DB	First Lieutenant
Pickering, Charles H.	F&S	Lieutenant Colonel
Ranson, Newton	GI	Second Lieutenant
Shafter, James N.	BE	First Lieutenant
Shafter, John N.	H	First Lieutenant
Shafter, William R.	F&S	Colonel
Shepard, Benjamin H.	F&S	Captain
Sommer, McKenzie	HK	Second Lieutenant
Springsteen, Theron J.	KE	First Lieutenant
Stivers, Edwin J.	IAC	Second Lieutenant
Sumner, McKenzie	HK	Second Lieutenant
Tupper, Joseph E.	F&S	Major
Van Hise, Orlando	I	First Lieutenant

18th REGIMENT INFANTRY

Organized in Missouri at large February 1 to September 28, 1864. Attached to District of St. Louis, Mo., Dept. of Missouri, to December, 1864. Unassigned, District of the Etowah, Dept. of the Cumberland, December, 1864. 1st Colored Brigade, District of the Etowah, Dept. of the Cumberland, to January, 1865. Unassigned, District of the Etowah, Dept. of the Cumberland, to March, 1865. 1st Colored Brigade, Dept. of the Cumberland, to July, 1865. 2nd Brigade, 4th Division, District of East Tennessee and Dept. of the Tennessee, to February, 1866. SERVICE.-Duty in District of St. Louis, Mo., and at St. Louis till November, 1864. Ordered to Nashville, Tenn., November 7. Moved to

Paducah, Ky., November 7-11, thence to Nashville, Tenn. Occupation of Nashville during Hood's investment December 1-15. Battles of Nashville December 15-16. Pursuit of Hood to the Tennessee River December 17-28. At Bridgeport, Ala., guarding railroad till February, 1865. Action at Elrod's Tan Yard January 27. At Chattanooga, Tenn., and in District of East Tennessee till February, 1866. Mustered out February 21, 1866.

Officer Roster

Name	Company	Rank
Ball, Artemas E.	I	First Lieutenant
Cartlidge, Charles W.A.	G	Captain
Cass, Charles L.C.	H	Captain
Clague, John J.	E	Captain
Darling, Ehud N.	H	First Lieutenant
Darling, Richard J.	ACK	First Lieutenant
Dodge, William H.	K	First Lieutenant/ Regimental Quartermaster
Dods, William B.	F&S	Assistant Surgeon
Douglass, Lewis M.	IB	Second Lieutenant
Drew, George J.	BD	First Lieutenant
Drew, Josiah R.	BK	Second Lieutenant
Goodier, Charles H.	F	First Lieutenant
Keith, W.B.	B	First Lieutenant
Kent, Eugene E.	DA	First Lieutenant
Knight, George W.J.	K	Second Lieutenant
Leissering, Otto	G	First Lieutenant
Lucas, Nathaniel B.	A	Captain
Martin, Daniel M.	A	Second Lieutenant
Martin, Leander	A	First Lieutenant
Martin, Leander	A	First Lieutenant
Millington, Augustus O.	F&S	Colonel
Murdock, Thomas B.	F	Second Lieutenant
Oakes, Thomas F.	G	Second Lieutenant

Ong, Jacob H.	F&S	Surgeon
Porter, Charles L.	D	Captain
Sears, John J.	F&S	Lieutenant Colonel
Sibley, Isaac D	BE	
Smith, Solomon	F	Captain
Snoddy, Lewellyn O	I	Adjutant
Turner, Joseph A.	EFD	Second Lieutenant
Warden, Horace		Chaplain
Wood, Edward H.	DC	Second Lieutenant
Worden, Horace		Chaplain

44th REGIMENT INFANTRY

Organized at Chattanooga, Tenn., April 7, 1864. Attached to District of Chattanooga, Dept. of the Cumberland, to November, 1864. Unattached, District of the Etowah, Dept. of the Cumberland, to December, 1864. 1st Colored Brigade. District of the Etowah, Dept. of the Cumberland, to January, 1865. Unattached, District of the Etowah, to March, 1865. 1st Colored Brigade, Dept. of the Cumberland, to July, 1865. 2nd Brigade, 4th Division, District of East Tennessee, July, 1865. Dept. of the Cumberland and Dept. of Georgia to April, 1866. SERVICE.-Post and garrison duty at Chattanooga, Tenn., till November, 1864. Action at Dalton, Ga., October 13, 1864. Battle of Nashville, Tenn., December 15-16. Pursuit of Hood to the Tennessee River December 17-28. Post and garrison duty at Chattanooga, Tenn., in District of East Tennessee, and in the Dept. of Georgia till April, 1866. Mustered out April 30, 1866.

Officer Roster

Name	Company	Rank
Billingsley, Lorenzo W.	A	Captain
Black, Wm. H.	G	First Lieutenant
Blackmer, Collins		First Lieutenant/ Regimental Quartermaster

Burnham, Hiram H.	HE	Second Lieutenant
Call, Francis L.	I	Lieutenant
Carmody, Charles H.	K	Lieutenant
Chatfield, Theodore C.	I	First Lieutenant
Christensen, Niels	H	Captain
Cleland, John E.	A	Lieutenant
Cooke, Samuel G.	A	First Lieutenant
Crampton, Hiram	D	Second Lieutenant
Eastman, Joseph A.	F&S	Assistant Surgeon
Elliott, J. Walter	BF	First Lieutenant
Garrett, Richard	C	Captain
Hall, M. Stuart	C	Second Lieutenant
Hinckley, Thaddeus W.	GK	Second Lieutenant
Holmes, David	D	Captain
Johnson, Levi O.	I	Lieutenant
Johnson, Lewis	F&S	Colonel
King, John W.	AD	Lieutenant
Kirby, Thomas B.	B	Captain
Kniffin, Ves W.	EG	Lieutenant
Knowles, Henry C.	F	Lieutenant
Lowe, John W.	G	Captain
Meeker, Henry W.	E	First Lieutenant
Michener, Wm. P.	D	First Lieutenant
Noe, William W.	C	First Lieutenant
Peck, Joseph H.	B	Lieutenant
Penfield, Charles G.	AE	Lieutenant
Railsback, Lysurgus	F&S	Chaplain
Squire, Erastus F.	F	First Lieutenant
Webster, Joseph R	F&S	Lieutenant Colonel
Wilcox, Roswell	HG	First Lieutenant

100th REGIMENT INFANTRY

Organized in Kentucky at large May 3 to June 1, 1864. Attached to defense of Nashville & Northwestern Railroad, Dept. of the Cumberland, to December, 1864. 2nd Colored Brigade, District of the Etowah, Dept. of the Cumberland, to January, 1865. Defenses of Nashville & Northwestern Railroad, Dept. of the Cumberland, to December, 1865. SERVICE.—Guard duty in Nashville & Northwestern Railroad in Tennessee till December, 1864. Skirmish on Nashville & Northwestern Railroad September 4. Action at Johnsonville November 4-5. Battle of Nashville, Tenn., December 15-16. Overton Hill December 16. Pursuit of Hood to the Tennessee River December 17-28. Again assigned to guard duty on Nashville & Northwestern Railroad January 16, 1865, and so continued till December, 1865. Mustered out December 26, 1865.

Officer Roster

Name	Company	Rank
Aldrich, Elias H.	F	Second Lieutenant
Barrett, Wm. H.	D	Second Lieutenant
Benshoof, John	BI	Second Lieutenant
Brooks, Willis	B	Captain
Callahan, John C.	AG	Second Lieutenant
Collahan, John C.	AG	Lieutenant
Cook, George	H	Lieutenant
Coulter, Will A.	B	Captain
Cox, Wm. Henry	G	Lieutenant
Dillenbach, Frank Cook	F&S	First Lieutenant/ Adjutant
Elliott, Justin C.	F&S	Surgeon
Essex, James F.	I	First Lieutenant
Farnham, Moses P.	C	First Lieutenant
Ford, Collin	F	Major
Gardner, Washington W.	AD	First Lieutenant
Grosvenor, David A.	K	First Lieutenant

Jones, George W.	B	First Lieutenant
Jones, Reuben D.	I	Second Lieutenant
Kaepestion, Gustav W.		First Lieutenant/ Regimental Quartermaster
Kilp, Anton		Captain
Lescher, Samuel B		Assistant Surgeon
Liscon, Francis	D	First Lieutenant
Lyman, Carl P.	G	Captain
Masterson, Jason N.	E	Second Lieutenant
Mason, Thomas	F	Captain
McCarthy, Daniel	CB	Second Lieutenant
Miler, Levi B.	F&S	Chaplain
Musson, Reuben D.	HK	Colonel
Rogers, William H.	GH	Second Lieutenant
Selders, Thomas B.	H	First Lieutenant
Smith, Alexander T.	D	Second Lieutenant
Smith, James A.	F	First Lieutenant
Stone, Henry	F&S	Lieutenant Colonel
Straight, David E.	I	Captain

1ST BATTERY KANSAS LIGHT ARTILLERY

Organized at Mound City July 24, 1861. Attached to Dept. of Kansas to August, 1862. 2nd Brigade, Dept. of Kansas, to October, 1862. 1st Brigade, 1st Division, Army of the Frontier, Dept. Missouri, to February, 1863. District of Rolla, Dept. of Missouri, to June, 1863. District of Columbus, Ky., 6th Division, 16th Army Corps, Dept. Tennessee, to November, 1863. Defenses of the Nashville & Northwestern Railroad, District of Nashville, Dept. of the Cumberland, and 2nd Brigade, 4th Division, 20th Army Corps, Dept. of the Cumberland, to November, 1864. 2nd Colored Brigade, District of the Etowah, Dept. Cumberland, to January, 1865. Reserve Artillery, District of Nashville, Dept. Cumberland, to July, 1865. SERVICE.-Attached to Lane's Kansas Brigade and operations about Fort Scott, and on line of the

Marmiton August and September, 1861. Actions at Ball's Mills August 28. Morse's Mill August 29. Dogwood Creek near Fort Scott September 2. Morristown September 17. Osceola September 21-22. Duty at Fort Scott till May, 1862. Expedition into Indian Country May 25-August 15. Action at Grand River June 6. Locust Grove July 3. Bayou Bernard July 27. Blunt's Campaign in Missouri and Arkansas September 17-December 3. Expedition to Sarcoxie September 28-30.Action at Newtonia September 29-30. Occupation of Newtonia October 4. Old Fort Wayne or Beattie's Prairie near Maysville October 22. Cane Hill November 28. Battle of Prairie Grove, Ark., December 7. Expedition over Boston Mountains to Van Buren December 27-31. Moved to Springfield, Mo., January, 1863, and duty there till February 17. Moved to Forsyth, Mo., thence to Fort Scott, Kansas. Duty In Missouri and Kansas, District of Rolla, till July, 1863. Ordered to St. Louis, Mo., July 5, thence to Cairo, Ill., July 18. Duty in District of Columbus, Ky., till November. Ordered to Nashville, Tenn., and assigned to duty on line of the Nashville & Northwestern Railroad till November, 1861. Moved to Nashville, Tenn. Battles of Nashville December 15-16. Post duty at Nashville till January, 1865, and at Chattanooga, Tenn., till July. Mustered out July 17, 1865. Regiment lost during service 2 Enlisted men killed and 1 Officer and 23 Enlisted men by disease. Total 26.

Officer Roster

Name	Company	Rank
Allen, Norman		First Lieutenant
Baldwin, Moses D.		Second Lieutenant
Beckerton, Thomas		Captain
Brown, Hartson R.		Second Lieutenant
Cook, John B.		Second Lieutenant
Kearney, Michael		Second Lieutenant
Kent, Alonzo H.		First Lieutenant
Nolan, James N.		Second Lieutenant
Stoneburner, John C.		First Lieutenant
Taylor, Thomas		Second Lieutenant
Tenney, Marcus D.		First Lieutenant
Woodruff, William		First Lieutenant

APPENDIX B

Uncommon Valor

Uncommon valor was a common virtue[1]

Another spectacular naval exploit was performed in May 1862 by Robert Smalls, *a slave living in Charleston, South Carolina. The following account is taken from a book about the Negro in the Civil War,* Camp-Fires of the Afro-American, *published in 1889:*

When Fort Sumter was attacked, [Smalls] and his brother John, with their families, resided in Charleston, and saw with sorrow the lowering of its flag, but they were wise enough to think much, while saying little, except among themselves, and hoped for a time to come when they might again live under its Government. The high-pressure side-wheel steamer *Planter,* on board which they were employed, Robert as an assistant pilot, and John as a sailor and assistant engineer, was a light-draught vessel, drawing only five feet when heavily ladened (sic), and was very useful to the Confederates in plying around the harbor and among the islands near Charleston . . . . On Monday evening, May 12, 1862, the *Planter* was lying at her wharf, the Southern, and her officers having finished their duties for the day, went ashore, first giving the usual instructions to Robert Smalls, to see that everything should be in readiness for their trip next morning. They had a valuable lot of freight for Fort Ripley and Fort Sumter, which was to be delivered the next day, but Robert thought to himself that perhaps these forts would not receive the articles after all, except as some of them might be delivered by the propulsion of powder out of Union guns. He did not betray his thoughts by his demeanor, and when the officers left the vessel he appeared to be in his usual respectful, attentive, efficient and obedient state of mind. He busied himself immediately to have the fires banked, and everything put shipshape for the night, according to orders. A little after eight o'clock the wives and children of Robert and John Smalls came on board. As they had sometimes visited the vessel, carrying meals, nothing was thought of this circumstance by the wharf guard, who saw them.

Somewhat later a Colored man from the steamer *Etowah* stepped past him, and joined the crew. Robert Smalls, for some time, had been contemplating the move which he was now about to make. He had heard that Colored men were being enlisted in the United States service at his old home [Beaufort], and that General Hunter was foreshadowing the mancipatory (sic) policy, giving kindly treatment to all contraband refugees. Now he was more anxious to get within the Union lines, and to join its forces. He had seen from the pilot-house, at a long distance, the blockading vessels, and thought over a plan to reach them with the *Planter,* and his desire was to run her away from the Confederates when she would have a valuable cargo. He had to proceed cautiously in the unfolding of his designs. First his brother was taken into confidence, and he at once approved the project. He, of course, could be trusted to keep the secret. Then the others were approached, gradually, after sounding with various lines the depths of their patriotism . . . . The brave men knew what would be their fate in the event of failure, and so, in talking over the matter together, just before cutting loose, they decided not to be captured alive, but to go down with the ship if the batteries of Castle Pinckney, Forts Moultrie and Sumter, and other guns should be opened upon them.

They also determined to use the *Planter's* guns to repel pursuit and attack, if necessary . . . . after midnight, when the officers ashore were in their soundest and sweetest slumbers, the fires were stirred up and steam raised to a high pressure, and between 3 and 4 o'clock Robert Smalls, the conceiver, leader and manager of this daring scheme, gave orders to "cast off," which was done quietly. To guard against a suspicion of anything being wrong in the movements of the *Planter,* he backed slowly from the wharf, blew her signal whistles, and seemed to be in no hurry to get away. He proceeded down the harbor, as if making towards Fort Sumter, and about quarter past 4 o'clock passed the frowning fortress, saluting it with loud signals, and then putting on all steam. Her appearance was duly reported to the officer of the day, but as her plying around the harbor, often at early hours, was not a strange occurrence, and she had become a familiar floating figure to the forts, she was not molested; and the heavy guns that easily could have sunk her, remained silent.

Passing the lower batteries, also, without molestation, the happy crew, with the greater part of the strain removed from their minds, now jubilantly rigged a white flag that they had prepared for the next emergency, and steered straight on to the Union ships. They were yet in great danger, this time from the hands of friends, who, not knowing anything concerning their escape, and on the lookout to sink at sight torpedo-boats and "rebel-rams," might blow them out of the water before discovering their peaceful flag. An eye-witness of the *Planter's* arrival, a member of the *Onward's* crew, and a war correspondent, gave a good account of it; and with some alterations it is here introduced: "We have been anchored in the ship channel for some days, and have frequently seen a secesh (sic) steamer plying in and around the harbor. Well, this morning, about sunrise, I was awakened by the cry of 'All hands to quarters!' and before I could get out, the steward knocked vigorously on my door and called: 'All hands to quarter, sah! de ram am a comin', sah!' I don't recollect of ever dressing myself any quicker, and got out on deck in a hurry. Sure enough, we could see, through the mist and fog, a great black object moving rapidly, and steadily, right at our port quarter . . . . Springs were bent on, and the *Onward* was rapidly warping around so as to bring her broadside to bear on the steamer that was still rapidly approaching us; and when the guns were brought to bear, some of the men looked at the Stars and Stripes, and then at the steamer, and muttered 'You! if you run into us we will go down with colors flying!' Just as No.3 port gun was being elevated, someone cried out, 'I see something that looks like a white flag;' and true enough there was something flying on the steamer that would have been *white* by application of soap and water. As she neared us, we looked in vain for the face of a white man. When they discovered that we would not fire on them, there was a rush of contrabands out on her deck, some dancing, some singing, whistling, jumping; and others stood looking towards Fort Sumter, and muttering all sorts of maledictions against it, and *'de heart of de Soul,'* generally. As the steamer came near, and under the stern of the *Onward,* one of the Colored men stepped forward, and taking off his hat, shouted, 'Good morning, sir! I've brought you some of the old United States guns, sir!'"

Congress granted half of the prize money for the Planter to Smalls and his men. Smalls became one of the most valuable assets of the Union blockade fleet in the South Atlantic.[2]

Robert Smalls[3]
Courtesy of the Library of Congress

The Medal of Honor (MOH) was established in 1861 by President Lincoln as the Nation's highest award for bravery, then and now. At first it was abused. For example, all members of the 27th Maine Infantry Regiment (864 troops) were awarded the MOH on the eve of Gettysburg. They were entitled to be discharged because their enlistment had expired, but they agreed to stay and fight the battle. A later review board chaired by General Nelson Miles rescinded hundreds of MOH awards as unworthy including those of 27th Maine.[4] None of the rescinded awards were for African Americans. Currently (2011) only 3,464 MOH have been awarded. Of these, twenty five African Americans in the Civil War were approved for the award and many others in the wars that followed.[5] Nineteen service men have received two MOH including African American Robert Augustus Sweeny who served in conflicts after the Civil War. In perhaps the final chapter of the Civil War, Andrew Jackson Smith an African American discussed below, was awarded the MOH in 2001, *137 years after the event.* The reason was a missing battle report. President Clinton pushed a bit to get this done.[6]

Listed below are Union African Americans who were awarded the Medal of Honor for bravery in the Civil War.[7] In many cases, as with white recipients, the below citations mention seizing or defending flags. Today, this may appear trivial to some, but at the time, performing this act was fraught with danger and many who attempted this did not survive. Capturing or defending the colors was a rallying point for the battle and in many cases determined its outcome. Most of these medals for African Americans were a result of the Battle of New Market Heights (also called Chaffin's Farm). These were based upon recommendations of General Butler (see Chapter 2 for discussion of Butler).

Aaron Anderson (AKA Sanderson) Served on board the U.S.S. *Wyandank* during a boat expedition up Mattox Creek, March 17, 1865. Participating with a boat crew in the clearing of Mattox Creek, Anderson carried out his duties courageously in the face of a devastating fire which cut away half the oars, pierced the launch in many places and cut the barrel off a musket being fired at the enemy.

Bruce Anderson, Private, Company K, 142d New York Infantry.

At Fort Fisher, N.C., 15 January 1865. Entered service at: Ephratah, N.Y. Born: Mexico, Oswego County, N.Y., 9 June 1845. Voluntarily advanced with the head of the column and cut down the palisading.

Private William H. Barnes, Company C, 38th U.S. Colored Troops.

At Chapins Farm, Va., 29 September 1864. Birth: St. Mary's County, Md. Date of issue 6 April 1865. Among the first to enter the enemy's works; although wounded.

Powhatan Beaty
Courtesy of the Library of Congress

First Sergeant Powhatan Beaty, Company G, 5th USC Infantry, September 29, 1864.

All his company officers being killed or wounded, he took control of his company, leading them gallantly throughout the battle at New Market Heights.

Robert Blake, Contraband, U.S. Navy. Entered service at: Virginia. G.O. No.: 32, 16 April 1864. Accredited to: Virginia. Citation: On board the U.S. Steam Gunboat Marblehead off Legareville, Stono River, 25 December 1863, in an engagement with the enemy on John's Island. Serving the rifle gun, Blake, an escaped slave, carried out his duties bravely throughout the engagement which resulted in the enemy's abandonment of positions, leaving a caisson and one gun behind.

First Sergeant James H. Bronson, Company D, 5th USC Infantry, September 29, 1864.

At New Market Heights, he took command of his company after all its officers were killed or wounded, and led them on to victory.

William H. Brown, Landsman, U.S. Navy.

Born: 1836, Baltimore, Md. Accredited to: Maryland. G.O. No.: 45, 31 December 1864. Citation: On board the U.S.S. Brooklyn during successful attacks against Fort Morgan rebel gunboats and the ram Tennessee in Mobile Bay on 5 August 1864. Stationed in an area which was twice cleared of men by bursting shells, Brown remained steadfast at his post and performed his duties in the powder division throughout the furious action which resulted in the surrender of the prize rebel ram Tennessee and in the damaging and destruction of batteries at Fort Morgan.

Wilson Brown, Landsman, U.S. Navy.

Born: 1841, Natchez, Miss. Accredited to: Mississippi. G.O. No.: 45, 31 December 1864. On board the flagship U.S.S. Hartford during successful attacks against Fort Morgan, rebel gunboats and the ram Tennessee in Mobile Bay on 5 August 1864. Knocked unconscious into the hold of the ship when an enemy shell burst fatally wounding a man on the ladder above him, Brown, upon regaining consciousness, promptly returned to the shell whip on the berth deck and zealously continued to perform his duties although 4 of the 6 men at this station had been either killed or wounded by the enemy's terrific fire.

William H. Carney
Courtesy of the Library of Congress

Sergeant William H. Carney, Company C, 54th Massachusetts, Colored Infantry, July 18, 1863. While storming the ramparts at Fort Wagner, the standard bearer was shot down. Sergeant Carney caught the banner and held it high throughout the battle. Though seriously wounded he carried the colors to the rear when retreat was ordered saying "the old flag never touched the ground, boys."

Sergeant Decatur Dorsey, Company B, 39th USC Infantry, July 30, 1864.

Planted his colors on the Confederate works in advance of his regiment, at Petersburg; when the regiment was driven back to the Union works, he carried the colors there and bravely rallied the men.

Christian A. Fleetwood
Courtesy of the Library of Congress

Sgt.-Major Christian A. Fleetwood, 4th USC Infantry, September 19, 1864.

At New Market Heights, he seized the colors after two color bearers had been shot down, and bore them "nobly" through the fight.

James Gardiner
Courtesy of the Library of Congress

Private James Gardiner, Company I, 36th USC Infantry, September 29, 1864.

At New Market Heights, he rushed in advance of his brigade, shot a rebel officer who was on the parapet rallying his men, then ran him through with his bayonet.

James H. Harris
Courtesy of the Library of Congress

James H. Harris, Company B, 38th USC Infantry, September 29, 1864.

Fought with great skill and courage in the assault at New Market Heights.

Thomas R. Hawkins
Courtesy of the Library of Congress

Sgt.-Major Thomas R. Hawkins, 6th USC Infantry, July 21, 1864.

At the battle of Deep Bottom, Va., at the risk of his life, he rescued the colors from the enemy.

Sergeant Alfred B. Hilton, Company H, 4th USC Infantry, September 29, 1864.

He carried the national colors at New Market Heights; when the regimental standard bearer fell, he caught the banner, struggled forward carrying both flags until badly wounded and fell. While on the ground and in great pain he continued to hold the colors aloft.

Milton M. Holland
Courtesy of the Library of Congress

Sergeant-Major Milton M. Holland, 5th USC Infantry, September 19, 1864.

Took command of Company C, after all its officers had been killed or wounded and led it through the battle.

Corporal Miles James, Company B, USC Infantry, September 30, 1864.

Having had his arm so badly mutilated that immediate amputation was necessary, he loaded and discharged his piece with one hand and urged his men forward—all within 30 yards of the enemy's works.

Alexander Kelly
Courtesy of the Library of Congress

First Sergeant Alexander Kelly, Company F, 6th USC Infantry, September 29, 1864.

At New Market Heights, seized the colors, which had fallen near the ramparts, raised them, and rallied his men at a time of confusion and a place of the greatest possible danger.

John Lawson
Courtesy of the Library of Congress

John Lawson, Landsman, U.S. Navy.

Born: 1837, Pennsylvania. Accredited to: Pennsylvania. G.O. No.: 45, 31 December 1864. On board the flagship U.S.S. Hartford during successful attacks against Fort Morgan, rebel gunboats and the ram Tennessee in Mobile Bay on 5 August 1864. Wounded in the leg and thrown violently against the side of the ship when an enemy shell killed or wounded the 6-man crew as the shell whipped on the berth deck, Lawson, upon regaining his composure, promptly returned to his station and, although urged to go below for treatment, steadfastly continued his duties throughout the remainder of the action.

James Mifflin, Engineer's Cook, U.S. Navy.

Born: 1839, Richmond, Va. Accredited to: Virginia. G.O. No.: 45, 31 December 1864. Citation: On board the U.S.S. Brooklyn during successful attacks against Fort Morgan, rebel gunboats and the ram Tennessee in Mobile Bay, on 5 August 1864. Stationed in the immediate vicinity of the shell whips which were twice cleared of men by bursting shells, Mifflin remained steadfast at his post and performed his duties in the powder division throughout the furious action which resulted in the surrender of the prize rebel ram Tennessee and in the damaging and destruction of batteries at Fort Morgan.

Joachim Pease, Seaman, U.S. Navy.

Born: Long Island, N.Y. Accredited to: New York. G.O. No.: 45, 31 December 1864. Citation: Served as seaman on board the U.S.S. Kearsarge when she destroyed the Alabama off Cherbourg, France, 19 June 1864. Acting as loader on the No. 2 gun during this bitter engagement, Pease exhibited marked coolness and good conduct and was highly recommended by the divisional officer for gallantry under fire.

Robert Pinn
Courtesy of the Library of Congress

First-Sergeant Robert Pinn, Company I, 5th USC Infantry, September 29, 1864.

After all company officers had been killed or wounded, he took command and led it through the entire battle.

First-Sergeant Edward Ratcliff, Company C, 38th USC Infantry, September 29, 1864. Thrown into command of his company by the death of his commanding officer, he was the first enlisted man in the enemy's works, leading his company with great gallantry.

Corporal Andrew Jackson Smith, of Clinton, Illinois, 55th Massachusetts Voluntary Infantry, distinguished himself on 30 November 1864 by saving his regimental colors, after the color bearer was killed during a bloody charge called the Battle of Honey Hill, South Carolina. In the late afternoon, as the 55th Regiment pursued enemy skirmishers and conducted a running fight, they ran into a swampy area backed by a rise where the Confederate Army awaited. The surrounding woods and thick underbrush impeded infantry movement and artillery support. The 55th and 54th regiments formed columns to advance on the enemy position in a flanking movement. As the Confederates repelled other units, the 55th and 54th regiments continued to move into flanking positions. Forced into a narrow gorge crossing a swamp in the face of the enemy position, the 55th's Color-Sergeant was killed by an exploding shell, and Corporal Smith took the Regimental Colors from his hand and carried them through heavy grape and canister fire. Although half of the officers and a third of the enlisted men engaged in the fight were killed or wounded, Corporal Smith continued to expose himself to enemy fire by carrying the colors throughout the battle. Through his actions, the Regimental Colors of the 55th Infantry Regiment were not lost to the enemy. Corporal Andrew Jackson Smith's extraordinary valor in the face of deadly enemy fire is in keeping with the highest traditions of military service and reflect great credit upon him, the 55th Regiment, and the United States Army. The award was made in 2001. Smith's descendents received the award from President Clinton.

Private Charles Veal, Company D, 4th USC Infantry, September 29, 1864.

After two color bearers had been shot down with the regimental colors, Private Veal seized them and bore them through the battle.

APPENDIX C

Summary of Significant Battles Fought by USCT

African Americans fought in many battles during the Civil War. The African American participation in battles for the Union is easily tracked since the African Americans were organized into segregated regiments. Not so in the South. African Americans who joined the Confederate army were integrated into Southern units and there was no great battle won for the Confederacy by African Americans: their participation in key battles is not visible, they fought in white units alongside their white fellow soldiers. The listing of battles below is not a complete list of Union African American battles, but only those that were significant and had a major impact on how the whites viewed African Americans as soldiers. The total list of all battles in which African Americans fought for the Union is impressive: 39 major battles and 449 engagements.

Port Hudson, 27 May 1863

The Battle of Port Hudson, Louisiana 27 May 1863. In cooperation with General Grant's attack on Vicksburg, General Banks moved against Post Hudson on the Mississippi. Two regiments of African American troops, 1st and 3rd Louisiana Regiments led the assault on the Confederate stronghold. At least six charges were made against Port Hudson and the regiments sustained heavy losses. After the attack failed, the Union army settled into a siege that ended on 9 July when the Confederates surrendered the fort. The attack by the African American regiments proved their effectiveness and courage.[1] As Banks wrote to Halleck, Lincoln's General-in-Chief. "Whatever doubt may have existed heretofore as to the efficiency [of the African American regiments] the history of this day proves conclusively . . . . no doubt of their ultimate success."[2] There were many other battles during this period that proved that African Americans could fight just as well if not better than their white counterparts. Battles such as Honey Springs in Indian Territory and Milliken's Bend in Louisiana proved African American's courage and determination to the Union army.[3]

Battle of Milliken's Bend, 7 June 1863

Milliken's Bend was a Union outpost on the Mississippi River above Vicksburg defended by white units and African Americans of the Ninth Regiment of the Louisiana Volunteers. Captain M. M. Miller of the ninth described the battle in a letter home to his aunt.

> Dear Aunt: We were attacked here on 7 June, about 3 o'clock in the morning, by a brigade of Texas troops about 2,500 in number. We had about 600 men to withstand them—500 of the negroes . . . Our regiment had about 300 in the fight . . . We had about 50 men killed in the regiment and 80 wounded; so you can judge of what part of the fight my company sustained . . . I never more wish to hear the expression, "the niggers won't fight." . . . The enemy charged us so close that we fought with our bayonets, hand to hand . . . . It was a horrble fight, the worst I was ever engaged in—not even Shiloh. The enemy cried "No quarter!" but some of them were very glad to take it when made prisoners.[4]

The Confederate commander General Henry McCulloch wrote "This charge was resisted by the negroe portion of the enemy's force with considerable obstinancy while the white or true Yankee portion ran like whipped curs almost as soon as the charge was ordered."[5] No African American soldier taken prisoner by the rebels during that fight was found alive.[6]

Battle of Honey Springs, 17 July 1863

In Indian Territory, General Blunt's Union command attacked and defeated Confederate General Cooper. It was the largest engagement in the territory and the African American regiments were instrumental in handing the Confederates a defeat.[7]

Battle of Fort Wagner, 18 July 1863: October 1863

The 54th Massachusetts African American regiment commanded by Colonel Robert Gould Shaw moved south for operations against Charleston, South Carolina. Fort Wagner was among the forts guarding Charleston and the 54th was given the task of leading the assault on the fort. Wagner had been under artillery fire for most of the day which did little good. The approach to the fort was a narrow sandy beach that forced the troops to bunch up and the Confederates opened fire with devastating effect.[8]

Baxter Springs, 6 October 1863

The Battle of Baxter Springs was fought in Kansas when raider Southern William Clark Quantrill attacked a Union column on a road near Baxter Springs. After some members of the column were captured and murdered, the rest fled to the nearby fort. The African Americans fought off the Quantrill attack.

Battle of Olustree, 20 February 1864

The Eighth Regiment, USCT and Seventh New Hampshire Regiment fought under General Truman Seymour near Ocean Pond in Florida. This was the major battle of the war in Florida. The Union was defeated by an equal force of Confederates under General Joseph Finegan. Both U.S. regiments suffered heavy casualties.[9]

The Fort Pillow Massacre, 12 April 1864

Nathan Bedford Forrest reported after the battle that of 500 African Americans and 200 white soldiers, 500 were killed in the battle.[10] A later investigation stated that 300 of the men were murdered in cold blood after they had surrendered. There were many examples of the murder of African American Union soldiers (and usually their white leaders, as well) by the Confederate Army. The Confederacy viewed African American Union soldiers as traitors and, as such, they should be killed. White officers of African American regiments were executed for "fermenting slave insurrection"[11] General Grant informed the Confederacy that for every African American murdered by the South, one white Confederate prisoner would be executed.[12] It was not an idle threat. Some of the white Confederate prisoners were shot in retaliation for the murders committed by the Confederacy. Unfortunately Southern Generals such as Pickett and Forrest were not charged for their war crimes after the war as they should have been.

Grant's order stopped the wholesale murder of Union African American soldiers by the Confederacy, but they were still mistreated.[13]

Battle of Petersburg, 15 June 1864

22nd USCT at Petersburg
Courtesy of the Library of Congress

The Federals attacked the Confederate line but a courageous Confederate defense saved Petersburg although a gallant charge by the 22d Regiment, USCT carried the first Confederate line.[14]

Battle of the Crater, 30 July 1864

The Crater
Courtesy of the Library of Congress

The concept was to dig a mine under the Confederate line, load it with explosives and blow the mine breaking the Confederate defenses. It was a risky plan. Two African American brigades were chosen to lead the attack after the mine was blown, but Grant changed that. He later said that if the African American brigades were slaughtered, it would be said that they had been sacrificed to save white soldiers.[15] As a result, white troops were put in first at the last minute. They were untrained for this operation and battle weary. As a result when the mine blew, the white troops spent time milling around in the crater accomplishing nothing for two hours and the two African American brigades were then ordered in. By that time the Confederates had recovered from the shock of the blast and had reformed their line. The African American brigades sustained heavy casualties.[16] The white troops broke and ran back to federal lines shortly followed by the African American troops. Total killed in the African American brigades was 195. By chance or Confederate design, many of the white officers in the African American regiments were killed or wounded adding to the chaos in the crater.[17]

Battle of Chaffin's Farm (Also called the Battle of New Market Heights), 29-30 September 1864

Chaffin's Farm was part of the defense system surrounding Richmond. Thirteen regiments of the USCT participated in the battle and fourteen Medals of Honor were awarded to African Americans. See Appendix B for details.[18] 870 African Americans were killed or wounded in the battle.[19]

Battle of Spanish Wells, 27 March to 8 April 1865

The Union army attacked Spanish Fort after a bombardment. The Union broke through the Confederate line but the Southern defenders escaped under cover of darkness.[20]

Battle of Fort Blakely, 9 April 1865

After four years of arduous service, marked by unsurpassed courage and fortitude, the Army of Northern Virginia has been compelled to yield to overwhelming numbers of resources . . . . By the terms of the agreement officers and men can return to their homes and remain until exchanged. You will take with you the satisfaction that proceeds from the consciousness of duty faithfully performed, and I earnestly pray that a Merciful God will extend to you His blessing and protection. With an increasing admiration of your constancy and devotion to your country, and a grateful remembrance of your kind and generous considerations for myself, I bid you an affectionate farewell.[21]

R. E. Lee

Robert E. Lee after the War
Courtesy of the Library of Congress

As a clear spring sun rose in Virginia, General Robert E. Lee surrendered the Confederate army in Virginia to U. S. Grant at Appomattox Court House. At the same time, in the West, the USCT and regiments of McArthur's Division were making the final assault on Fort Blakely in Alabama on 9 April 1865. This was the last major battle of the Civil War.[22]

Grant's objective in January of 1865 was to end the war as soon as possible with minimum loss of life. The Confederacy was defeated and this was clear to people on both sides. Grant had key elements in his plan. He would continue to confront Lee. Sherman intended to invade South Carolina to seize Port Royal. General Sheridan would move in Virginia with the objective of Lynchburg and destroying railroads and locks. General Stoneman's cavalry would raid in Tennessee and move into North Carolina and Virginia. General Canby who was in New Orleans was ordered to attack several key objectives including Mobile, one of the few remaining Confederate ports that was also a rail hub. To do all of this, Grant had 900,000 troops including 300,000 reserves that he could call in. The Confederacy could muster only about 160,000 men. The author Shelby Foote, labeled this "Grant's Close-Out Plan." Very few Confederates wanted to be the last casualty of the Civil War dying for the "lost cause". Absenteeism was about forty-nine per cent in the Army of Tennessee, sixty percent in the Army of Northern Virginia and Jefferson Davis stated that one-quarter of a million deserters were on the rolls of the War Department.[23] The end was near. Lincoln was very clear: there would be no discussions or negotiations among generals about political matters.[24] Lincoln did not want to fritter away at any conference table of generals what had been won on the battlefield at the cost of hundreds of thousands of lives. The terms would be unconditional surrender. The Union would be reunited. With this backdrop, the last major battle of the Civil War was fought.

The Battle of Spanish Fort in Alabama took place from 27 March through 8 April 1865. After the Union navy victory at the Battle of Mobile Bay, the city of Mobile, Alabama remained in the hands of the Confederate army. As a major port and railroad hub, it was necessary to take Mobile and Union forces including A. J. Smith's XVI Corps under General Canby[25] advanced to take Spanish Fort, a major stronghold defending Mobile. While Grant was trapping R. E. Lee in Virginia, General Canby was preparing for the attack on Mobile, Alabama. This would be trench warfare with the Union troops slowly digging their way to the Confederate Spanish Fort defenses. The battle was fought from 27 March to 8 April 1865. This was a formidable defensive position but the other regiments reduced casualties by digging at night and throwing up dirt and logs to protect them from the enemy fire which followed each morning. The trench followed a zig-zag pattern toward the fort that afforded opportunity to bring in Union artillery, but these guns were unable to penetrate the fort's defenses. By the 7th of April, the Union troops had dug their way to the stronghold of Spanish Fort and were now ready for the final assault. That night a heavy bombardment was started by several hundred Union guns that continued the next day and into the evening of 8 April.

The Union troops rushed in and overwhelmed the Spanish Fort defenders only to find that the Confederates had spiked their guns and fled to nearby Fort Blakely seven miles away. One soldier entering the fort described the scene. "Our shells had converted the ground into a striking resemblance to a hog yard that had been rooted over and over. We had avoided the torpedoes by having gotten our trench higher than they were. Spanish Fort with its heavy armaments was ours."[26]Fort Blakely was a smaller fort and not well defended. While R. E. Lee was surrendering to Grant at Appomattox on Palm Sunday, 9 April 1865 the Union army was assembling before Fort Blakely. By that afternoon, the troops that had been surrounding Fort Blakely launched their attack. Fort Blakely and two thousand Confederate prisoners were taken. Total cost in Union casualties for this two week campaign was about fifteen hundred dead and wounded or about one in ten of those engaged.[27]

Battle of Palmetto Ranch, 15 May 1865

Palmetto Ranch was the last battle of the Civil War and occurred after the Confederate surrender and Lincoln's assassination.[28]

APPENDIX D

The Price They Paid

Beans killed more soldiers than bullets.[1]

Some describe medical treatment during the Civil War as "at the end of the medical Middle Ages."[2] One out of three soldiers in the Civil War died of disease and battle wounds.[3] Little was known of the causes of diseases and even less about the necessity for clean instruments or to maintain a sterile environment when operating on the wounded even if the surgeons had time for these measures. While many surgeons were aware of the relationship between cleanliness and low infection rates, they did not have the time or means to sterilize instruments and often went days without "fresh water" to wash hands or instruments. In this way infection was spread from one patient to another and many died of what was then called "surgical fevers". The treatment of the wounded was considered by some to be barbaric. One witness described the situation: "Tables about breast high had been erected upon which the screaming victims were having legs and arms cut off. The surgeons and their assistants, stripped to the waist and spattered with blood, stood around, some holding the poor fellows while others, armed with long bloody knives and saws, cut and sawed away with frightful rapidity, throwing the mangled limbs on a pile nearby as soon as removed."[4] In spite of all of the horror stories, 75% of the amputees survived and anesthetics such as chloroform were available to kill pain.[5]

Wounds, diseases and treatment of the wounded were similar in the South and the North during the Civil War. The greatest differences between the two were that the South lacked surgeons, drugs due to the Union blockade, and resources to adequately care for the casualties. Joseph Jones, a Confederate medical officer, estimated that the South mobilized more than 600,000 fighting men and of these nearly 200,000 died from all causes.[6] On average, each soldier fell victim to wounds or disease six times during the war.[7] Jones also concluded that three quarters of the deaths were from disease.[8] This was a similar figure to the Union's experience, but the statistics for the South are suspect since many records were lost during and after the war and the numbers may have been much higher.[9] By comparison, two out of three Union deaths were from disease.[10]

Added to the Confederate medical workload was the number of Union prisoners that also required treatment. Admissions at the Andersonville prison hospital were 17,875.[11] For the most part, African Americans were not included in the list of casualties since they were not formally mustered into Confederate units but were body servants or those impressed to perform labor.

The South had few doctors to cope with this high number of patients. By 1861, the South had twenty-one medical schools. Quality of the schools was similar to those found in the North.[12] They ranged from diploma mills to schools that maintained high academic standards such as Virginia.[13]

Chloroform was first used by Dr. James Young Simpson of Edinburgh in 1847.[14] It was used by both sides during the Civil War, but ether was also used. Death from either anesthetic was rare. Curiously, the fatality rate among wounded Union soldiers was higher than the Confederates although the Union had more doctors, facilities and drugs than did the Confederates.[15]

This difference is not explained, but it may come down to record keeping and the fact that the Union tracked casualties more thoroughly than the Confederates and after the war many Confederate records were lost. For example, the records of the Confederate Surgeon General were destroyed by fire in 1865.

The Confederate army was always on the lookout for medical supplies. When Stonewall Jackson captured a Union supply train near

Winchester, Virginia on 24 May 1862 it was the medical stores including 1,500 cases of chloroform that were quickly liberated.[16] The number of cases of chloroform was probably an exaggeration. Many rosters only identified those killed in action or died of wounds because the death by disease was not recorded. A total of approximately 620,000 men died during the Civil War of all causes—360,000 Union and 260,000 Confederate.[17] This is more than the total deaths of all other wars in the history of the United States.

Two causes for this disastrous death toll can be identified. First, the Civil War was being fought with 18th Century tactics and 19th Century technology. By the 1860s, the rifled musket was available to both the North and the South. These rifles extended the range and accuracy of the infantry weapon and coupled with the Minie bullet invented by a French officer, Claude Etienne Minie. The Minie bullet first saw service in the Crimean War a few years before the U. S. Civil War. The Minie bullet increased the speed with which the single shot muzzle loading rifle could be reloaded. The hollow base of this .58 caliber bullet expanded when fired and enabled the bullet to spin providing greater accuracy. The shock of a Minie bullet was far greater than a round ball and created more severe wounds.[18]

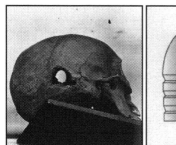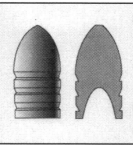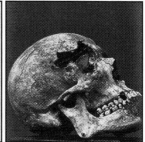

The Minie
Courtesy of the Library of Congress

Rapid fire breech loading cartridge rifles such as the Spencer rifle (test fired and approved by Lincoln) appeared during the Civil War. The Spencer rifle could fire eight rounds as fast as the soldier could operate the lever and cock the rifle. This may have provided the Union victory at Gettysburg when Buford's Cavalry delayed Lee's advance while Union forces were brought up. When hit by a Minie bullet in the head or body, the results were usually fatal since this heavy lead bullet tore a huge hole with an enormous impact.[19] Other nasty weapons and ammunition played a role in this war. Surgeons noticed that many of the casualties had multiple wounds including a lead ball and buckshot.[20] The ammunition was call "buck and ball" and was used by both sides. The concept was that the paper cartridge used during the Civil War included powder, a lead ball (to seal the barrel) with buckshot in front of it. When fired, the ball was lethal, but the buckshot would spread and create more wounds. Confederate General Patrick Cleburne who was killed at the battle of Franklin, Tennessee in 1864 was hit by forty-nine projectiles:[21] a classic case of over-kill. A Southern officer wounded at Shiloh wrote to his son. "My son, I am wounded in the arm, in the leg, in the head, in the body, and in another place which I have a delicacy in mentioning."[22]

As the war progressed, surgeons developed treatments for these wounds that somewhat reduced fatalities, but surgery as we know it today was not practiced. Opening of the body cavity during the Civil War was almost always fatal.[23] Those that survived the initial impact succumbed to infection that followed since there were no antibiotics to treat the infections. Unfortunately, surgeons were faced with a major problem: the body had already been opened by a gunshot wound and the surgeons had to deal with the consequences. Many times these wounded were left to die without any medical treatment since the wounds were considered to be mortal.[24] When hit in the extremity, the result was usually amputation.

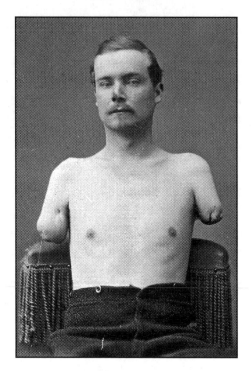

The Amputees
Courtesy of the Library of Congress

Astonishing statistics came out of the Civil War. While many veterans told of fear and the terrible toll inflicted by artillery, it was insignificant. 94 percent of casualties were caused by small arms (nearly always the .58 caliber rifled musket). Only 5.5 percent were caused by artillery. Compare this with World War I: three-quarters of casualties were caused by artillery.[25] The reason for the disparity was blurred areas indicating that more were lost to artillery than thought. For example, an artillery round of canister (small bullets) could not be distinguished from a musket bullet. A body disintegrated by a cannon blast would not make the statistics. The fact that the Confederacy had far less artillery than the Union also drove up losses from rifle fire by the Union side. The result is that cannon fire caused more casualties than indicated in the Civil War statics, but far less than the veterans remembered. The point is that the terrifying effect of massed artillery upon the troops was far greater than the wounds inflicted and led to battles lost due to panic among the troops.

Against these weapons traditional infantry tactics proven over several hundred years were employed. Soldiers advanced shoulder to shoulder against modern weapons and were shot down by the thousands. The problem was massed formations used to get into position and within range of the enemy. Once engaged, the troops would find cover when they could. One study of 44,000 men killed in action found that 82 percent were hit in the head, chest or neck.[26]

Second, on the medical side, neither the North nor the South were prepared for the war. At the start of the war, the Union had a total of 98 medical officers and the Confederates had twenty-four. By the end, the Union had 13,000 and the South had 4,000. More important, few surgeons on either side had treated a gunshot wound before the war started.[27] The numbers tell us of the need for doctors and why so many soldiers died from the beginning to the end of the conflict.[28] In Europe, doctors across the continent were discovering the causes of disease, treatment, and preventative measures such as sanitation. Unfortunately these discoveries had not reached the North American continent that was still in the middle ages of medicine.

Civil War physicians had a better grip on the treatment of wounds and diseases than most recognize today, but there were many unknowns. Infection caused by lack of sterilization was understood at the time, but surgeons did not have the time or resources to fix the problem.

Some common-sense things today did not appear to occur to the surgeons at the time such as boiling instruments and washing hands in whiskey although much less satisfying than drinking it.

The Physical Examinations

Each recruit was given a physical and many African Americans were found unfit for service due to the abuse by slaveholders and the rigors of life as a slave. Those unfit for service could volunteer for the Invalid Corps (later renamed Veteran Reserve Corps). This offered service and they would be given light duty such as guarding facilities. Many unfit volunteers joined. As with whites, African American conscripts reported for the physical examine claiming a variety of illnesses, real and imagined. Some limped into the medical facility on crutches recently cut from a nearby woods. A volunteer doctor recalled. "The stubbornness with which they persist in shamming disease, in order to escape soldiering is truly wonderful."[29] Most that enlisted when a regiment was being formed were committed to three years service while those enlisting in the field had a one year obligation.[30]

The first factor to consider is the health of the African Americans when they enlisted. Obviously the slaves were poorly fed and often beaten. Southerners Robert Fogel and Stanley Engerman dispute this in their book *Time on the Cross*. Their conclusion was that the slaves had an adequate and nutritious diet, a conclusion challenged by many critics.[31] A more relevant metric is height of the soldiers. African Americans were nearly one and one half inches shorter that their white fellow soldiers indicating malnutrition when they were young.[32] Add to this is the fact that in many cases they had traveled long distances and endured hardships in order to reach Union lines. An extreme example is found in the 65th USCT regiment. Thirty men died after they arrived and before they could be mustered.[33] A common practice at the time was to photograph African Americans when they reached Union lines and after they had been equipped. Scars on their backs from floggings is ample evidence of their treatment in the South. This was in part for Union propaganda purposes but was also very revealing about the condition of the recruits when they arrived. All recruits were supposed to undergo a surgeon's examination so that individuals unfit for service could be weeded out (perhaps saving their lives since they would be more likely to die from disease than a healthy person). Unfortunately, only about 11% of the African American recruits were examined when they enlisted.[34] Of those examined, one out of four were rejected. Whites fared no better and one survey found that one out of three whites were rejected.[35] There was an aspect of malingering in all of this. A conscripted white would be more likely to fake illness than an African American who may have traveled hundreds of miles to enlist.

Union Surgeon General Barnes was faced with old problems. Inadequate physical exams of recruits had led to an influx of old people many with degenerative diseases. These had burdened Grant's army in 1862 when a USSC report found a large number of patients with degenerative diseases occupying beds in the Department of the Gulf.[36] The list of disabilities was impressive: imbecility, insanity, epilepsy, paralysis, atrophy of a limb, tuberculosis, secondary syphilis and many other disabling diseases.[37] The cause was that many of these unfit people were pursuing bounties and others were being paid as substitutes in the subscription system in place at that time. They attempted to hide their disabilities and local politicians would persuade the examiners to be lenient.[38] At the other end of the spectrum were the very young people who had felt compelled to answer the call in defense of the nation. Young people age thirteen or younger were enlisting. Undoubtedly many who enlisted reported an age much older than they really were. It was generally agreed at that time that soldiers under the age of twenty (29 % of the soldiers were twenty or younger) were a liability to the army.[39] They had not developed immunity to common camp diseases. They were the first to sicken and die because their bodies had not matured and they could not withstand the rigors of service in the very hostile environment of war. Many of these deaths could have been avoided if adequate recruiting standards and an adequate system of examining recruits had been in place.

The Confederate experience was similar to the Union's. Medical regulations directed that surgeons strip and examine each recruit screening out those who were unfit,[40] but by the time these regulations were in place, many had already been accepted into service. As time went on and additional recruits were needed, the standards were lowered. In February 1863 examining surgeons were informed that "general debility . . . . slight deformity . . . . speech impediments . . . . functional heart trouble, muscular rheumatism . . . . loss of one eye . . . . loss of one or two fingers . . . . were not deemed sufficient and satisfactory for exemption."[41]

Diet of the Soldiers

The Union Army's diet was also a cause of casualties. Twelve ounces of salt pork or one pound four ounces of salt beef and one pound two ounces of flour was the basic diet. To that was added one vegetable, navy beans, peas or 1.6 ounces of rice. This was a skimpy diet and scurvy resulted.[42] Quality of the food was also a problem and beef was frequently bad in spite of efforts to pickle it and prevent decay.[43] The troops called it "salt horse" and sometimes it was a mystery meat of unknown origin. As one soldier described "It was black as a shoe; on the inside often yellow with putrefaction."[44] The troops called the hard bread "worm castles."[45] They preferred eating the bread at night so that they did not have to look at the maggots. Fortunately this bad diet was supplemented by food sent by relief organization and funds made available to purchase additional items, especially vegetables if the unit was in a location where such items were available. More often than not, the troops used their own pay to buy more rations. Foraging (stealing food from the locals) also added to the diet.

Cooking was a disaster and, as one surgeon put it, "Beans killed more soldiers than bullets." The problem was that the troops preferred to cook their own rations rather than use the unit cook. As a result, filthy disease ridden utensils and pans were used to cook up the beans and other food. People got sick from the practice. Pressure increased to force the troops to use the unit cook and enough cooks were hired to provide one cook per company, usually an African American. Surgeons and line officers were made jointly responsible for supervision and instruction.[46] This reduced illness, but many soldiers continued to cook on their own. Old habits die slow.

Science entered the scene to find a way to increase the quantity of potatoes available to the troops. "Desiccated potatoes" [dried potatoes] were introduced to fix the problem of potatoes rotting in shipment. Desiccated potatoes came in large, disgusting slabs that when boiled resembled, as one soldier put it "A dirty brook with all the dead leaves floating around promiscuously."[47] They were strongly loaded with pepper to make them "antiseptic." The result was indigestible by any creature and surgeons were surprised to find that scurvy reappeared even though soldiers who were hungry enough would eat anything even this product. What was not known until many years later was that the act of drying to produce desiccated potatoes removed the Vitamin C. Vitamin C prevented scurvy.

Other grand experiments followed. The "Horsford ration" invented by a Harvard professor of that name provided the bread and meat rations to give a Union soldier everything he needed. The meat was "sausage" consisting of such items as heart, liver, tongue and kidney and "varnished" with gelatin. The bread was coarsely ground wheat with salt and sugar added. The motivation was that this would save the government $10,000,000 per year.[48] A test was tried in Texas in 1864. The bread arrived loaded with vermin, the meat was spoiled and the troops got sick.[49] Many of these were African Americans. There is no record to indicate that Professor Horsford ever tried his own product. He is remembered for his reformulation of baking powder which was more successful than his Civil War efforts.

Poor rations accounted for many of the Confederate casualties. General Lee was constantly on the march to locate food for his forces and Lafayette Guild, Lee's medical director, stated in 1864 ". . . . the improvised ration, without vegetables or vegetable acids is in my opinion, the prime source of disease."[50] Rations in the Confederate army were always short, more so than the Union's units. This led to threats of mutiny and desperate measures. Lieutenant Nat Wood in Lee's army recalled that he and several fellow officers boiled a cat for two days only to find in frustration that it was too tough to carve. One North Carolinian recalled in his diary "Had fried rat for breakfast & never ate better meat."[51]

Poor preparation of food also took its toll. Unlike the Union that organized cooks on an army-wide level and enforced the use of company cooks, the Confederate approach was decentralized. The soldiers enjoyed bragging that "We can cook as good as any women."[52] until people continued to fall sick from dirty pans and utensils and poorly prepared food. The Confederate government response was "American soldiers have not the inherent taste for cooking like the Frenchman and certainly, until they are taught how to prepare their food so as to make it healthy and palatable, they ought to be furnished with cooks competent to attend to this department."[53] That was the extent of government help. Often the troops were fortunate enough to find an African

American to cook for them. Others would escape the government food and take meals at a friendly farmhouse. Like the Union army and its bread called "worm castles" the Confederates suffered from bad bread. The bread problem did not escape Confederate congressional scrutiny. In January 1864, a congressional committee condemned the food preparation and especially the bread. "The cooking especially of the bread was condemned . . . . bread hastily made up of flour and water and imperfectly baked [no mention of yeast], almost incapable of being digested, was deemed a most fruitful source of disease."[54] There was a difference in approach between the armies. In the North, "worm castles" were shipped to the troops from distant sources while in the South, the government poisoned its troops locally with unit cooks and poorly prepared bread.

The Union Mess Hall. Very often Supported by African American Cooks
Courtesy of the Library of Congress

Medical Organization
The Surgeon General

Eight days after Jefferson Davis was inaugurated the "Act for the Establishment and Organization of a General Staff for the Confederate States of America" was passed on February 26, 1861. This included a medical department with one Surgeon General and ten other surgeons.[55] When large scale epidemics entered the Confederate ranks early in the war, additional officers were added to the medical department.[56] The navy program was included and authorized physicians for the fleet.[57]

Samuel Preston Moore, a native of Charleston, South Carolina was selected to be acting Surgeon General with the rank of Colonel on 30 July 1861.[58] Moore was a graduate of the Medical College of South Carolina in 1834.[59] He would preside over the Confederacy's Medical Department for the duration of the war including over one hundred hospitals scattered throughout the Confederate states with a surgeon in charge of each.[60]

Other laws followed that authorized one surgeon and one assistant surgeon for each of the newly formed Confederate regiments.[61] There was much quarrelling within the Confederacy when proposals were made to increase assistant surgeons to two. President Davis vetoed the measure on the grounds that one was sufficient to meet regimental needs.[62] As a result, the Confederacy fought the war with the one assistant regimental surgeon while the Union had two. It appears that Jefferson Davis had the same problem shared with others: their frame of reference: service in the Mexican war when troops were few and weapons were less lethal.

Incompetence in the Union Medical Department soared to new heights in 1861. Commanders in the field and the younger surgeons supported the efforts to establish such things as a system of admittance and discharge of patients that was lacking. The problem was seniority in the Medical Department. As Frederick Law Olmsted, the Executive Secretary of the United States Sanitary Commission (USSC) put it, "It is criminal weakness to entrust such responsibilities . . . to a self-satisfied, supercilious, bigoted block-head, merely because he is the oldest of the old mess-room doctors of the frontier guard of the country. He knows nothing and does nothing, but quibble about matters of form and precedent."[63]

Frederick Olmstead in Later Years
Courtesy of the Library of Congress

The "old guard" had never seen a modern war of the enormous proportions that now faced the nation. Instead of an army of a few thousand troops serving on the frontier or in Mexico, the Civil War mushroomed the number of soldiers to hundreds of thousands. Old solutions did not work.

Finally, it became apparent to all that the Union Surgeon General Clement A. Finley needed to be removed and retired. Finley was an entrenched bureaucrat who had served in the army since 1818. Unlike Lawson his predecessor who had conveniently died at age seventy two, it appeared that Finley would live on forever. However, in a confrontation with the Secretary of War, he was finally removed and retired in early 1862. Finley died at age 82 in 1879. The problem with these people was their frame of reference. Both Lawson and Finley thought that it was quite all right for seven out of eight soldiers to die of disease in the Mexican War[64] without asking the question of why or what we can do about it. More important, this establishment of

Medical Department senior citizens could not adjust to reality. They were dealing with a Union army of unprecedented size; hundreds of thousands of troops not the few thousand that had served in conflicts in the early nineteenth century that they were familiar with. As a consequence the senior citizens in the Medical Department were pinching pennies and were unable to figure out what needed to be done. As a result, while Congress appropriated a meager $2.4M in 1862, the Medical Department could not figure out how to spend this amount of money.[65] It will never be known how many Union soldiers lost their lives because of this Medical Department bureaucracy.

Reform of the medical department was needed. On 25 April 1862 William Alexander Hammond was appointed as Surgeon General and embarked upon a plan to modernize the medical department and the treatment of the soldiers. He replaced ancient medical directors with younger men "not quite so thickly incrusted with the habits, forms and traditions of the service."[66] Among his better appointments was Jonathan Letterman as medical director of the Army of the Potomac.[67]

Jonathan Letterman seated at left with his staff at Warrenton, Virginia
Courtesy of the Library of Congress

Letterman moved without national authority to reorganize the ambulance corps using the authority of his commander, General McClellan. His system became the model for world armies for the next two generations.[68] Hammond moved forward with other improvements but unfortunately lacked the tact and social skills needed to successfully push changes through Congress. He was removed and replaced in November 1963 by Colonel Joseph K. Barnes.[69]

Southern medical records are fragmentary, so little is known about the treatment of white soldiers and less is known about the African Americans serving the Confederacy since they were integrated into the Southern units and they were not singled out in descriptions of medical treatment. Nevertheless, much can be related regarding the treatment.

Advances in medical treatment in the Confederate army are largely attributed to Surgeon General Samuel Preston Moore, but surgeon Julian John Chisolm also made major contributions.

Julian John Chisolm
Courtesy of the Library of Congress

Chisolm developed a pocket-sized chloroform inhaler that helped conserve the precious supply of this drug. He was a practicing surgeon during the war and was an organizer of hospitals, a designer of medical laboratories, and an improver of medical devices.[70] Chisolm was born in Charleston, South Carolina on 16 April 1830 and earned his M. D. at the Medical College of the state of South Carolina in 1850. His skill and forward thinking may be attributed to his studies abroad in Paris and time spent observing military hospitals in Milan during the Second Italian War of Independence.[71] His *Manual of Military Surgery, for the Use of Surgeons in the Confederate Army* was based in part upon his European experience.[72] His manual also covered public health which lay at the root of the death of soldiers by disease. Some attribute the reduction in death by disease to Chisolm's manual which was widely used and reprinted three times. During the Crimean war the statistic was six out of seven deaths were from disease while the Civil War found two out of three.[73] He offered endless advice to hospitals and surgeons. On the use of whiskey for medicinal purposes he said ".... I cannot conceive why whiskey should become the favorite remedy in measles. I would ask your authority to limit its use. Patients enter the hospital sober and leave it drunkards."[74] He might have added that they leave happier than when they entered.

The Search for Competent Physicians

A problem faced by both the North and the South was the qualifications of the physicians. At the start of the war, physicians in the army had to choose sides between North and South. Of the 122 physicians in the army, 24 joined the Confederacy and 98 remained with the Union. Very few on either side had experience in treating mass casualties. Only those physicians serving on the frontier had ever seen a gunshot wound and if so it was a novelty. Those who had served in the Mexican war were senior citizens by 1861 and were likely to do more harm than good. New physicians joining either army were generally young and inexperienced with poor qualifications. In the North the best surgeons took the exam for surgeon of volunteers. Others settled for the less stressful jobs such as examining recruits. Examining boards for surgeons turned this around. The boards got rid of incompetent surgeons and others resigned rather than face a board. Medical degrees at that time were in many cases meaningless, presented by "diploma mills." Even Harvard medical school was backward. It had no stethoscope (invented in France in 1816) until 1868 and no microscope until 1869. States had no licensing systems. By spring of 1864, incompetent surgeons had nearly disappeared from Union ranks.[75]

Finding an African American with a medical degree during the Civil War was probably harder than finding a hen with teeth, but there were a few out there. These faced the problem of racism on the part of those empowered to make appointments and many were rejected, but it was a numbers game. Even if every African American physician who applied was enlisted, it would not have made a dent in the requirement for surgeons in African American regiments. The story of African American Dr. Alexander Augusta is a relevant case. Dr. Augusta was assigned to the 7th Regiment USCT and had seniority over white surgeons that followed him. They created a cause célèbre complaining all the way up the chain of command to Lincoln that they could not be subordinate to an African American. There is no record of a Lincoln reply, but Augusta was later reassigned to a recruitment center in Baltimore.[76] As a brevet Lieutenant Colonel, August became the highest ranking African American to serve in the war.[77]

One of the best colleges in the United States was the Medical College of Virginia (MCV) in Richmond. As war approached, many Southern medical students left Northern medical schools such as the Jefferson Medical College and the University Pennsylvania. This provided an influx of students to MVC. This college attracted the best professors and students but as the war wore on, lack of funding curtailed the number of students and patients that could be cared for by MCV. While battles raged around Richmond, the college lacked cadavers for education while thousands of dead soldiers from both sides were piling up near the college. In the end, the college had to sell its one horse (that towed ambulances) in order to keep classes going.[78] By June of 1864, the MCV was closed and the rooms of the hospital were made available for rent.[79]

During the war, the buildup of surgeons was impressive. A survey in 1916 identified a total of 3,237 Confederate surgeons who had served in the Army and 107 in the navy.[80] The North had over 13,000.

Medical Boards

Qualifications of the surgeons assigned to the regiments was a key factor that would in some cases lead to enormously high death rates. There was no Federal control as the rush to create new regiments occurred early in the war. The states enlisted and assigned surgeons to their own regiments. The horror stories started to appear. While Massachusetts, Vermont and Ohio maintained the highest standards and examinations for surgeons appointed to their regiments, other states were not so diligent. Indiana regiments had a large number of incompetent surgeons whose sole qualifications were service in the field as a hospital steward and one year of reading in a doctor's office.[81] The soldiers from Indiana paid a high price for their governor's incompetence and failure to bring competent surgeons into the Indiana regiments. Statistics compiled after the war show that Indiana soldiers suffered far greater death rates than other states.

Confederate Surgeon General Moore started weeding out incompetent medical personnel soon after he assumed duty and he established a reporting system designed to inform him of all problems.[82] Medical boards were established that did not receive high marks. An assistant surgeon in South Carolina described the examinations as a "complete farce".[83] One physician who was examined, Aristides Monteiro, described the board: one member was from the University of Virginia who had not received a degree. "Another member was eccentric" while another "owed his promotion to nepotism—a very common disease at that time. A fourth member was very drunk."[84] In spite of all of the criticism of the boards, they did improve and in general were held in high esteem.[85]

United States Sanitary Commission

Lincoln authorized the creation of the U. S. Sanitary Commission (USSC) in June 1861. The USSC was similar to the Red Cross formed years later. The USSC was a volunteer association that helped by fundraising, collecting and distributing medicine, food and other supplies to the soldiers. It provided nursing and hospital care for wounded servicemen. It also inspected and helped provide advice on improvements in sanitation in the camps.[86] There was nothing comparable to the USSC in the Confederacy. Instead, they relied on volunteer efforts within their states which provided neither the quality nor scale of the USSC.

Historian George Worthington Adams described the USSC as "a gadfly in stinging the moribund department [medical] into more effective activity."[87] It was born by chance. Early in the war in a sidewalk encounter between two New Yorkers, the Rev. Henry W. Bellows, a prominent Unitarian minister and Dr. Elisha Harris had heard of the horrors of the Mexican War in which seven out of eight soldiers died from disease rather than battle wounds. A public meeting was held where a society was organized and this evolved into the USSC.

The USSC covered a wide range of activities. It inspected camps and made recommendations to improve sanitation. It collected food, drugs and clothing to supplement what was provided by the Union army. The fund raising effort to support these endeavors was enormous. Dr. John Strong Newberry, Secretary West, USSC, in 1863 estimated that in the Western theatre alone, $1,000 in cash and ten thousand items of clothing and drugs were distributed daily.[88] In reply to a politician's query, Newberry also identified the extent of USSC support that was not often identified: The USSC established soldier's homes in the West to provide quarters and care for disabled soldiers on their way home. He stated that 60,000 soldiers were aided in this way.[89] Newberry also identified steamers on the Mississippi contracted to move supplies and railroad cars equipped to care for the wounded on hospital trains.[90] On the home front in both the North and the South, citizens were involved by the millions in watching the activities of their governments, the army and organizations such as the USSC. They were not reluctant to voice complaints or concerns since their relatives were involved in the fight. In 1862, the President of the Soldier's Aid Society of Cleveland, Ohio, complained that gifts to soldiers were not received or were misappropriated by surgeons, nurses, etc.[91] Newberry in a lengthy reply stated that 99% of supplies were properly delivered but that there were many supplies consigned by the aid society to independent organizations separate from the USSC. These may have been misappropriated.[92] The point is that the USSC and other organizations on both sides employed a vast number of people, controlled vast resources, and most were voluntary organizations. They were watched by the citizens: everyone who had a son, a father or husband in the war were themselves fully involved.

Members of the USSC
Courtesy of the Library of Congress

Rebuffed is the best word to describe the early efforts of the USSC to assist the Medical Department. In answer to questions by the USSC as to how they could assist the Medical Department, the Surgeon General, Colonel Thomas Lawson (over eighty years old) replied that the department was "fully aroused" (whatever that meant) and "fully competent". Lawson went on to point out the stellar performance of his department during the Mexican War where only seven out of eight soldiers died from disease. Fortunately, Lawson was slowly dying at his home in Norfolk and the Acting Surgeon General R. C. Wood met with members of the USSC who suggested revolutionary measures to reduce the death rate in the war,[93] the most important of which was better examination of recruits, many of whom were medically unfit to serve and would die soon if inducted into the army due to the rigors that go with service. Other important proposals included the training of cooks and the use of nurses and attendants.[94] Wood endorsed the proposals to Secretary of War Cameron. Lincoln was skeptical when approached, but he did agree to the establishment of the USSC. He feared that it would be a "fifth wheel to the coach."[95]

Trying to access the impact of the USSC and medical support on the health of the Union regiments is difficult, but some statistics are available. During the first year and a half of the war, 2.01 per cent of Union soldiers died of disease compared to 3.81 percent of the Confederates.[96] In the West, Union mortality was far greater. Diarrhea was always a major complaint and while medical authorities continued to urge that company cooks be used, the troops preferred to cook their own food frying everything. One surgeon proclaimed that "beans killed more than bullets".[97] Lack of fresh vegetables added to the problem. Camp sanitation or lack of it was always a major killer. One report examined two Illinois regiments living in camps side by side near St. Louis. One was clean and had a listing of six patients while the other was dirty with a water supply that looked "black and disgusting." Here the sick list was 250 crammed into a small hospital capable of handling twenty-five patients.[98] At the army field sites in 1861 Washington, D.C. the reports were alarming.

> Most objectionable was the dearth of latrines and the reluctance of men to use them. Some regiments had dug no latrines at all. The men of one such regiment had gone on for eight days 'Relieving themselves anywhere within a few feet of their tents' The usual sink as the army called it, was a straddle trench thirty feet long, into which fresh earth was supposed to be thrown once a day., but frequently was not. It was so malodorous and so befouled at the edges that soldiers often ignored it, despite orders. Dysentery

and typhoid inevitably followed, and among the civilian population as well.[99]

In one of General Buell's regiments, men refused to use the latrines and were contaminating the ground leading to the water supply.[100] The USSC organized inspectors to go to the field and examine the sanitation in the units. A manual for inspectors outlined responsibilities and protocols such as: "On arriving at the camp of a regiment, ask for the officer of the day, and, stating your business, request him to present you to the colonel or commanding officer. Exhibit your credentials to the latter, and, if the opportunity is favorable, endeavor at once to obtain his confidence and co-operation in your business."[101] This was a "how to" manual that each inspector carried with detailed instructions that told the inspector what to look for. For example: "83. Are the rations found in sufficient quantity? . . . . 86. About how often is fresh meat served?"[102] The inspector was to cause things to be fixed as he proceeded, prepare a report of his findings presenting them to the local commander with a copy sent to the USSC. By the end of the year, a report was submitted indicating that there were poor latrine arrangements for 20% of the units, ineffective regulations for their use at 32% of the units, and 35% of the men were permitted to urinate in the camp streets during the night.[103] The USSC blamed lack of discipline for the problem which was not the entire answer.[104] Lack of education and training was the real problem. The officers were as ignorant as the troops regarding the consequence of poor sanitation. After a year of focus on the preventative aspects seen above, the USSC enlarged the relief aspects. These included the provision of food, drugs and clothing to supplement that provided by the government.[105]

As the war progressed and more doctors, nurses and attendants were brought onboard, casualties declined especially with efforts to improve camp sanitation when it became recognized as the cause of much of the disease.

The Confederacy had no organization comparable to the USSC. Instead, the South relied upon volunteers from each of the states to augment support such as drugs provided by the medical department. Soldier's aid and hospital relief organizations sprang up all over the South. The Confederate government finally assumed jurisdiction over these in late 1862.[106]

Confederate Surgeon General Moore ordered "frequent inspections" by medical personnel each month.[107] One inspector at Petersburg reported ". . . . offensive to the sight as well as the smell . . . . there was evident and inexcusable neglect."[108] A Union medical director examining Confederate field hospitals in the 1864 Shenandoah Valley Campaign reported seeing ". . . . the most extreme filth and positive indications of neglect."[109]

As in the North, the Confederacy relied upon inspections of medical facilities to assure adequacy. The difference was that in the North, both the surgeon and the local commander were jointly responsible. In the South, the medical director was responsible to inspect and provide *suggestions* to the military commander.[110] This was a small difference, but it relied upon the commander to do something about a suggestion which he usually did not. As an example, Confederate General Earl Van Dorn in Texas was accused of retaining Texas volunteers in an unhealthful location until all were sick.[111]

Impure Water

Bad water was a common cause of disease such as typhoid fever. As one Confederate soldier campaigning in Virginia put it. "We drank more mud and wiggle tails [tadpoles] than water.[112] Confederate surgeon J. Julian Chisolm advised that water should be boiled or filtered through straw. A more popular approach among the troops was serving blackberry cordial to the victims of bad water.[113]

Nurses

Dorothea Dix was appointed as Superintendent of Women Nurses for the Union in June 1861.[114] She established the nursing standards.

Dorothea Dix
Courtesy of the Library of Congress

She was widely respected for her work in insane asylum reform before the war. Dix had also studied Florence Nightingale's work during the Crimean War.

Florence Nightingale
Courtesy of the Library of Congress

Dix wrote.

> No young ladies should be sent at all, but some who . . . are
> sober, earnest, self-sacrificing, and self-sustained; who
> can bear the presence of suffering and exercise entire
> self-control of speech and manner; who can be calm,
> gentle, quiet, active, and steadfast in duty. All nurses are
> required to be plain looking women. Their dresses must
> be brown or black, with no bows, no curls, no jewelry, and
> no hoop-skirts.[115]

From Nightingale's *Notes on Nursing*, Dix extracted philosophy and tasks for nurses: Do no harm and let nature take its course.[116]

— Regulate what the convalescent soldier could eat.

— Distribution of supplies: most provided by USSC.

— Assist in the spiritual and emotional care of the soldier.

Union records show that approximately 5,600 women were listed in hospital records as "nurse".[117] This does not include male nurses or African Americans who were assigned to this duty.

As with all things bureaucratic, there were limits to her authority. Nurse Jane Stuart Woolsey described the system.

> There never was a system. Hospital nurses were of all sorts,
> and came from various sources of supply; volunteers paid
> and unpaid; soldiers' wives and sisters who had come to see
> their friends and remained without any clear commission or
> duties; women sent by State agencies and aid societies; women
> assigned by the General Superintendent of Nurses; sometimes
> the wife or daughter of a medical officer drawing rations.[118]

The control that Dix had did not override the authority of surgeons to appoint their own nurses. Some nurses simply made their way to hospitals to enlist. When questioned by a Union officer after her arrival nurse, Mary Bickerdyke replied "I have received my authority from the Lord God Almighty."[119] There is no record of the officer's reply, but she immediately went to work in the hospital. Clara Barton lobbied for weeks to obtain a position as a nurse and receiving no reply gathered supplies and headed for the front.[120] Barton went on to found the American Red Cross.

Clara Barton
Courtesy of the Library of Congress

Dix was overextended in trying to establish a centralized control over nursing. Her management style was faulted. Her records were haphazard. She traveled extensively arguing with surgeons that opposed her and had a large number of contacts. By comparison, Nightingale worked with only thirty-eight women during the Crimean War.[121]

Hospital care was a patchwork of sources. After Gettysburg in July 1863, Confederate soldiers were paroled to work in Union hospitals as nurses. This may have caused some Union soldiers' concern when seeing a Confederate soldier standing over them, but the record of Confederate soldiers working as nurses in Union hospitals indicated that they did as good if not better than most other nurses.

Wounded from the Battle of the Wilderness
Courtesy of the Library of Congress

Women nurses contributed greatly to the recovery of wounded soldiers and also provided a morale boost to hospitals.[122]

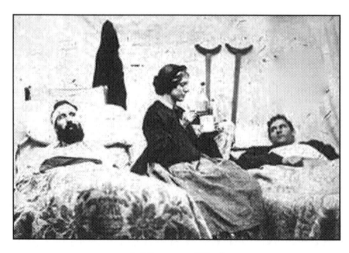

A Nurse at Work
Courtesy of the Library of Congress

For the Union, use of African American women in the wards was legalized in 1864.[123] Before then, runaway slaves were obtained from the Quartermaster Corps for use in the Union hospitals as nurses.[124] While African American women served as nurses in Union hospitals throughout the war, their exact number is not known since they were frequently carried on the rosters as "laundress" or "cook".[125] Sojourner Truth and Susie King Taylor are clearly documented cases of African American women who served as nurses.[126] Sojourner Truth was also an abolitionist, author, and activist.

Sojourner Truth
Courtesy of the Library of Congress

The Confederacy had different problems and approaches to nursing. Competent nurses were hard to find and it was recognized, as in the North, that women were better than men at nursing.[127] One surgeon described the male nurses as "rough country crackers who have not enough sense to be kind . . . . [They did not] know castor oil from a gun rod nor laudanum from a hole in the ground."[128] African American women were brought in to nurse and these were usually hired by the year in hospitals.[129]

There was no centralized government approach toward organizing nurses in the Confederacy but the government passed legislation in September 1862 that provided that soldiers should be detailed as ward masters and nurses if sufficient qualified nurses were not available. The number of matrons per hospital was also specified. This was followed, later, by directions that only disabled soldiers were to be detailed for hospital duty.[130] This produced a different set of problems. Surgeon Edmund Burke Haywood complained to the Surgeon General. "It will be impossible to keep a hospital in fine order and the patients well cared for with broken down men. Nurses who are detailed on account of permanent disability know that they are not likely to be returned to the field, and therefore do not exert themselves to please. They are generally . . . discontented at being detailed . . . instead of being furloughed or discharged."[131] Hospitals were on their own to accrue and manage the nurses that they needed.

Other Help

The *Scientific American Magazine* provided an enormous amount of information available to both sides on instruments, splints, improved sanitation and many other useful topics. It even provided diagrams of a device to show how lizards could be filtered out of drinking water.[132] Unfortunately, it was organisms much smaller than lizards that were causing the problem. The *Scientific American Magazine* provided advice called "Hints to Volunteers" such as put a cork in the muzzle of your rifle to keep out rain.[133] It struck pay dirt when it started a series of articles aimed at the military leadership of the army, but available for all soldiers to read. These titles speak for themselves "Protection of Troops from Sunstroke", "Sanitary Measures for Soldiers," "Purifying Water for Soldiers," and a full page article entitled "Malaria and its Remedies."[134] While the validity of some the advice might be questioned (lizards?) the point is that it focused attention on problems not considered earlier. Much of the advice is still valid, today "proper ventilation, scrupulous personal cleanliness, ... moderate use of fresh vegetables and fruits, especially oranges and lemons [to prevent scurvy], regular rations and abstinence from spirits."[135] The magazine also dabbled in weaponry with some rather crazy ideas such as a cannon ball that had knives included in it that would expand after the ball was fired and mow down the enemy (not a new idea).[136] It also got into chemical warfare which is very chilling given its introduction during World War I, over half a century after the *Scientific American* article. Advice included use of ordnance to distribute clouds of cayenne pepper, cyanide or acid among enemy troops as well as chloroform to put fort defenders to sleep. To defend against this, *Scientific American* suggested breathing apparatus (gas masks) to protect the troops.[137] Today it is a fact of life in the army, 150 years ago it was science fiction. The advice to "develop an arrangement of reflectors and lenses which would send a focus of light and heat two or three miles without diminishing its intensity, so that it would set objects on fire with the same facility as ordinary sunglass".[138] is amazing given the work on lasers 150 years later. The *Scientific American* produced a mixture of advice that on the one hand suggested ways to protect the health of soldiers and on the other hand how to kill them in greater numbers: a sort of potpourri designed to interest any reader.

In the South, the *Southern Medical and Surgical Journal* was established in 1836 in Augusta, Georgia. Theses of medical students were published in this and other Southern journals.[139]

Medical Evacuation
Ambulances

In the first battle of the Civil War, Bull Run, the Union loss was compounded by the performance of the Union Medical Department which left much to be desired. In the confusion and Union flight from the battlefield, regimental surgeons refused to treat soldiers who were not members of their regiment.[140] The union losses were 2,000 killed and wounded. How many of these died due to medical neglect and incompetence is not known. In the words of Assistant Surgeon W. W. Keen, who found himself on his own during the fighting and made his own decisions, "The days when there was no King in Israel and every man did that which was right in his own eyes."[141] A major deficiency was the ambulances that had been issued to the army. Most were the two wheeled version that were inferior to four wheeled ambulances that were issued on a basis of one out of four.[142] It did not matter. Many of the ambulances were seized by officers for their travel and most of the rest were taken by soldiers in their flight back to Washington. The wounded were on their own to walk back to Washington, a distance of twenty-seven miles.[143] Later, when properly organized, the medical department would determine that for the critically wounded the two wheeled ambulance should be used and those with minor wounds should use four wheeled ambulances. These were usually manned by African Americans.

The Ambulance Corps
Courtesy of the Library of Congress

Dr. Tripler was responsible for many advances in medical evacuation.

Dr. Charles S. Tripler
Courtesy of the Library of Congress

Bandsman (usually African Americans) were trained in the duties of stretcher men.[144]

The 107th USCT Band
Courtesy of the Library of Congress

These would move the casualties quickly to a hospital or an ambulance. Tripler, Letterman, Mayo, and other talented surgeons and administrators would make their mark on the medical profession. Ambulances were under the control of the Quartermaster Corps, not the Medical Corps, and this was a problem.[145] An officer who issued beans and blankets had no clue about the medical requirements associated with ambulances. Tripler did the math and was astonished to find that for an army of 100,000 people, the ambulance train would be twenty-five miles long.[146] He reduced the requirement to 250 ambulances only to find that the Quartermaster Corps could not meet this reduced requirement.[147] Of the 228 two-wheelers delivered by the Quartermaster Corp between 1 July and 1 October 1861, many disappeared. These were either breakdowns or confiscated for other uses such as general utility vehicles. The troops must have cheered as the two-wheeled ambulances continued to disappear. They were too light and uncomfortable for patients who referred to them as "avalanches".[148] The situation was compounded by teamsters who had been hired by the Quartermaster Corps. During the Battle of Second Manassas in August 1862 these frequently ran away when exposed to gunfire, a common ingredient of all battles, and they left the wounded behind.[149] The Medical Corps pressed for control of an ambulance corps.

Dr. Jonathan Letterman replaced Tripler as Surgeon General and had the good fortune to have the Battle of Antietam on 17 September 1862, a Union victory, as his first test.[150] Letterman had persuaded the Union commander, General McClellan to create a separate ambulance corps manned by soldiers selected by the Medical Corps.[151] With McClellan's support, the effort to establish an ambulance corps of 12,000 men continued but was not supported by the General-in-Chief Halleck or by Congress.[152] As the parade of failed generals passed into history and were replaced by Lincoln, General Hooker appeared to be one who cared about the welfare of the troops. While he failed in battle, he had the sense to improve the living conditions of the troops. He added vegetables to their diets and added furloughs for the troops. He also supported Letterman's efforts to improve ambulance service.

Under Hooker, the ambulance service drilled daily.

Ambulance Corps at Training
Courtesy of the Library of Congress

The battle of Gettysburg in July 1863 was a success story from the view point of the Medical Service. Letterman had assembled an organization that included 650 medical officers. With 1000 ambulances and nearly 3,000 ambulance drivers and stretcher men, the battlefield was cleared of Union wounded the day after the battle: an impressive feat.[153] About 14,500 Union and 6,000 Confederate wounded needed to be treated. Since General Lee abandoned the field and fled South leaving many of his wounded, the U. S. Army was responsible for the treatment of all wounded on the field. At this point, Letterman made a tactical error. The Union army started South in pursuit of Lee. Another battle was expected so Letterman left few surgeons behind to care for nearly 21,000 patients at Gettysburg. He wanted another maximum effort by the Medical Corps at the next battle (the next battle did not happen). This meant a patient load at Gettysburg of nearly 900 for each surgeon.[154] Undoubtedly many died because of the lack of care that resulted.

On 23 December 1863, work started in the Senate on the Ambulance Corps Bill. This was designed to create specially trained enlisted corps and ambulances under the Medical Department and not the Quartermaster Department. A system would be applied throughout the Union army that would save lives. There were other advantages. Up to then, a soldier slightly injured could wander off the battlefield for medical treatment to avoid gunfire. Many soldiers frequently helped a wounded comrade off of the battlefield for the same reason.

One soldier found himself with eight comrades to carry his stretcher. Union General Dan Sickles who lost a leg at Gettysburg found himself surrounded by forty men who were "helping" him to Chambersburg for medical treatment. With a professional corps of stretcher bearers and ambulance drivers, this loss of manpower on the battlefield could be avoided. The Ambulance Corps Act of 1864 enacted on 11 March provided most of the changes needed to apply Letterman's system throughout the army. The Quartermaster Corps would continue to control the ambulances and horses, but the use of ambulances for other purposes was prohibited.[155] This ambulance organization within the Union army would be copied by other military organizations throughout the world until World War I.[156] Small improvements continued throughout the war. These meant the difference between life and death to many soldiers. During the Wilderness Campaign in 1864 the medical supply train was only five miles behind the troops, not the twenty-five miles at Gettysburg.

The Confederacy never had an adequate number of ambulances.[157] Surgeon Lafayette Guild complained that the wagons were made of inferior materials and the "horses appear to be broken down before turned over to the ambulance train."[158] The Confederacy had slightly different rules from the Union: each regiment was authorized two of the two-wheeled ambulances and two of the four.[159] These were controlled by the units rather than an army ambulance corps. Like the Union, the needed ambulances failed to appear.

Guild reported the aftermath of Gettysburg: two ambulance trains were attacked by enemy raiding parties. The raiders destroyed many wagons, paroled the wounded soldiers (it is not clear what a badly wounded Confederate soldier would do with his parole after he was ejected from an ambulance), and took with them all of the officers who fell into their hands."[160] The wounded were finally moved to railroad trains that removed most to Richmond while many remained in the Shenandoah Valley for treatment. The rules of war enacted in the twentieth century were not in place and what would be called an atrocity today was accepted behavior by some during the Civil War. Jonathan Letterman the Union army's medical director expressed the sentiment of most surgeons and soldiers during the Civil War. "Humanity teaches us that a wounded and prostate foe is not our enemy."[161]

The Confederacy used a different approach to collect their wounded from the battlefield. Each regiment had an infirmary corps of about thirty men, usually these were those that were the least effective in combat.[162] They were not allowed to engage in any action other than their primary duty. Other soldiers were severely punished if they tried to evacuate soldiers from the field.[163] This was no place for cowards. The infirmary corps was charged to follow the battle closely. John Casler, a member of the infirmary corps, described the scene during the battle of the Wilderness. "On the left side of our lines . . . . the scene beggars description. The dead and badly wounded from both sides were lying where they fell. The woods, taking fire that night from the shells, burnt rapidly and roasted the men alive. As we went to bury them we could see where they had tried to keep the fire from by scratching the leaves away as far as they could reach. But it availed not; they were burnt to a crisp. The only way we could tell to which army they belonged was by turning them over and examining their clothing where they lay close to the ground."[164]

African Americans were called to perform the duties in the ambulance corps and infirmary corps and years later both Union and Confederate African American veterans would relate their duties that they bravely performed.

Hospitals

Patient care was important and a good surgeon would make sure that the hospital wards were clean, with adequate warm bedding, needed medicines and food for his patients. Whites and African Americans were segregated into different wards in hospitals. In St. Louis, Ira Russell, the Massachusetts surgeon, was tired of surgeons telling him that the reason for high mortality in their wards "was the inherent weakness of the colored patients."[165] He converged on Dr. James M. Martin who was one of the most attentive and competent physicians whose ward had the lowest mortality rate. He reassigned Martin to the ward that had the worst death rate and found that in a remarkably short amount of time that ward had the least death rate.[166] At Nashville, care of the wounded and those suffering from disease was abominable after the two day battle that cost the lives of thousands of Union and African American soldiers (See Chapter 6). General Lorenzo Thomas inspected the white and African American wards after the battle. He found the white wards adequate but the African American wards deplorable. He noted that "One soldier had been wounded with leg amputated, [who] was on a bed, the clothing of which had not been changed up to yesterday, and he was still in the dress [uniform] in which he had been carried from the battlefield, everything saturated with blood—he [the African American soldier] complained that the lice were eating him up. Had these men been white soldiers, think you this would have been their condition?"[167] It is not clear that any reforms were instituted.

Surgeon W. W. Keen described surgery.

> We operated in old blood-stained and often pus-stained coats, the veterans of a hundred fights. We operated with clean hands in the social sense, but they were undisinfected hands (sic) . . . . We used undisinfected (sic) instruments from undisinfected (sic) plush-lined cases, and still worse used marine sponges which had been used in prior pus cases and had been only washed in tap water. If a sponge or an instrument fell on the floor it was washed and squeezed in a basin of tap water and used as if it were clean.[168]

Surgery in the Field Hospital
Courtesy of the Library of Congress

This is remarkable since antiseptics such as carbolic acid were used to clean the wounds and protect against infections, yet no one thought to use these same antiseptics to clean instruments.[169] Unfortunately, the African American regiments suffered more because they had no state advocate to promote adequate medical support.

Where a person got sick was a major factor. African Americans stationed on the East coast of the United States were well off because they had been recruited in regions close to where they were stationed and acquired immunity was an important factor.[170] It was not that simple. The white troops had as many as 30% of their unit strengths down due to fevers found in the region of the Carolinas. Since the whites were down with disease, the African Americans had to pick up their work duties. The extra labor caused additional illnesses in the African American regiments. One African American regimental commander complained. "My sick list has increased from 4 or 5 to nearly 200 in a little over one month."[171] Not all of the African Americans were recruited from this region. Others came from Massachusetts. One observer noted "The white troops suffer from fever and dysentery in the summer, the colored from lung diseases in the winter and Northern colored regiments suffer from both."[172] In the west mostly along the Mississippi River the mortality rate of the African Americans was nearly twice that found in the East. Other factors played here. Recruiting standards were much higher in the East than those who were enlisted in the West where many more should have been rejected. Many of the recruits came from Missouri, Kentucky and Tennessee where the incidence of malaria was less than locations where these troops were stationed such as Louisiana. Therefore, acquired immunity to malaria was less. Skill of the surgeons also played a part. Most surgeons believed that African Americans were immune to malaria. Therefore when a soldier appeared with malaria, quinine was withheld and his illness was misdiagnosed often with deadly consequences. Generally figures suggest that medical treatment in the East was better than the West.[173]

Benton Barracks in St. Louis is often mentioned as center of diseases due largely to overcrowding in inadequate barracks especially in the winter of 1863-64. Five large barracks had been constructed, each 750 feet long and 40 feet wide. A physician described the horror upon his arrival there in late 1861.

> The quarters of the rank and file were erected one story high, of rough material, and washed with lime on the exterior. The floors, also rough, were loosely laid and in many instances lower than the surrounding surface." The only ventilation was provided by small apertures out into the walls "for the admission of air and light, and closed by a door, or a shutter made to slide to and fro." Since "these apertures opened upon the upper bunks, whose occupants at night closed them to exclude the currents of cold air from their persons," the nighttime atmosphere became quite fetid. Adding to the fragrance were emanations from nearby sinks and deposits of kitchen offal, so that "during the whole night, therefore, these quarters were filled with a hot, foul, and poisonous breath, without due means of escape." Into these rough quarters some 30,000 men crammed.[174]

Ira Russell was ordered to St. Louis and placed in charge of a new general hospital at Benton Barracks. Russell had graduated from a New York medical college in 1844. By August 1863, Russell fell ill from diarrhea and returned home to Massachusetts in order to recover.[175] When he returned, he continued to stress cleanliness in the barracks and improved treatment in the hospital. He was aided by his chief nurse Emily Parsons a thirty-nine year old from Massachusetts who had trained at one of Boston's best hospitals before joining the army. They made a good team.[176] He continued to work to improve medical treatment of the African Americans but the mortality rates continued to climb as more troops arrived.

Both whites and African Americans suffered equally at Benton Barracks with the African Americans suffering a slightly higher mortality rate. One white regiment, the 10th Minnesota Volunteers recorded details of their stay at Benton Barracks. Comments seemed slightly blasé such as enjoying a winter carnival but dozens were sick and were not counted in regimental records. Five died of disease. Three were in their teens. Several died of misadventure such as drowning in the river. Unit strength at that time was about one thousand people.[177]

Facilities

In the Confederacy as in the Union, hospitals and medical treatment were divided between the field where casualties were treated by units close to the front and general hospitals further back designed to treat all casualties. For the Confederacy, Surgeon General Moore directed the activities of both.[178] Moore established one story pavilion hospitals that became the model for modern general hospitals. These provided forty-five to sixty huts of twenty-five to fifty patients each and became independent wards within the hospital.[179]

Surgeon General Moore
Courtesy of the Library of Congress

Each Confederate patient was allocated eight hundred cubic feet in the hospital and it was to be kept scrupulously clean.[180] This was easier said than done. The Confederate patients were notoriously nonchalant about sanitation as were their counterparts in the North. They would use anything but the sinks (latrines) to "evacuate the contents of their bowels."[181] Comments about patients seemed to focus on their state of origin, more so than in the North. Texans like to drink and gamble (a comment that could be applied to all soldiers before and since). Kate Cummings described the Louisianan's as "the most unruly and dastardly in our hospitals"[182] Nurse Phoebe Pember described Virginians as "intelligent, manly, and reasonable with more civilized tastes and some desire to conform to rules that were conducive to their health." (she was probably from Virginia).[183] She described North Carolinians thus: ". . . . were certainly [the] most forlorn specimens" their drawls were "insufferable"[184] On a broader scale then hospitals, the North appeared to be a more integrated society with less focus on individual states.

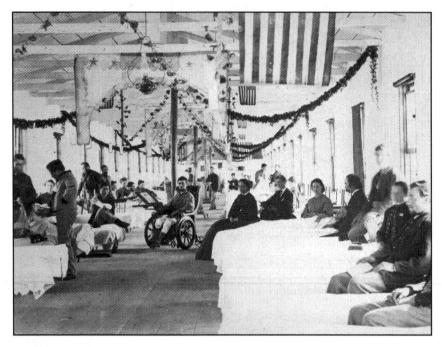

The Union General Hospital
Courtesy of the Library of Congress

The South by its nature, a confederacy of individual states, appeared to have no desire for a strong central government or an integrated society. Each state could leave the Confederacy at will and there are examples of Southern counties seceding from the Confederacy after their state had seceded from the Union. West Virginia is the most famous, but there were others.[185]

Nevertheless, the early picture of the general hospitals was confusing at best. The Confederacy appropriated only $50,000 in 1861 for the hospitals that were swamped after a battle.[186] After the first clash at Manassas, fifteen hundred patients were being cared for by twelve Richmond hospitals which handled only a fraction of those sick and wounded.[187] Churches, courthouses and private home were pressed into service. Nearly every home in Richmond sheltered one to four of the wounded.[188] Confederate Surgeon General Moore favored the construction of larger hospitals to handle the load and smaller hospitals were shut down as new larger hospitals were constructed. From September 1862 to March 1864, thirty-five hospitals were closed in Richmond, alone and the larger hospitals were opened to better cope with mass casualties.[189]

The problem of attendants needed to be fixed. Early on, volunteers and Confederate soldiers recovering from wounds were used in the hospitals but this proved unsatisfactory. Volunteers departed and soldiers recovering from wounds left leaving the problem of replacing them with people who were largely untrained. The hiring of hospital attendants both white and African Americans was authorized by the law of 21 August 1861.[190] Of course, there were many complaints by the hospital staff about the time they needed to spend training the slaves. Nurse Kate Cummings complained that she needed to spend more time supervising her African American attendants then working with detailed soldiers.[191] This is hardly a surprise since the South denied education to African Americans and most could not read. Others put the situation in a more logical perspective. Surgeon James B. McCaw stated in May 1862 that it would be "impossible to continue the Hospitals" without the 256 slaves employed at Chimborazo hospital in Richmond.[192] Later in September 1862 another positive step was taken. A new law provided for six matrons per ward.[193]

Large numbers of Confederate wounded were furloughed and sent home to recover. "Way hospitals" were established along major railroad lines.[194] These would furnish rations and quarters to wounded soldiers on their way home. The problem was that many were called back before they had fully recovered. Vice President Alexander H. Stephens estimated that thousands had died because of this.[195] Another problem was that at home they did not receive the professional medical care that they needed and they died at home. Many of these were sent home because beds were needed in the hospitals when there was a large influx of casualties after a battle. An attempt was made to solve this by establishing a board of examiners composed of surgeons to review applicants for furloughs.[196]

Innovation was the characteristic of the care for the Union wounded. In the West, special hospital trains were organized to transport the wounded. The cabs were painted brilliant scarlet and at night three red lanterns were hung beneath the head lamp. In an era before the Red Cross and its symbol these warned the Confederate army and train wreckers that wounded were on board.[197] It is said that Confederate cavalry leaders such as Forrest and Morgan ordered that these trains should not be interfered with.[198] Throughout the war, both Union and Confederate hospitals were protected by "hospital flags" these were yellow material with an "H" added in the center by the Union late in the war. All of the Union advances in medical treatment were far superior to anything the Confederacy could do for its wounded. The difference was that the Union could bring to bear enormous resources that the Confederacy did not have.

Throughout the Civil War, surgeons stressed ventilation not only in hospitals but the tents of the troops.[199] This was a valid concern for contagious airborne diseases such as tuberculosis, but other threats such as "effluvia's [sic] from the ground" that could cause such diseases as typhoid were imaginary. What followed was an effusion of different designs to provide the best ventilated quarters for the troops. For the Union, among these was the "pup tent" as the troops called it which were two pieces of canvas joined together that would keep the rain and snow off of two soldiers. Pup tents would survive the war and remain in the army inventory for nearly 150 years.

Diet

The Confederate Congress established a hospital fund of $1 a day for each patient in September 1862. The hospital fund was to be used for the purchase of perishables such as fruits and eggs.[200] The fund was increased over time as inflation set in. Hospital gardens were also employed to increase food for patients.

Surgeon General Moore wanted to establish a standard diet for patients. Similar to the Union, diets were full, standard or low depending upon the condition of the patient. Full diet was beef and cawn (sic) bread and other items such as vegetables when available. Half diet was soup and toast while low diet was rice and milk.[201] As always, the troops complained about the food. An inspection directed by Congress found that the sick were provided with poorly cooked rations.[202] At the Confederate Winder hospital in Richmond the patients revolted after an endless diet of dried peas every day. These were used to decorate the floors and ceilings of the wards and the bakery was torn down by the patients because they wanted bread and got none. Miss Emily V. Mason a matron at Winder recalled that she quelled the riot by reminding the men of her many acts of kindness that included stewing the rats that they had captured when the cook refused to do so.[203]

Medicine

Lack of medical supplies in the South accounted for many of the deaths. The primary source of shortages was the Federal blockade that prevented supplies from reaching the Confederacy while the North had an unlimited supply.[204] Fortunately, the Southern supply of drugs was augmented by Confederate blockade runners and drugs smuggled in from the North.[205] Nevertheless, the South was short of drugs. As a consequence, the South turned to the use of plants for medicine. There is nothing new in this except the unprecedented scale of the demand. The first step was when the Surgeon General Moore released a pamphlet on 21 March 1862 promoting the use of native flora. It listed sixty-seven of the South's more important medicinal plants. Moore directed medical officers to collect these and send them to medical purveyors so that they could be processed and distributed.[206] Next, Moore ordered Dr. Francis Peyre Porcher to enlarge Moore's 1862 pamphlet. In a classic case of overkill, Porcher produced a 601 page book in March 1863 entitled *Resources of Southern Fields and Forests.*[207] It was not user friendly, but medical officers were impressed because of Porcher's academic credentials. Most important, it convinced them that the use of native flora was a viable alternative to drugs blocked by the Federal blockade.[208] Newspaper articles and hand bills promoted the collection of plants. In some cases, the soldiers collected these for their own use and in others, handed them in for processing.[209] Flora were funneled to medical laboratories (drug manufacturers) where they were processed for delivery to the field.[210] How effective was this flora drill? We do not know. Surviving records cannot identify lives saved or suffering allayed,[211] but it appears that death rates would have been much higher without it.

Confederate physicians had a standard routine. They had a ball of opium and a ball of blue mass on hand to treat many ailments, especially diarrhea and dysentery. William H. Taylor, a medical office described his procedure. "How are your bowels? If they were open I administered a plug of opium. If they were shut I gave a plug of blue mass."[212] Blue mass was a sort of "cure all" with varying ingredients, but it nearly always included mercury which over time could be deadly.

It was said that Lincoln took blue mass for melancholy, but there is no evidence that he suffered from mercury poisoning.

Stupidity was a major factor in the Civil War. It was not just the generals, but the surgeons that caused the troops to throw away medicine preferring instead folk medicine. The problem was that the African American soldiers did not trust their white surgeons. The surgeons were unable to diagnose illnesses of the African Americans. One disparaged his regimental surgeon. "The doctor having charge of seven cases of small-pox, as is supposed, has acknowledged his ignorance of the true character of the disease, alleging that he never saw black folks with small pox and consequently is unable to decide upon the treatment.[213]

Battle Wounds

Most surgeons agreed that surgery should be performed as soon as possible after the wound was received. Confederate surgeon Chisolm asserted "All needful operations must be performed within twenty-four hours, or the wounded will suffer from neglect."[214] In a situation of mass casualties, this was not always possible. A war correspondent after the Battle of Second Manassas described the scene.

> The casualties were lying upon the ground awaiting their turn with patience, some dead and some dying, but the great majority with only painful wounds in the extremities. The operating tables . . . were slimy with blood . . . and as fast as one patient was removed another took his place to be anethized (sic) by the merciful chloroform and undergo the necessary surgical treatment. The men all appeared to bear their wounds cheerfully, and it was only now and then when the knife cut deep that a smothered groan revealed the sharp pang of pain.[215]

After the Battle of Gettysburg, Confederate Surgeon Simon Barach recalled that he spent two days and two nights in constant surgery,

> The tail gate of a wagon, the communion table of a church, a door laid upon barrels or boxes, and other such makeshifts, were often employed as operating tables. A distinguishing feature of all field hospitals at such times, according to one veteran surgeon, was "that ineffable smell of gore which no man can fail to recognize who has passed through the experiences of four years of a bloody war."[216]

Amputation

Amputation in a Field Hospital
Courtesy of the Library of Congress

Southern surgeons classed amputations as primary and secondary. A primary amputation occurred within twenty four hours of the gunshot wound while a secondary was greater than twenty four hours after. Mortality for the former was less than a third and for the later over half. Location of the amputation was also significant. An amputation just below the hip was considered fatal, but statistics showed that nearly half of these treated within twenty four hours survived.[217] Phoebe Pember, the matron at the Chimborazo hospital in Richmond recalled that secondary amputations were nearly always fatal because the soldiers were weakened by poor food and "thinned blood." Mrs. Pember remarked that she could only recall two cases of people surviving secondary amputations. "[They] were two Irishmen and it was really difficult to kill an Irishman . . . . and [because they were Irish] there was little cause for boasting on the part of the officiating surgeons."[218]

Nerve Damage

Nerve damage was a common injury during the Civil War and soldiers knew that they had a problem immediately or weeks after a gunshot wound when various parts of their bodies were still numb or withering. Battlefield doctors were not much help since the nerve damage could not always be detected and there was no time to treat it if suspected. Repair of a severed nerve was rarely, if ever, a surgical priority.[219] The only cure was to remove a projectile that was pressing on a nerve.[220] Dr. Silas Weir Mitchell, a graduate of Jefferson Medical College and his colleagues concentrated on nerve damage.[221] As a consequence, other surgeons began referring cases of nerve injury to Mitchell and his colleagues. This led to the establishment of the first hospital in the United States devoted to injuries and diseases of the nervous system at the U. S. Army Hospital, Christin Street in Philadelphia.[222] There were no great breakthroughs during the Civil War to reduce paralysis, but the work of Mitchell and others set the stage for progress many years later.

Dressings

Dressings were a horror story from the Civil War. Both sides used lint to dress wounds. It was stuffed into wounds to slow bleeding. Lint was produced by scraping old dresses, linens and other worn goods with a knife.[223] The infections that followed were predictable and often lethal. No one thought to boil lint to kill germs, but other dressings such as raw cotton were boiled. Horse hair was also used and boiled extensively to make it pliable. In doing that they also sanitized the horse hair and this limited infections.[224]

Larval Therapy

From the Napoleonic wars and perhaps hundreds of years earlier, it was known that flies produce maggots and on wounds the larva eat the dead tissues, but not the living. The result was faster healing and in some cases, patient survival. These earlier lessons were lost to the Civil War. All sorts of remedies were produced to kill the maggots, but the maggots prevented gangrene. A few surgeons such as Joseph Jones noticed that larva killed the gangrene and promoted healing: a lesson lost before and after the Civil War.[225]

Surgical Fevers

"Surgical fevers" was the term used to describe infections that followed surgery. These included tetanus, gangrene and a host of other post-operative infections. There was no treatment for tetanus. People died. There was a general consensus among surgeons that soldiers who suffering from exposure, scurvy and other common camp diseases were more likely to accrue Surgical Fevers.[226] It did not take much brain power to figure that out. Treatment included cleanliness, proper ventilation and a nutritious diet.[227] To the delight of the troops (those conscious) large doses of brandy and opium were prescribed.[228]

Nervous Diseases and PTSD

Combat neuroses or "nervous diseases" also claimed many victims sometimes years after the war. Over time this has been called shell shock, combat fatigue and more recently post-traumatic stress disorder (PTSD). During the Civil War, this injury was not understood or treated. An example of PTSD was the Lang case.[229] Lang was a Union medic and among his experiences is one he recalled after the Battle of Gettysburg ".... In one place I counted 16 [bodies] in a spot no larger than your kitchen. In going over I saw one man who did not look like the rest. He was not black or swollen. He was still alive .... I went up to him and saw that the top of his head was blown off. I gave him a little water-got some help—put him on a blanket and carried him to an old barn where he got attention .... I have seen men torn in pieces in almost every shape and mind nothing of it, but not so with this one."[230] Back home, his wife noticed that he had mood swings and was pensive. He attacked her without warning and she escaped with a divorce.

Monotony and boredom also appeared to generate sickness. These surfaced when units were stationary for an extended period of time. An army on the move generally did not suffer from this complaint.[231] One Confederate surgeon when his sick list was increasing, put the troops to work on projects. Where there were none, he set up make-work projects and was amply rewarded by a diminishing sick list.[232]

Diseases

Battle wounds were most feared by soldiers but were not the primary cause of death. Three out of five Union deaths were from disease while two out of three Confederate dead were from disease.[233] Part of the problem was that enlisted soldiers on both sides were often in poor health as seen earlier. Also in the desperate search for manpower over-aged and under-aged men were enlisted and these would be most susceptible to disease. From the standpoint of disease, it is easy to understand why a farm boy from either side did not have an immune system equipped to counter the many diseases that were endemic to camp life such as measles, chicken pox, and whooping cough.[234] The biggest killers were intestinal disorders and other diseases such as typhoid fever, malaria, diarrhea and dysentery which accounted for about half of the deaths and the rest were mostly lung diseases such as tuberculosis, pneumonia and other diseases. Dr. Alfred Jay Bollet[235] has suggested that typhoid fever caused the majority of deaths during the Civil War but this is just not true. All of the other diseases mentioned above and combined caused the high death rate The Union army reported that 995 out of every 1,000 soldiers contracted chronic diarrhea or dysentery sometime during their service. Confederate statistics were similar.[236] A key factor in all of this was sanitation in the camps on both sides. We see soldiers downstream drinking water that was used upstream to dump offal and other waste. Piles of waste littered the camps and were breeding places for flies and dysentery that followed. Few understood at that time the connection between diseases, death and camp sanitation.

Diagnosis was very imperfect. A surgeon made a guess and treated the patient accordingly, often for the wrong disease. The statistics that were gathered were based on what was many times a bad diagnosis and some patients were logged into the statistics for several different diseases. Hundreds of thousands were counted with diarrhea, but this was usually a secondary cause of their hospitalization for more deadly diseases such as pneumonia.

Most of diseases are recognized today but some appear obscure based upon the terminology of the Civil War. These are explained. John Julian Chisolm, the South Carolina surgeon assessed the problem of disease faced by the Confederacy. "Continued exposure and fatigue, bad and insufficient food, salt meat, indifferent clothing, want of cleanliness, poor shelter, exposure at night to sudden changes in temperature, infected tents and camps, form a combination of causes which explains the fatality of an army in the field."[237] For the Union, Charles Tripler attributed disease "To bad cooking, bad police, bad ventilation of tents, inattention to personal cleanliness, and unnecessarily irregular habits we are to attribute the greater proportion of the diseases that actually occurred in the army."[238] Both sides stressed items such as infected tents and bad ventilation. At the time, many diseases were thought to be a result of vapors emanating from the ground that needed to be dispelled: a theory that was long ago discarded. Most of the other causes are recognized as valid and are related to sanitation.

Diarrhea and Dysentery

Intestinal diseases produced the greatest number of casualties, both North and South, African Americans and whites. The annual average was 73.8 percent. Soldiers nicknamed it "the Tennessee's quick-step." and remarked that "bowels are of more consequence than brains" in the army.[239]

One Confederate surgeon stated that when a soldier was admitted to the hospital "No matter what else he had, he had diarrhea."[240] The causes were thought to be inadequate ration, poor cooking, impure water, fatigue, and exposure.[241] A Southern minister observed that "The disease that seemed to break down the will power more than any other was chronic diarrhea, and the patients seemed to lose not only the desire to live but all manliness and self-respect. They whined and died in spite of all we could do."[242] Blue mass and a number of other drugs such as nitrate of silver were prescribed.

Typhoid Fever, Typhus and Common Continued Fevers

Willie Lincoln died in the White House at age eleven in 1862. The most probable cause of death was typhoid fever caused by contaminated drinking water. It gives pause for thought: if the President's son in the White House could die from drinking contaminated water, it is not surprising that thousands of soldiers suffered the same fate.

Typhoid fever was one of the most deadly of diseases. Isolating the victims in well ventilated rooms appeared to reduce the outbreaks. Use of oil of turpentine reduced the effects of the disease. These appear to be rather meager treatments which may account for the large number of deaths.

Malaria and Yellow Fever

Malaria and yellow fever were a plague during the Civil War. It was not until nearly a half a century later that Dr. Walter Reed and others discovered that mosquitoes were a cause of these diseases. The ventilation theory of the Civil War also invited malaria since mosquitoes had more easy access to the troops. Quinine was the most used preventive measure. Medical authorities at the time ascribed malaria to sleeping in wet blankets and bad water as well as other nonsensical theories. It appeared that no one connected mosquitoes to malaria and yellow fever until years later. Sometimes hospitals were located near latrines and kitchens with the result that hordes of flies and mosquitoes invaded the wards. To protect the soldiers some mosquito netting was provided in hospitals. This was for the comfort of the troops to protect them from mosquito bites. No one realized that it also protected them from malaria, yellow fever and other insect-borne diseases,[243] although some surgeons were suspicious about the cause of malaria/yellow fever and mosquitoes. The troops did not like the nets since they cut down on air flow and as soon as they were well enough, the nets came down.[244]

The General Hospital with its Nets
Courtesy of the Library of Congress

Some say that the differences in the biology of the races had an effect of their susceptibility to diseases but it is difficult to find any evidence to support this. Built-in immunity is another cause for differences in mortality between the races, but this argument frequently falls apart. As an example, because of environment, many African Americans in the deep South had built up immunity to malaria.[245] Whites in the same environment would also have built up immunity to the disease. Nevertheless, malaria mortality rates for African Americans were actually higher than white.[246] Many of the African Americans came from areas not known for malaria such as Kentucky so these enjoyed no built-in immunity to malaria.[247] Surgeons were convinced that African

Americans were immune to malaria and so when an African American appeared at sick call with symptoms of malaria, the surgeon would ascribe the symptoms to some other disease; this misdiagnosis could be fatal. The conclusion would be that the high death rate among African Americans was caused by other factor such as poor diet or lack of the medical care (and quinine) that the whites enjoyed.

Yellow fever is another case to consider. It is a product of environment so much so that the South was convinced that yellow fever would become the "scourge of the Yankees" as they moved South.[248] The built in immunity of the African Americans appears to have been a factor considered by Union commanders when they sent African American troops into areas with a high incidence of yellow fever. While the yellow fever mortality among whites was higher than African Americans, the disease resulted in very few deaths in the Civil War (23 African Americans and 409 whites) and was not significant to the health of the Union army.[249]

Malaria and yellow fever were caused by mosquitoes but this was not understood. "I have been having chills & fevers & I tell you that I don't like the chaps at atol (sic)" wrote a soldier in Salisbury, North Carolina, in the fall of 1862. "I had one yesterday," he continued "that like to shook me clean out of the garrison."[250] Another Confederate veteran recalled insects seemed "born with national prejudices against all Southern flesh."[251] Another remarked that "they seem resolved to take me dead or alive."[252] Medical authorities attributed malaria to "miasmas" emanating from areas covered by stagnant waters: a rather vague concept of some sort of evil thing rising from the ground or water. Burning of tar in the vicinity of hospitals was recommended to prevent the malady,[253] and this would prove more effective than other preventive measures since it would also repel mosquitoes. A few physicians seemed to understand the role of insects in spreading yellow fever and malaria. South Carolinian Josiah Clark Nutt reached the conclusions that mosquitoes transmitted the disease and he recommended that the drainage of swamps as a prophylactic measure. Communities that followed his advice and others who agreed found a reduction in the disease.[254] Quinine was isolated by a French chemist in 1822. It was used as a treatment and also a prophylactic. The incidence of malaria among Confederate troops was slightly higher than the Union's.[255]

Pneumonia

Of the respiratory ailments that attacked soldiers, pneumonia was the most deadly. The mortality rate was about 25%. Confederate surgeon Joseph Jones estimated that between 17,209 and 21,474 deaths resulted from pneumonia during the period January 1862 through August 1863.[256] He also stated that 17% of Confederate soldiers suffered from pneumonia. How he came up with his numbers is anyone's guess since the deaths could have been caused by multiple diseases of which pneumonia was only one. Soldiers exposed to bad weather and bad food were susceptible. On the bright side, Confederate surgeons prescribed a number of drugs to counter pneumonia. The troops were delighted to find brandy, whiskey and opium on the list.[257]

Tuberculosis

Pulmonary tuberculosis was a sequelae to measles, a disease that ravaged both armies. Mortality rate was high, from 20-30%.[258] Since it is a contagious disease, closeness of camp life added to those infected.

Small Pox

There was nothing new about this disease during the Civil War. During the American Revolution and before, it was recognized that vaccination would prevent the disease. The use of pus from a victim to vaccinate others worked with less efficiency than today, but it did work and caught on with soldiers self-vaccinating themselves to the point that entire regiments had to be taken off-line while the troops recovered from self-vaccination. General George Washington finally banned the practice of self-vaccination in favor of vaccination controlled by physicians.

Small pox was one of the most dreaded diseases in the Confederacy. Medical authorities appeared unaware of the danger of small pox outbreaks and the sudden epidemics had a high mortality rate.[259] In late 1862, the small pox hospital in Richmond recorded 250 admissions and 110 deaths from the disease.[260] Treatment consisted of saline purgatives, cooling drinks and enema to reduce the fever.[261]

Spurious Vaccinia

An unwelcome by-product of small pox was spurious vaccinia. It was caused by impure vaccine and produced large ulcers that would not heal. It was not a trivial problem. At the battle of Chancellorsville Lee's army had over 5,000 soldiers unfit for duty due to the disease.[262]

Scurvy

The cause of scurvy had been known since the eighteenth century and the cure was simple: adequate fruits and vegetables, a fact known by the British navy for over one hundred years thanks to Dr. James Lind. An augmented ration went into effect that increased the flour ration by six ounces and provided four ounces of hard bread and three pounds of potatoes per man per week.[263] The potatoes were an important addition since they contain vitamin C. These were the rations normally provided but during some campaigns such as Atlanta, rations went short and the troops suffered. Surgeon Joseph Jones estimated that 90% of the deaths at Andersonville prison were due to scurvy.[264] A strange result of scurvy was nyctalopia or night blindness. It reached epidemic proportions late in the war. One Confederate soldier recalled the scene. "Men led by the hand all night . . . . go into battle with the command the next morning."[265]

Rheumatism

Rheumatism infected many soldiers. The Confederate army east of the Mississippi had 59,772 cases in the first two years of the war. The treatment when it was applied had little effect on the symptoms of the disease. For chronic cases, no treatment at all was tried.[266]

Measles

Measles generally thought to be a childhood disease was a great scourge during the Civil War. The Union army reported 76,318 cases of which 5,177 died.[267] Since it is highly infectious it spread wildly in camps especially among those from rural areas and the younger soldiers.

Improving hygienic conditions helped reduce outbreaks, but there was little available to reduce the length of the sickness.

Camp Itch

One of the most annoying diseases was camp itch that effected thousands. It was a non-parasitic skin irritation caused by filth, lice and lack of bathing. Surgeons prescribed sulfur, arsenic or alkaline baths, but it is not clear that the soldiers preferred camp itch or the prescribed treatment. Assistant Surgeon S. R. Chambers claimed to have a remedy that never failed. It was an ointment of inner bark of the elder, lard, sweet gum, basilica ointment, olive oil and sulfur flour.[268] It sounded more like a cooking recipe than an ointment but worked if the patient could stand the smell.

Alcoholism

"George Slone died last Wednesday wit (sic) delearam (sic) tremens."[269] The writer was a soldier from North Carolina in 1861.[270] Life and death with and from alcohol was a way of life in the nineteenth century and beyond. Combat merely enhanced the dependency. Captain Raphael Semmes of the Confederate raider *Alabama* complained that some of his crew got drunk at every opportunity and could be trusted "with everything but whiskey."[271] Drunkenness got so out of hand that the Confederate Congress got involved and passed "An Act to punish drunkenness in the Army."[272] Under the provisions of the act, all officers found guilty were to be "cashiered or suspended from the service of the Confederate States."[273] The Union had similar experience, but the statistics from both armies show very few deaths from drunkenness. The Union army had fewer than a thousand deaths from alcoholism during the war.[274] The deaths came later.

Alcoholism was rampant throughout both armies and helped the individual face up the to the horrors of this war. It also destroyed the effectiveness of the soldiers and officers who were engaged. A war correspondent in Virginia summarized the problem in the Southern army and reported that surgeons were in a state of intoxication even during the course of an engagement and when operating.

> Engaged at the amputation table many of them feel it to be their solemn duty, every time they administer brandy to the patient, to take a drink themselves. This part of the work is performed with great unction and conscientiousness . . . . Surgeons were so stupefied by liquor that they could not distinguish between a man's arm and the spoke of a wagon wheel, and who would just as soon have sawed off the one as the other.[275]

Venereal Disease

Soldiers did not write home about venereal disease then or now. Many acquired the disease and some died but more took it home with them to infect others. Some such as historian Bell Irvin Wiley concluded that there was little venereal disease in the Confederate army.[276] This may have been wishful thinking. One regiment, the Twenty-first North Carolina listed 59 cases of venereal disease from April 1862 through April 1864.[277] Others claimed that it was used by some soldiers to get out of battle and into a hospital[278]: a very difficult way out. Remedies included many different roots and berries. Also, mercury was prescribed for syphilis.

Veteran Reserve Corps

During the Civil War, Union soldiers who were wounded or ill from disease could be assigned to the Veteran Reserve Corps or Invalid Corps as it was at first called to perform light duty freeing able bodied soldiers to fight. General Orders defined the Corps.

War Department General Orders No. 105, issued by the Adjutant General's Office on April 28, 1863, authorized the creation of the Veteran Reserve Corps (VRC) originally called the Invalid Corps.[279] The Corps consisted of companies and battalions made up of :

- Officers and enlisted men unfit for active field service because of wounds or disease contracted in the line of duty, but still capable of performing garrison duty.
- Officers and enlisted men in service and on the Army rolls otherwise absent from duty and in hospitals, in convalescent camps, or otherwise under the control of medical officials, but capable of serving as cooks, clerks, orderlies, and guards at hospitals and other public buildings.
- Officers and enlisted men honorably discharged because of wounds or disease and who wanted to reenter the service.[280]

The Invalid Corps was renamed the Veteran Reserve Corps because of confusion with the damaged goods stamp "I.C." (inspected-condemned—used on material ordered by the army), that affected volunteer morale.

This was an individual decision. For example, Sergeant Major Eicher of the Tenth Minnesota Volunteers who lost an arm at Nashville continued to serve until the end of his three year enlistment (August, 1865).[281] He could have entered the Veteran Reserve Corps after he was wounded. The system was not perfect and some cases of the assignment to the Veteran Reserve Corps cannot be explained. More numerous were the discharges for disability which could have been anything from a fever, dysentery, recurring infection or the aftermath of a battle wound.

Nearly 60,000 Union soldiers served in the Veteran Reserve Corps during the Civil War. At the hanging of the prisoners convicted of Lincoln's murder, members of the VRC were given the honor of knocking out the post at the scaffold causing the condemned to drop to their deaths.

The Confederacy followed suit when the Confederate Congress responded with "An Act to provide an Invalid Corps" which was signed into law on 17 February 1864.[282] The rules were similar to those of the Union. Since the measure was enacted late in the war, the number of soldiers on the roles were a fraction of those in the Union's VRC. The registers indicated that 1,063 officers and 5,139 enlisted men served in the Invalid Corps.[283]

African American Casualties

Death entered the ranks of African American regiments from very unlikely sources. Robert Cowden described the first summer with the Union recruits.

> During the months of July and August, the condition of the health of the regiment was very discouraging,—more than forty dying in July, and nearly as many in August. The principal cause, doubtless, was that meal, from which the corn-bread to which they were accustomed was made, could not be obtained, and they were obliged to live on wheat-bread. Their superstitions may also have increased mortalities, for so frightened were they that, going to the regimental hospital was considered equivalent to death. As soon as corn-meal was obtained and the hot weather was past, health was restored. Meantime panic had seized upon many and they had absented themselves from camp for a time, but most of them returned, and after slight punishment were restored to duty."[284]

The death rate among African Americans was considerably higher than their white counterparts during the war. Slaves were often in poor health, more so than their white colleagues because of poor diet and mistreatment. The mortality rate in the Union camps for African Americans was twenty five percent.[285] This was much higher than whites.

Historian Margaret Humphreys stated that of the nearly 200,000 African Americans that served for the Union, 33,000 died including 29,000 from disease and only four thousand from battle wounds.[286] On the other hand, Joseph T. Wilson stated that the total deaths from all causes was 68,178 and he provided a state by state breakdown of the deaths[287] which is close to estimates of other authors. Statistics from the war are often confusing. In the case, above, Humphreys was counting Union casualties while Wilson was counting all on both sides. According to Humphreys whites sustained a 4.5% death rate from battle wounds while the African Americans fared much better and lost only 1.8%.[288] This is easily explained. African Americans were assigned garrison duty in order to free up white regiments to fight battles. Garrison duty was a death sentence in many respects. Disease was rampant in the camps for such reasons as poor sanitation. While far fewer African Americans died in combat or as a result of wounds, the death by disease was much more than that of the whites. From all causes, battle and disease, 13.5 % of white soldiers died during the Civil War; but the African American death toll was 18.5 %.[289] The difference may have been much higher depending upon which historian's numbers one wishes to trust. The 65th Regiment USCT had no combat deaths but lost nearly half of its strength due to disease.[290] Subsequent to the war, the 65th was scrutinized because it had no combat deaths, but had the highest mortality rate of any Union regiment in the war.[291] Some ascribe this high death rate to the locations of the camps to which they were assigned, Benton Barracks in St. Louis and the Mississippi camps in Louisiana.[292]

Other diseases were examined by the USSC to determine if susceptibility had anything to do with race, but the results were inconclusive. The higher death rates of African Americans were not a result of any susceptibility to disease but other factors such as medical care.

African Americans in the Civil War received second-class medical care.[293] A part of the problem was the surge to recruit African American regiments in 1863-64. While white regiments were already in place with medical staff, the African Americans were new. The much studied 65th regiment USCT shows that out of 20,000, Union regiments, it had a higher death rate than any other regiment, nearly half of its strength did not survive the war. More important, the regiment never fought in a battle: in addition to casualties, a battle produces a host of deadly disease such as pneumonia. The 65th experienced none of that, yet had the highest death rate in the war. All of the benefits of the sick such as better food, clothing and shelter were not available to the men of the 65th and other African American regiments.[294] As a result of high mortality rates, surgeons serving African American regiments blamed it on racial deficiencies rather than the poor level of care that they provided to those in their keeping. Regiments were authorized a surgeon and two assistant surgeons, but few of the African American regiments had their full complement, and those that did, had surgeons and assistant surgeons assigned late in the war. Some regiments had none. See *Official Army Register of the Volunteer Force of the United States*

Army for the Years 1861, '62 '63 '64, '65 Volume 8 for a listing of surgeons and assistant surgeons assigned to African American regiments.[295] The point is that in the surge to create new African American regiments, medical doctors were offered an opportunity for promotion and good pay, but there were not enough qualified people to assign to this duty. As a consequence, unqualified people were assigned. As an example, The First Regiment USCT had a physician appointed who did not want to go South when the regiment was assigned there. He was replaced by a surgeon who disliked the duty, did nothing and was fired. Third, a private stepped forward claiming that he had medical experience (he did not). It appears that his motivation was the ample supply of medicinal alcohol which he greatly enjoyed. Finally, a competent surgeon stepped forward, but inspectors found that he also had a liking for medicinal whiskey and on the day of the inspection found him with a black eye and bruised nose from his previous night's activities.[296] The army did its best to find qualified surgeons for the African American regiments with uneven results. Calls to medical colleges were put out to enroll medical students. While some colleges had excellent curriculum others were merely diploma factories that inflicted more medical incompetence on the troops. The soldiers called these student's work "the poison of the scholars".[297] General Lorenzo Thomas, who was given the task of forming the new African American regiments by Secretary of War Stanton, refused to appoint anyone without a medical degree.[298] It was a hopeless situation; and, in the end, the troops paid the price for the Union army's inability to find qualified surgeons.

Even cultural differences and language had roles in the high mortality rates. If a white surgeon did not understand his African American patient, it would be difficult to diagnose and treat the disease.[299] The consequence of all of these problems with the white surgeons was the creation of a gulf between the soldiers and their surgeons.[300] This caused the soldiers to avoid treatment which further drove up the death rate.

As the war progressed, Union forces were ordered East and South from Benton Barracks to fight a number of campaigns that neither the whites nor African Americans were acclimated for. They entered into one of the most unhealthy regions of the United States. There was a buildup of African American regiments in Louisiana and the plan was to replace whites who were thought to be more susceptible to disease such as malaria and yellow fever. It was thought that African Americans with their acquired immunity were better suited to defending forts in this area.[301] While this approach reduced African American battle casualties, death by disease increased because of inadequate food and lack of adequate shelter and the heavy labor that had to be performed in building fortifications,. The high water table in the region served as excellent breeding grounds for mosquitoes and the water was frequently contaminated with fecal matter.[302] While the official policy was that white and African Americans would divide the labor, in fact the division was less than equal with the African Americans doing the vast majority of the work. Three of the African American regiments in Louisiana lost four men in combat and 1,374 to disease. James E. Yeatman of the Western Sanitary Commission visited Youngs Point, Louisiana in late 1863. The camp housed about 2,100 people. "There appears to be more squalid misery and destitution here than any other place that I have visited. The sickness and deaths were most frightful. During the summer from thirty to fifty died in a day and some days as many as seventy-five."[303]

As the war ended, 25,000 African American troops were ordered to Texas.[304] The rationale was that first: they went to defeat the Confederate general Kirby Smith. Even after Lee and Johnston had surrendered and Jefferson Davis had been captured, Kirby Smith refused to give up the fight.

General Kirby Smith
Courtesy of the Library of Congress

Second: Union forces there were intended to secure the border with Mexico which was in a state of upheaval with warfare between Benito Juarez and the French Emperor Maximilan.

Benito Juarez Emperor
Courtesy of the Library of Congress

Maximilan of Mexico
Courtesy of the Library of Congress

Last: they were intended to deal with recalcitrant Texans who wanted to continue the war and Texans were always difficult to deal with. This last point was not valid. By the summer of 1865, even Texans were war weary and wanted no further part in fighting. Scurvy now became the major killer of African American troops. Scurvy continued unabated because of poor planning in setting up a system to supply the troops, but more important, white Union officers were diverting supplies and funding to their own use. Surgeon Charles Radmore in charge of Brownsville Hospital ordered "certain quantities of Brandy, Whiskey, Claret Wine, Champaign, Hostetters Bitters and Malt Liquors for the Gov't Service, almost none of which ever found its way to the sick in Hospital or elsewhere."[305] The result of this sad affair in Texas was that about 2,500 African Americans perished from scurvy in the summer and fall of 1865. In a case of underreporting the Union army listed 128

African American soldiers who had died.[306] The USSC commission had done much during the war to supplement the diets of Union soldiers but by late 1865 it was shutting down so the soldier's "safety net" was not available when it was needed the most in Texas.

Summary

As seen above, throughout the war there appeared to be trends that caused more deaths among African Americans than should have occurred. First, at all levels of the Army, the accepted cause of high death rates was the racist view that African Americans were an inferior race that could not survive. As a result, when the high death rates occurred, they were accepted as yet another proof of the inferior race without looking further. Second, the African American regiments were supported by incompetent surgeons and some white officers who were determined to profit from the war at the expense of the troops. Third, as with whites, many volunteers were enlisted in the army without adequate physicals or no examinations at all. As a result, people with diseases and disabilities were accepted into the Union army and it was their death sentence.

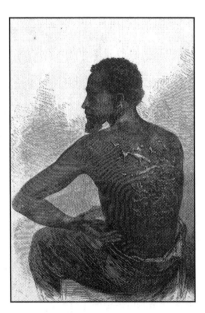

An African American Recruit
Courtesy of the Library of Congress

Fourth: African American regiments were singled out as the bottom of the supply chain that received rations and all other supplies after white regiments had been served. Finally, the Union army moved troops without regard to their background or acquired immunity (except for the Louisiana assignments of African Americans). No one suggests that they had the time to consider this, but preventive measures would have helped. As an example, the 10th Minnesota Regiment was moved from Minnesota South to Benton Barracks at the same time as the influx of African American regiments. The Minnesota troops had winter clothing and knew how to survive in cold weather. They may also have had built in immunity to counter some of the diseases at Benton Barracks. The African Americans were brought in from southern climates where they had been raised. Whether or not they had cold weather clothing is not known. What is known is that while hundreds of African Americans were dying at Benton Barracks from pneumonia and dysentery a total of five Minnesotan's lost their lives. Another factor has to be entered into the equation. Throughout the war African Americans generally had living quarters far less satisfactory then the white troops. Russell described the quarters assigned to the African Americans. "One hundred men were crowded into rooms originally meant for fifty, necessarily rendering the air very impure; and this evil was rendered greater by faulty construction of the barracks and imperfect ventilation."[307] The result was a perfect breeding ground for TB, pneumonia and other diseases. While this was going on, members of white regiments were writing home about winter sports, guard duty and a winter fair.

Historian and MD Margaret Humphreys summarized, best. "Had they [African Americans] received even the minimal care meted out to white troops, the same (though still inadequate) diet, the same amount of fatigue duty, the same uniforms, the same tents, and had they been led by experienced, caring officers, much of the disease that mowed them down could have been prevented."[308]

BIBLIOGRAPHY

Primary Sources
Books

Athearn, Robert G. *Soldier in the West, The Civil War Letters of Alfred Lacey Hough*. Philadelphia: University of Pennsylvania Press, 1957.

Brown, William Wells. *Narrative of William W. Brown, An American Slave*. Memphis: General Books, 2009.

Christie, Thomas and William. *Brother of Mine*. St. Paul: Minnesota Historical Society Press, 2010.

Cox, Jacob D. *The March to the Sea: Franklin and Nashville*. New York: Charles Scribner's Sons, 1882.

Cullum, George Washington. *Biographical Register of the Officers and Graduates of the U. S. Military Academy at West Point from its Establishment, in 1802, to 1890 with the Early History of the United States Military Academy*. Boston: Houghton, Mifflin and Company, 1891

Cummings, Kate. *Kate The Journal of a Confederate Nurse*. Baton Rouge, Louisiana State University Press, 1987.

Douglass, Frederick. *The Life and Times of Frederick Douglass*. Mineola: Dover Publications, 2003.

Dyer, Frederick H. *A Compendium of the War of the Rebellion, Vol.1-3*. New York: Thomas Yoseloff, 1959.

Eggleston, George Cary. *A Rebel's Recollections*. Baton Rouge: Louisiana University Press, 1966.

Grant, Ulysses S. *Memoirs and Selected Letters, Personal Memoirs of U. S. Grant, Selected Letters 1839-1865*. New York: Literary Classics of the United States, Inc., 1990.

The Great Impeachment and Trial of Andrew Johnson, President of the United States. Philadelphia: T. B. Peterson & Brothers, 1868.

Harpers Weekly. 14 June 1862, 372, March-June 1868.

Howe, Samuel Gridley. *The United States Sanitary Commission*. Boston: Crosby and Nichols, 1864.

Johnston, Joseph E. *Narrative of Military Operations During the Civil War*. New York: Da Capo Press, 1959.

Long, A. L. *Memoirs of Robert E. Lee*. Secaucus: The Blue and Grey Press, 1983.

Marsh, Roswell. *Defence of Edwin Stanton*. Steubenville: W. R. Allison's Printing Establishment, 1873.

Newberry, John Strong. *What The U.S. Sanitary Commission is Doing in the Valley of the Mississippi*. Louisville: U. S. Sanitary Commission, 1863.

Nightingale, Florence. *Notes of Nursing, What It Is and What It Is not*. New York: D. Appleton and Company, 1860.

Post, Lydia Minturn. *Soldiers' Letters, from Camp, Battle-field and Prison*. New York: Bunce & Huntington, Publishers, 1865.

Reynolds, Thomas C. *General Sterling Price and the Confederacy*. St. Louis: University of Missouri Press, 2009.

Ross, Edmund G. *History of the Impeachment of Andrew Johnson, President of the United States*. Teddington: The Echo Library, 2007.

Sherman, William Tecumseh. *Memoirs of General W. T. Sherman*. New York: Literary Classics of the United States, Inc., 1990.

Townsend, E. D. *Anecdotes of the Civil War in the United States*. New York: D Appleton & Company, 1883.

United States Sanitary Commission. *The Sanitary Commission of the United States Army; A Succinct Narrative of its Works and Purposes*. New York: Published for the Benefit of the United States Sanitary Commission, 1864.

United States Military Academy. *Register of the Officers and Cadets of the U. S. Military Academy, June 1820*. West Point: Headquarters, U. S. Military Academy, 1884.

United States Military Academy. *Register of the Officers and Cadets of the U. S. Military Academy, June 1821.* West Point: Headquarters, U. S. Military Academy, 1884.

United States Military Academy. *Register of the Officers and Cadets of the U. S. Military Academy, June 1822.* West Point: Headquarters, U. S. Military Academy, 1884.

United States Military Academy. *Register of the Officers and Cadets of the U. S. Military Academy, June 1823.* West Point: Headquarters, U. S. Military Academy, 1884.

United States Military Academy. *Sixth Annual Reunion of the Association of Graduates of the United States Military Academy at West Point, New York June 17, 1875.* New York: A. S. Barnes & Company, 1875.

Wormeley, Katherine Prescott. *The United States Sanitary Commission: A Sketch of its Purposes and Its Works.* Boston: Little, Brown and Company, 1863.

Articles

New York Independent, December 12, 1867.
Washington Daily Morning Chronicle, June 23,1863.

Public Documents

Delaware Public Archives. *Baptism: Lorenzo Thomas (Adult).* V. 87, p.130, 9/25/1836.

Delaware Public Archives. *Marriage: Lorenzo Thomas to Elizabeth Colesberry.* V. 11, p.181, 12/4/1832.

U. S. War Department. *The War of Rebellion: A Compilation of the Official Records of the Union and Confederate Armies.* Series 1, vols. 13, 22, 34, 41, 48, Washington D.C., 1880-1901.

U. S. War Department. *Official Army Register of the Volunteer Force of the United States Army for the Years 1861, 1862, 1863, 1864; Volume 8.* Washington: Adjutant General's Office, 1867.

U.S. Department of War. *General Order Number 105.* Washington, D.C.: Government Printing Office, 28 April 1863.

Online Databases

Ancestry. http://www.ancestry.com.

National Park Service. *Civil War Soldiers & Sailors System.* http://www.
civilwar.nps.gov/cwss/

Slave Narratives, Federal Writers' Project Multiformat 1936-1938,
United States Library of Congress http://memory.loc.gov/ammem/
snhtml/snhome.html

U. S. Army. http://www.history.army.mil/moh.html

http://www.archives.gov

http://www.archives.gov/exhibits/featured_documents/emancipation_
proclamation/transcript.html

Unpublished Sources

Curran, John A. *The Civil War Diary of an Iowa Soldier July 1864-
February 1865.* Undated.

Letter, Lorenzo Thomas to Irving McDowell, 14 January 1858.

Letter, Lorenzo Thomas to A. S. Johnston, 18 February 1858.

Secondary Sources
Books

Ambrose, Stephen E. Duty, Honor, Country, A History of West Point.
Baltimore: Johns Hopkins University Press, 1966.

Adams, George Worthington. *Doctors in Blue. The Medical History of the
Union Army in the Civil War.* New York: Henry Schulman, 1952.

Alotta, Robert I. *Civil War Justice, Union Army Executions Under
Lincoln.* Shippensburg: White Mane Publishing Company, 1989.

Association of Graduates, United States Military Academy. *The Register
of Graduates and Former Cadets of the United States Military, 2010.*
West Point: Association of Graduates, 2010.

Barrow, Charles Kelly. *Black Confederates.* Gretna: Pelican Publishing
Company, 1995.

Barrow, Charles Kelly, J. H. Sefars and R. B. Rosenbur. *Forgotten
Confederates, An Anthology About Black Southerners.* Atlanta:
Southern Heritage Press, 1995.

Bell, Andrew McIlwaine, *Mosquito Soldiers. Malaria, Yellow Fever, and the Course of the American Civil War.* Baton Rouge: Louisiana State University Press, 2010.

Benedict, Michael Les. *The Impeachment and Trail of Andrew Johnson.* New York: W. W. Norton & Company, Inc., 1973.

Bessler, John D. *Legacy of Violence, Lynch Mobs and Executions in Minnesota.* Minneapolis: University of Minnesota Press, 2003.

Blackmon, Douglas A. *Slavery by Another Name, the Re-enslavement of Black Americans from the Civil War to World War II.* New York: Doubleday, 2008.

Boatner, Mark M, III. *The Civil War Dictionary.* New York: Vintage Books, 1991.

Bobrick, Benson. *The Battle of Nashville.* New York: Alfred A. Knopf, 2010.

Bonner, Robert E. *Mastering America, Southern Slaveholders and the Crisis of American Nationhood.* Cambridge: Cambridge University Press, 2009.

Boritt, Gabor S. *Lincoln's Generals.* Lincoln: University of Nebraska Press, 1994.

Burchard, Peter. *One Gallant Rush: Robert Gould Shaw and His Brave Black Regiment.* New York: St. Martin's Press, 1965.

Carnegie, Andrew. *Edwin M. Stanton Address by Andrew Carnegie on Stanton Memorial Day at Kenyon College.* New York: Doubleday, Page and Company 1906.

Carnes, Mark C. and John A. Garraty. *American Destiny, Narrative of a Nation, Volume I to 1877, Second Edition.* New York: Pearson Longman, 2006.

Castel, Albert. *General Sterling Price and the Civil War in the West.* Baton Rouge: Louisiana State University Press, 1996.

Catton, Bruce. *The Civil War.* New York: The Fairfax Press, 1980.

_____. *A Stillness at Appomattox, The Fateful Last Chapter of the Army of the Potomac's Dramatic Saga.* New York: Doubleday & Company, 1957.

Channing, Steven A. *Crisis of Fear, Secession in South Carolina.* New York: W. W. Norton & Company, 1974.

Cimprich, John. *Fort Pillow, A Civil War Massacre, and Public Memory (Conflicting Worlds: New Dimensions of the American Civil War.* Baton Rouge: Louisiana State University Press, 2005.

Clinton, Catherine & Nina Silber. *Divided Houses, Gender and the Civil War.* New York: Oxford Press, 1992.

Civil War Society. *Civil War Society's Encyclopedia of the Civil War: The Complete and Comprehensive Guide to the American Civil War.* Princeton: Wing Books, 1997.

Claxton, Melvin and Mark Puls. *Uncommon Valor A Story of Race, Patriotism, and Glory in the Final Battles of the Civil War.* Hoboken: John Wiley and Sons, Inc., 2006.

Collins, Donald E. *The Death and Resurrection of Jefferson Davis.* New York: Rowman & Littlefield Publishers, 2005.

Cornish, Dudley Taylor. *The Sable Arm, Negro Troops in the Union Army, 1861-1865.* New York: W. W. Norton & Company, Inc, 1956.

Cowley, Robert and Thomas Guinzburg. *West Point Two Centuries of Honor and Tradition.* New York: Warner Books, 2002.

Cunningham, H. H. *Doctors in Gray. The Confedereate Medical Service.* Baton Rouge: The Louisiana State University Press, 1958.

Current, Richard Nelson. *Lincoln's Loyalists, Union Soldiers from the Confederacy.* New York: Oxford University Press, 1992.

Davis, William C. *The Image of War, 1861-1865 Volumes I-VI.* New York: Doubleday & Company, Inc., 1983.

Dishman, Christopher D. *A Perfect Gibraltar, The Battle of Monterry, Mexico, 1846.* Norman: University of Oklahoma Press, 2010.

Dobak, William A. *Freedom by the Sword The U. S. Colored Troops 1862-1867.* Washington: Center for Military History United States Army, 2010.

Durden, Robert Franklin. *The Gray and the Black: The Confederate Debate on Emancipation.* Baton Rouge: Louisiana State University Press, 1972.

Eggleston, Larry G. *Women in the Civil War, Extraordinary Stories of Soldiers, Spies, Nurses, Doctors, Crusaders, and Others.* Jefferson: Mcfarland & Company, Inc., Publishers, 2003.

Eggleston, Michael A. *10th Minnesota Volunteers, A History of the Action in the Sioux Uprising and the Civil War with a Regimental Roster.* Jefferson: McFarland Publishers, 2012.

Eicher, John H. and David J. Eicher. *Civil War High Commands.* Stanford: Stanford University Press, 2001.

Eisenhower, John S. D. *Agent of Destiny The Life and Times of Genral Winfield Scott*. Norman: University of Oklahoma Press, 1997.

Ellis, Richard N. *General Pope and U. S. Indian Policy*. Albuqerque: University of New Mexico Press, 1970.

Faust, Drew Gilpin. *This Republic of Suffering, Death and the American Civil War*. New York: Alfred A. Knopf, 2008.

Field, Ron. *The Seminole Wars 1818-1858*. New York: Osprey Publishing, 2009.

Field, Ron and Alexander Bielakowski. *Buffalo Soldiers. African American Troops in the U. S. Forces 1866-1945*. Oxford:Osprey Publishing, 2008.

Flower, Frank Abial. *Edwin McMasters Stanton: The Autocrat of Rebellion, Emancipation and Reconstruction*. Boston: George M. Smith & Company, 1905.

Foner, Eric. *Free Soil, Free Labor, Free Men, The Ideology of the Republican Party Before the Civil War*. Oxford: Oxford University Press, 1995.

_____. *Reconstruction, America's Unfinished Revolution, 1863-1877*. New York: Perennial Classics, 2002.

Foreman, Amanda. *A World on Fire*. New York: Random House, Inc., 2010.

Foster, Gaines M. *Ghosts of the Confederacy, Defeat, the Lost Cause, and the Emergence of the New South*. New York: Oxford University Press, 1987.

Frassanito, William A. *Grant and Lee, The Virginia Campaigns of 1864-1865*. New York: Charles Scribner's Sons, 1983.

Freehling, William W. *The South vs. The South, How Anti-Confederate Southerns Shaped the Course of the Civil War*. New York: Oxford University Press, 2001.

Gallagher, Gary W. and Alan T. Nolan. *The Myth of the Lost Cause and Civil War History*. Bloomington: Indiana University Press, 2000.

Garrison, Nancy Scripture. *With Courage and Delicacy, Civil War on the Penninsula, Women in the U. S. Sanitary Commission*. New York: Da Capo Press, 1999.

Garrison, Webb, Jr. *Strange Battles of the Civil War*. Naperville: Cumberland House, 2001.

Giesberg, Judith Ann. *Civil War Sisterhood, The U. S. Sanitary Commission and Women's Politics in Transition.* Boston: Northwestern University Press, 2000.

Gladstone, William A. *United States Colored Troops 1863-1867.* Gettysburg: Thomas Publications, 1990.

Glatthaar, Joseph T. *Forged in Battle: The Civil War Alliance of Black Soldiers and White Officers.* New York: The Free Press, 1990.

Greenberg, Martin H. and Charles G. Waugh. *The Price of Freedom, Slavery and the Civil War.* Nashville: Cumberland House,

Greene, Jerome A. *Indian War Veterans, Memories of Army Life and Campaigns in the West, 1864-1898.* New York: Savas Beatie, 2007.

Grimsley, Mark. *The Hard Hand of War, Union Military Policy Toward Southern Civilians, 1861-1865.* New York: Cambridge University Press, 1995.

Hafendorfer, Kenneth A. *Nathan Bedford Forrest, A Distant Storm. The Murfreesboro Raid, July 13, 1862.* Louisville: KH Press, 1997.

Hargrove, Hondon B. *Black Union Soldiers in the Civil War.* Jefferson: McFarland & Company, Publishers, 1988.

Harrington, Arthur Elliot. *Edmund G. Ross A Man of Courage.* Franklin: Providence House Publishers, 1997.

Hattaway, Herman and Archer Jones. *How the North Won, A Military History of the Civil War.* Urbana: University of Illinois Press, 1991.

Hearn, Chester G. *The Impeachment of Andrew Johnson.* Jefferson: McFarland & Company, Inc., 2000.

Higginson, Thomas Wentworth. *Army Life in a Black Regiment.* Boston: Fields, Osgood, & Company, 1870.

Holland, Mary Gardner. *Our Army Nurses, Stories from Women in the Civil War.* St. Paul: Edinborough Press, 1998.

Horn, Stanley F. *The Decisive Battle of Nashville.* Knoxville, University of Tennessee Press, 1978.

Humphreys, Margaret. *Intensely Human: The Health of the Black Soldiers in the American Civil War.* Baltimore: Johns Hopkins University Press, 2008.

Hurst, Jack. *Nathan Bedford Forrest, A Biography.* New York: Vintage Books, 1994.

Jenkins, Sally and John Stauffer. *The State of Jones, The Small Southern County that Seceded from the Confederacy.* New York: Anchor Books, 2010.

Johnson, Timothy D. *Winfield Scott, The Quest for Military Glory.* Lawrence: The University Press of Kansas, 1998.

Jones, Madison. *Nashville, 1864. The Dying of the Light.* Nashville: J. S. Sanders & Company, 1997.

Jones, Robert Huhn. The *Civil War in the NorthWest, Nebraska, Wisconsin, Iowa, Minnesota and the Dakotas.* Norman: University of Oklahoma Press, 1960.

Jordan, Ervin L. Jr. *Black Confederates and Afro-Yankees in Civil War Virginia.* Charlottesville: University Press of Virginia, 1995.

Jordan, General Thomas and J. P. Pryor. *The Campaigns of Lieut.-Gen N. B. Forrest and of Forrest's Cavalry.* Dayton: Morningside Bookshop, 1977.

Josephy, Alvin M., Jr. *The Civil War in the American West.* New York: Alfred A. Knopf, 1991.

Kennedy, John F. *Profiles in Courage.* New York: Harper Collins, 1955.

Lardas, Mark. *African American Soldier in the Civil War USCT 1862-1866.* Oxford: Osprey Publishing, 2006.

Lemann, Nicholas. *Redemption, The Last Battle of the Civil War.* New York: Farrar, Straus and Giroux, 2006.

Levine, Bruce. *Confederate Emancipation: Southern Plans to Free and Arm Slaves during the Civil War.* New York: Oxford University Press, 2006.

Lewis, Felice Flanery. *Trailing Clouds of Glory, Zachary Taylor's Mexican War Campaign and His Emerging Civil War Leaders.* Tuscaloosa: The University of Alabama Press, 2010.

Logsdon, David R. *Eyewitnesses at the Battle of Nashville.* Nashville: Kettle Mill Press, 2004.

Long, E. B. *The Civil War Day by Day, An Almanac 1861-1865.* New York: Doubleday & Company, Inc., 1971.

Lounsberry, Colonel Clement A. *Early History of North Dakota, Essential Outlines of American History.* Washington, D. C.: Liberty Press, 1919.

Manning, Chandra. *What This Cruel War Was Over, Soldiers, Slavery, and the Civil War.* New York: Vintage Books, 2007.

McDonough, James Lee. *Chattanooga—Death Grip on the Confederacy*. Knoxville: The University of Tennessee Press, 1984.

_____. *Nashville. The Confederacy's Last Gamble*. Knoxville: The University of Tennessee Press, 2004.

McFeely, William S. *Grant*. New York: W. W. Norton & Company, 1981.

McMurry, Richard M. *John Bell Hood and the War for Southern Independence*. Lincoln: University of Nebraska Press, 1982.

McPherson, James M. *For Cause and Comrades, Why Men Fought In The Civil War*. New York: Oxford University Press, 1997.

_____. *The Negro's Civil War: How American Blacks Felt and Acted During the Civil War*. New York: Vintage Books, 1965.

McWhitney, Grady and Perry D. Jamieson. *Attack and Die, Civil War Military Tactics and the Southern Heritage*. University: University of Alabama Press, 1982.

Merriam-Webster Collegiate Dictionary, Eleeventh Edition. Springfield: Merriam-Webster, Incorporated, 2003.

Miller, Edward A. Jr. *Lincoln's Abolitionist General: The Biography of David Hunter*. Columbia: University of South Carolina Press, 1997.

Moe, Richard. *The Last Full Measure*. New York: Henry Holt and Company, 1993.

Monaghan, Jay. *Civil War on the Western Border 1854-1865*. Boston: Little, Brown and Company, 1955.

Nagel, Paul C. *John Quincy Adams A Public Life, A Private Life*. New York: Alfred A. Knopf, 1957.

Nolan, Alan T. *Lee Considered, General Robert E. Lee and Civil War History*. Chapel Hill: University of North Carolina Press, 1991.

Nolan, Dick. *Benjamin Franklin Butler: The Damnedest Yankee*. Novato: Presidio Press, 1991.

Oates, Stephen B. and Charles J. Errico. *Portrait of America Ninth Edition Volume 1 From the European Discovery of America to the End of Reconstruction*. Boston: Houghton Mifflin Company, 2007.

_____. *Portrait of America Ninth Edition Volume 2 From 1865*. Boston: Houghton Mifflin Company, 2007.

Oates, Stephen B. *With Malice Toward None, The Life of Abraham Lincoln*. New York: Harper & Row, Publishers, 1977.

Packard, Randall M. *The Making of a Tropical Disease A Short History of Malaria*. Baltimore: The John Hopkins University Press, 2007.

Paulsen, Gary. *Soldier's Heart Being the Story of the Enlistment and Due Service of the Boy Charley Goddard in the First Minnesota Volunteers*. New York: Dell Laurel-Leaf, 1998.

Poland, Charles P, Jr. *The Glories of War, Small Battles and Early Heroes of 1861*. Bloomington: Author House, 2004.

Powell, William Henry. *A History of the Organization and Movements of the Fourth Regiment of Infantry, United States Army*. Washington City: McGill & Witherow, Printers and Steretypers, 1871.

Pratt, Fletcher. *Stanton Lincoln's Secretary of War*. New York: W. W. Norton, Inc., 1953.

Quarles, Benjamin. *The Negro in the Civil War*. Boston: Little, Brown, and Company, 1953.

Redkey, Edwin S. *Black Exodus: Black Nationalists and Back-to-Africa Movements, 1890-1910*. Newhaven: Yale University Press, 1969.

Reid, Richard M. *Freedom for Themselves: North Carolina's Black Soldiers in the Civil War Era*. Chapel Hill: University of North Carolina Press, 2008.

Reynolds, Thomas C. *General Sterling Price and the Confederacy*. St. Louis: University of Missouri Press, 2009.

Robertson, James. *The Untold Civil War Exploring the Human Side*. Washington, D.C.: The National Geographic, 2011.

Rodriguez, Ricardo J. *Black Confederates in the U. S. Civil War: A Compiled List of African—Americans Who Served the Confederacy*. Charleston: Create Space, 2010.

Rollins, Richard. *Black Southerners in Gray: Essays on Afro-Americans in Confederate Armies*. Murfreesboro: Southern Heritage Press, 1994.

Russell, Andrew J. *Russell's Civil War Photographs*. New York: Dover Publications, Inc., 1982.

Rybczynski, Witold. *A Clearing in the Distance, Frederick Law Olmsted and the America in the Nineteenth Century*. New York: Scribner

Sandburg, Carl. *Abraham Lincoln, The War Years, Volumes I-IV*. New York: Harcourt, Brace & Company, 1939.

Sateren, Shelley Swanson. A *Civil War Drummer Boy, The Diary of William Bircher, 1861-1865*. Mankato: Blue Earth Books, 2000.

Schmidt, James M. and Guy R. Hasegawa. *Years of Change and Suffering: Modern Perspectives on Civil War Medicine*. St. Paul: Edinborough Press, 2009.

Schultz, Jane E. *Women at the Front, Hospital Workers in Civil War America*. Chapel Hill: The University of North Carolina Press, 2004.

Segars, J. H. *Black Southerners in Confederate Armies: A Collection of Historical Accounts*. Gretna: Pelican Publishing Company, 2007.

Shea, William L. and Earl J. Hess. *Pea Ridge Civil War Campaign in the West*. Chapel Hill: University of North Carolina Press, 1992.

Smith, Derek. *In The Lion's Mouth. Hood's Tragic Retreat from Nashville, 1864*. Mechanicsburg: Stackpole Books, 2011.

Palmer, Dave Richard. *The River and the Rock, A History of Fortress West Point. 1775-1783*. New York: Hippocrene Books, 1969.

Speer, John. *Life of Gen. James H. Lane, "The Liberator of Kansas": With Corroborative Incidents of Pioneer History*. Garden City: John Speer, Printer, 1896.

Stern, Philip Van Doren. *Secret Missions of the Civil War*. New York: Wing Books, 1959.

Stewart, David O. *Impeached: The Trial of President Andrew Johnson and the Fight for Lincoln's Legacy*. New York: Simon & Schuster Paperbacks, 2009.

Streeter, James, Jr. *The Civil War, The Struggle for Tennessee, Tupelo to Stones River*. Alexandria: Time-Life Books, 1985.

Stockdale, Paul H. *The Death of an Army: The Battle of Nashville & Hood's Retreat*. Murfreesboro: Southern Heritage Press, 1992.

Stoker, Donald. *The Grand Design Strategy and the U. S. Civil War*. New York: Oxford University Press, 2010.

Stout, Harry S. *Upon the Altar of the Nation*. New York: The Penguin Group, 2007.

Sully, Langdon. *No Tears for the General, The Life of Alfred Sully, 1821-1879*. Palo Alto: American West Publishing Company, 1974.

Sword, Wiley. *Embrace an Angry Wind, The Confederacy's Last Hurrah. Spring Hill, Franklin, & Nashville*. New York: Harper Collins Publishers, 1992.

Symonds, Craig L. *A Battlefield Atlas of the American Civil War*. London: Ian Allan, Ltd., 1985.

Thomas, Benjamin P. and Harold M. Hyman. *Stanton The Life and Times of Lincoln's Secretary of War*. New York: Alfred A. Knopf, 1962.

Thomas, Emory M. *The Confederate Nation, 1861-1865*. New York: Harper & Row Publishers, 1979.

Tindall, George Brown & David Emory Shi. *America, A Narrative History, Seventh Edition, Volume Two*. New York: W. W. Norton & Company, 2007.

Trudeau, Noah Andre. *Southern Storm, Sherman's March to the Sea*. New York: Harper Perennial, 2009.

Vincent, Thomas MacCurdy. *Abraham Lincoln and Edwin M. Stanton*. Washington, D. C.: Commandery of the District of Columbia, 1892.

Wakefield, John F. *The Battle of Nashville, 1864*. Florence: Honors Press, 2001.

Ward, Geoffrey C. *The Civil War, An Illustrated History*. New York: Alfred A. Knope, Inc., 1990.

Warner, Ezra J. *Generals in Blue Lives of the Union Commanders*. Baton Rouge: Louisiana State University Press, 1964.

Wheeler, Richard. *Voices of the Civil War*. New York: Thomas Y. Crowell Company, 1976.

West, Nathaniel. *The Ancestry, Life, and Times of Hon. Henry Hastings Sibley, L.L.D.* St. Paul: Pioneer Press Publishing Company, 1889.

Wiley, Bell Irvin. *The Life of Johnny Reb, The Common Soldier of the Confederacy*. Baton Rouge: Louisiana State University Press, 1943.

_____. *The Life of Billy Yank, The Common Soldier of the Union*. Baton Rouge: Louisiana State University Press, 1952.

_____. *Southern Negroes, 1861-1865*. Baton Rouge: Louisiana Stat University, 1938.

Wills, Brian Steel. *The Confederacy's Greatest Cavalryman, Nathan Bedford Forrest*. Lawrence: University of Kansas, 1992.

Wilson, Joseph T. *The Black Phalanx African American Soldiers in the War of Independence, the War of 1812 and the Civil War*. Memphis: General Books, 2010.

Woodworth, Steven E. *Decision in the Heartland The Civil War in the West*. Westport: Praeger Publishers, 2008.

_____ *Jefferson Davis and his Generals The Failure of Confederate Command in the West.* Lawrence: University of Kansas Press, 1990.

_____ *Civil War Generals in Defeat.* Lawrence: University Press of Kansas, 1999.

Wyatt-Brown, Bertram. *Honor and Violence in the Old South.* New York: Oxford University Press, 1986.

Wyeth, John Allan. *That Devil Forrest, The Life of General Nathan Bedford Forrest.* Baton Rouge: Louisiana State University, 1989.

NOTES

Cover

[1] This statue was completed in 1997. A major feature is the inscribed panel that surrounds the statue and contains the names of over two hundred thousand African Americans who fought for the Union. The inscription on the memorial reads "Civil War to Civil Rights and Beyond. This memorial is dedicated to those who served in the African American units of the Union Army in the Civil War. The 209,145 names inscribed on these walls commemorate those fighters for freedom."

Preface

[1] James M. McPherson, *The Negro's Civil War: How American Blacks Felt and Acted During the Civil War.* (New York: Vintage Books, 1965).

[2] David R. Logsdon, *Eyewitnesses at the Battle of Nashville* (Nashville: Kettle Mill Press, 2004).

[1] Hondon B. Hargrove, *Black Union Soldiers in the Civil War.* (Jefferson: McFarland & Company, Publishers, 1988), ix.

[2] *Ibid.*, x.

[3] Logsdon, *Eyewitnesses at the Battle of Nashville,*70.

[4] Michael A. Eggleston, *10th Minnesota Volunteers, A History of the Action in the Sioux Uprising and the Civil War with a Regimental Roster.* (Jefferson: McFarland Publishers, 2012).

[5] National Park Service. *Civil War Soldiers & Sailors System.* http://www.civilwar.nps.gov/cwss/

[6] The number of USCT regiments varies between 166 and 175 according to which reference one is reading. Some of the confusion is because some

of the state regiments were converted to USCT and others were not. If one counts all regiments including USCT and state regiments the higher number would be more appropriate.

7   Cunningham, *Doctors in Gray. The Confederate Medical Service*, 27.

8   William A. Gladstone, *United States Colored Troops 1863-1867.* (Gettysburg Thomas Publications, 1990), 120.

9   McPherson, *The Negro's Civil War: How American Blacks Felt and Acted During the Civil War,* 160.

10   Joseph T. Wilson, *The Black Phalanx African American Soldiers in the War of Independence, the War of 1812 and the Civil War.* (Memphis: General Books, 2010), 80.

11   McPherson, *The Negro's Civil War: How American Blacks Felt and Acted During the Civil War.* (New York) Vintage Books, 1965), Appendix A.

12   Hargrove, *Black Union Soldiers in the Civil War,* 3.

13   McPherson, *The Negro's Civil War: How American Blacks Felt and Acted During the Civil War,* Appendix A.

14   Wilson *The Black Phalanx African American Soldiers in the War of Independence, the War of 1812 and the Civil War,* 60.

15   *Ibid.,* 70.

Introduction

1   Dudley Taylor Cornish, *The Sable Arm, Negro Troops in the Union Army, 1861-1865.* (New York: W. W. Norton & Company, Inc, 1956), 114.

2   McPherson, *The Negro's Civil War: How American Blacks Felt and Acted During the Civil War,* 3.

3   *Ibid.,* 12.

4   Hondon B. Hargrove, *Black Union Soldiers in the Civil War.* (Jefferson: McFarland & Company, Publishers, 1988), 17.

5   McPherson, *The Negro's Civil War: How American Blacks Felt and Acted During the Civil War,* 19.

6   Ibid., 22.

7   Ibid., 31.

8   Ibid., 34.

9   Ibid., xvi.

10   *Ibid.,* 40.

11   Charles Kelly Barrow, *Black Confederates.* (Gretna: Pelican Publishing Company, 1995), 38.

12　*Ibid.*, 10.

13　McPherson, *The Negro's Civil War: How American Blacks Felt and Acted During the Civil War*, xvii.

14　Richard Rollins, *Black Southerners in Gray: Essays on Afro-Americans in Confederate Armies.* (Murfreesboro: Southern Heritage Press, 1994), 76.

15　Barrow, *Black Confederates*, 12.

16　Rollins, *Black Southerners in Gray: Essays on Afro-Americans in Confederate Armies*, 130-131.

17　Hargrove, *Black Union Soldiers in the Civil War*, x.

18　McPherson, *The Negro's Civil War: How American Blacks Felt and Acted During the Civil War*, 243.

19　Wilson, *The Black Phalanx African American Soldiers in the War of Independence, the War of 1812 and the Civil War.* (Memphis: General Books, 2010), 80.

20　McPherson, *The Negro's Civil War: How American Blacks Felt and Acted During the Civil War*, 241.

21　*Ibid.*, 160.

22　Wilson, *The Black Phalanx African American Soldiers in the War of Independence, the War of 1812 and the Civil War*, 84.

23　Barrow, *Black Confederates*, 3.

24　George Washington Adams, *Doctors in Blue. The Medical History of the Union Army in the Civil War.* (New York: Henry Schulman, 1952), 213.

25　Lardas, *African American Soldier in the Civil War USCT 1862-1866*, 4.

26　Gladstone, *United States Colored Troops 1863-1867*, 9.

27　*Ibid.*, 10-11.

28　*Ibid.*, 39.

29　Rollins, *Black Southerners in Gray: Essays on Afro-Americans in Confederate Armies*, 26.

Chapter 1

1　*Why We Fight* was a seven episode series by film director Frank Capra produced during the Second World War. These war information training films were commissioned by the U. S. Government to explain to soldiers the reasons for the U. S. involvement in the war. The focus of the series is similar to what is presented in this chapter for the Civil War, hence the title of this chapter.

2   Mark Lardas, *African American Soldier in the Civil War USCT 1862-1866.* (Oxford: Osprey Publishing, 2006), 43.

3   Rollins, *Black Southerners in Gray: Essays on Afro-Americans in Confederate Armies*, 49.

4   *Ibid.*, 10.

5   *Ibid.*, 7.

6   *Ibid.*, 65.

7   Barrow, *Black Confederates*, 38.

8   Rollins, *Black Southerners in Gray: Essays on Afro-Americans in Confederate Armies*, 58.

9   Ricardo J. Rodriguez, *Black Confederates in the U. S. Civil War: A Compiled List of African-Americans Who Served the Confederacy.* (Charleston: Create Space, 2010), 2-224.

10   Rollins, *Black Southerners in Gray: Essays on Afro-Americans in Confederate Armies*, 68.

11   *Ibid.*, 78.

12   Hargrove, *Black Union Soldiers in the Civil War*, 5.

13   *Ibid.*, 5.

14   McPherson, *The Negro's Civil War: How American Blacks Felt and Acted During the Civil War*, 245.

15   Barrow, *Black Confederates*, 46.

16   McPherson, *The Negro's Civil War: How American Blacks Felt and Acted During the Civil War*, 245.

17   Hargrove, *Black Union Soldiers in the Civil War*, 6.

18   McPherson, *The Negro's Civil War: How American Blacks Felt and Acted During the Civil War*, 248.

19   Robert Franklin Durden, *The Gray and the Black: The Confederate Debate on Emancipation.* (Baton Rouge: Louisiana State University Press, 1972), 277.

20   Hargrove, *Black Union Soldiers in the Civil War*, 6.

21   McPherson, *The Negro's Civil War: How American Blacks Felt and Acted During the Civil War*, 24.

22   Barrow, *Black Confederates*, 38.

23   McPherson, *The Negro's Civil War: How American Blacks Felt and Acted During the Civil War*, 24.

24   *Ibid.*

25   Barrow, *Black Confederates*, 127.

26   McPherson, *The Negro's Civil War: How American Blacks Felt and Acted During the Civil War*, 55.

27   Barrow, *Black Confederates*, 7.

28   Philip Van Doren Stern, *Secret Missions of the Civil War*. (New York: Wing Books, 1959), 190.

29   Lardas, *African American Soldier in the Civil War USCT 1862-1866*, 42.

30   *Ibid.*, 42.

Chapter 2

1   McPherson, *The Negro's Civil War: How American Blacks Felt and Acted During the Civil War*, 34-35.

2   Melvin Claxton and Mark Puls. *Uncommon Valor A Story of Race, Patriotism, and Glory in the Final Battles of the Civil War*. (Hoboken: John Wiley and Sons, Inc., 2006), 1.

3   Hargrove, *Black Union Soldiers in the Civil War*, 10.

4   *Ibid.*, 10.

5   *Ibid.*, 8.

6   *Ibid.*, 9.

7   Barrow, *Black Confederates*, 10.

8   *Ibid.*, 10.

9   Wilson, *The Black Phalanx African American Soldiers in the War of Independence, the War of 1812 and the Civil War*, 62.

10   Wilson, *The Black Phalanx African American Soldiers in the War of Independence, the War of 1812 and the Civil War*, 60.

11   Rollins, *Black Southerners in Gray: Essays on Afro-Americans in Confederate Armies*, 76.

12   For details of the USSC, see Appendix E.

13   Rollins, *Black Southerners in Gray: Essays on Afro-Americans in Confederate Armies*, 76.

14   Barrow, *Black Confederates*, 111.

15   Rodriguez, *Black Confederates in the U. S. Civil War: A Compiled List of African-Americans Who Served the Confederacy.*

16   Adams, *Doctors in Blue. The Medical History of the Union Army in the Civil War*, 45.

17   Wilson, *The Black Phalanx African American Soldiers in the War of Independence, the War of 1812 and the Civil War*, 59.

18   *Ibid.*, 59.

19 *Ibid.*, 317.

20 Barrow, *Black Confederates*, 62.

21 Wilson, *The Black Phalanx African American Soldiers in the War of Independence, the War of 1812 and the Civil War*, 318.

22 Cornish, *The Sable Arm, Negro Troops in the Union Army, 1861-1865*, 16.

23 Wilson, *The Black Phalanx African American Soldiers in the War of Independence, the War of 1812 and the Civil War*, 60.

24 McPherson, *The Negro's Civil War: How American Blacks Felt and Acted During the Civil War*, 38-39.

25 *Ibid.*, 57.

26 Barrow, *Black Confederates*, 15.

27 *Ibid.*, 17.

28 *Ibid.*, 18.

29 *Ibid.*, 25.

30 *Ibid.*, 47-48.

31 *Ibid.*, 48.

32 Wilson, *The Black Phalanx African American Soldiers in the War of Independence, the War of 1812 and the Civil War*, 322.

33 Barrow, *Black Confederates*, 48.

34 *Ibid.*

35 *Ibid.*, 51-54.

36 McPherson, *The Negro's Civil War: How American Blacks Felt and Acted During the Civil War*, 67.

37 *Ibid.*, 163.

38 Cornish, *The Sable Arm, Negro Troops in the Union Army, 1861-1865*, 5.

39 *Ibid.*, 7.

40 *Ibid.*, 10.

41 *Ibid.*, 13.

42 McPherson, *The Negro's Civil War: How American Blacks Felt and Acted During the Civil War*, 41.

43 *Ibid.*

44 Cornish, *The Sable Arm, Negro Troops in the Union Army, 1861-1865*, 110.

45 McPherson, *The Negro's Civil War: How American Blacks Felt and Acted During the Civil War*, 47.

46 Hargrove, *Black Union Soldiers in the Civil War*, 15.

47 Cornish, *The Sable Arm, Negro Troops in the Union Army, 1861-1865,* 17-18.

48 *Ibid.,* 18.

49 *Ibid.,* 5.

50 *Ibid.,* 20.

51 *Ibid.,* 23.

52 McPherson, *The Negro's Civil War: How American Blacks Felt and Acted During the Civil War,* 23.

53 Lardas, *African American Soldier in the Civil War USCT 1862-1866,* 4.

54 *Ibid.,* 5.

55 Wilson, *The Black Phalanx African American Soldiers in the War of Independence, the War of 1812 and the Civil War.* (86.

56 *Ibid.,* 64-65.

57 Cornish, *The Sable Arm, Negro Troops in the Union Army, 1861-1865,* 38.

58 Edward A. Miller, Jr., *Lincoln's Abolitionist General: The Biography of David Hunter.(* Columbia: University of South Carolina Press, 1997), 102.

59 *Ibid.,* 110.

60 *Ibid.*

61 Gladstone, *United States Colored Troops 1863-1867,* 22.

62 Wilson, *The Black Phalanx African American Soldiers in the War of Independence, the War of 1812 and the Civil War,* 94.

63 Miller, Jr., *Lincoln's Abolitionist General: The Biography of David Hunter,* 122.

64 Wilson, *The Black Phalanx African American Soldiers in the War of Independence, the War of 1812 and the Civil War,* 94.

65 McPherson, *The Negro's Civil War: How American Blacks Felt and Acted During the Civil War,* 48.

66 Cornish, *The Sable Arm, Negro Troops in the Union Army, 1861-1865,* 46.

67 *Ibid.,* 51.

68 McPherson, *The Negro's Civil War: How American Blacks Felt and Acted During the Civil War,* 300.

69 Miller, Jr., *Lincoln's Abolitionist General: The Biography of David Hunter,* 111.

70 Wilson, *The Black Phalanx African American Soldiers in the War of Independence, the War of 1812 and the Civil War,* 115.

71 Cornish, *The Sable Arm, Negro Troops in the Union Army, 1861-1865*, 60-61.

72 Ibid., 65.

73 Lardas, *African American Soldier in the Civil War USCT 1862-1866*, 5.

74 *Ibid.*

75 Cornish, *The Sable Arm, Negro Troops in the Union Army, 1861-1865*, 65.

76 McPherson, *The Negro's Civil War: How American Blacks Felt and Acted During the Civil War*, 167.

77 Cornish, *The Sable Arm, Negro Troops in the Union Army, 1861-1865*, 69.

78 *Ibid.*, 73.

79 *Ibid.*, 75.

80 *Ibid.*, 77.

81 *Ibid.*, 80.

82 *Ibid.*, 86.

83 *Ibid.*, 93.

84 Civil War Society, *Civil War Society's Encyclopedia of the Civil War: The Complete and Comprehensive Guide to the American Civil War.* (Princeton: Wing Books, 1997), 405-406.

85 Cornish, *The Sable Arm, Negro Troops in the Union Army, 1861-1865*, 96.

86 McPherson, *The Negro's Civil War: How American Blacks Felt and Acted During the Civil War*, 50.

87 Cornish, *The Sable Arm, Negro Troops in the Union Army, 1861-1865.* 99.

88 McPherson, *The Negro's Civil War: How American Blacks Felt and Acted During the Civil War*, 50.

89 *Ibid.*, 52.

90 Cornish, *The Sable Arm, Negro Troops in the Union Army, 1861-1865*, 101.

91 *Ibid.*, 102.

92 *Ibid.*, 107.

93 *Ibid.*, 105.

94 McPherson, *The Negro's Civil War: How American Blacks Felt and Acted During the Civil War*, 176.

95 *Ibid.*, 176-177.

96 *Ibid.*, 176

[97] *Ibid.*, 181.

[98] *Ibid.*, 185.

[99] Association of Graduates, United States Military Academy. *The Register of Graduates and Former Cadets of the United States Military, 2010.* (West Point: Association of Graduates, 2010), 360.

[100] Cornish, *The Sable Arm, Negro Troops in the Union Army, 1861-1865,* 113.

[101] *Ibid.*

[102] *Ibid.*, 117.

[103] McPherson, *The Negro's Civil War: How American Blacks Felt and Acted During the Civil War,*173.

[104] Cornish, *The Sable Arm, Negro Troops in the Union Army, 1861-1865,* 118.

[105] *Ibid.*

[106] *Ibid.*, 114.

[107] McPherson, *The Negro's Civil War: How American Blacks Felt and Acted During the Civil War,* 130.

[108] *Ibid.*, 130-131.

[109] *Ibid.*, 132.

[110] Wilson, *The Black Phalanx African American Soldiers in the War of Independence, the War of 1812 and the Civil War,* 68.

[111] Cornish, *The Sable Arm, Negro Troops in the Union Army, 1861-1865,* 128.

[112] McPherson, *The Negro's Civil War: How American Blacks Felt and Acted During the Civil War,* 171.

[113] Cornish, *The Sable Arm, Negro Troops in the Union Army, 1861-1865,* 129.

[114] McPherson, *The Negro's Civil War: How American Blacks Felt and Acted During the Civil War,* 173.

[115] Cornish, *The Sable Arm, Negro Troops in the Union Army, 1861-1865,* 130.

[116] *Ibid.*, 138.

[117] *Ibid.*, 139.

[118] *Ibid.*, 140.

[119] Lardas, *African American Soldier in the Civil War USCT 1862-1866,* 6.

[120] *Ibid.*

[121] *Ibid.*, 9.

122 Some historians indentify the border slave states to include West Virginia and delete Delaware.

123 Lardas, *African American Soldier in the Civil War USCT 1862-1866*, 12.

124 *Ibid.*, 11.

125 *Ibid.*, 6.

126 *Ibid.*, 7.

127 Cornish, *The Sable Arm, Negro Troops in the Union Army, 1861-1865*, 251.

128 *Ibid.*, 288.

Chapter 3

1 Hunt, *Observations of T. J. Hunt in the Civil War: A Narrative of the Military Life of T. J. Hunt in the Sioux Indian and Civil Wars of 1862-1865*, 19.

2 *Ibid.*

3 Adams, *Doctors in Blue. The Medical History of the Union Army in the Civil War*, 215.

4 Eggleston, *10th Minnesota Volunteers, A History of the Action in the Sioux Uprising and the Civil War with a Regmental Roster.*

5 Adams, *Doctors in Blue. The Medical History of the Union Army in the Civil War*, 16.

6 *Ibid.*, 224-225.

7 Eggleston, *10th Minnesota Volunteers, A History of the Action in the Sioux Uprising and the Civil War with a Regmental Roster.*

8 Lardas, *African American Soldier in the Civil War USCT 1862-1866*, 25.

9 *Ibid.*

10 *Ibid.*, 14.

11 *Ibid.*, 15.

12 Cornish, *The Sable Arm, Negro Troops in the Union Army, 1861-1865*, 218.

13 Lardas, *African American Soldier in the Civil War USCT 1862-1866*, 15.

14 Cornish, *The Sable Arm, Negro Troops in the Union Army, 1861-1865*, 207.

15 *Ibid.*, 214.

16 *Ibid.*, 217.

17 Lardas, *African American Soldier in the Civil War USCT 1862-1866*, 15.

18 Cornish, *The Sable Arm, Negro Troops in the Union Army, 1861-1865*, 203.

19　Lardas, *African American Soldier in the Civil War USCT 1862-1866*, 15.

20　*Ibid.*, 17.

21　McPherson, *The Negro's Civil War: How American Blacks Felt and Acted During the Civil War*, 134.

22　Cornish, *The Sable Arm, Negro Troops in the Union Army, 1861-1865*, 240-1.

23　McPherson, *The Negro's Civil War: How American Blacks Felt and Acted During the Civil War*, 215.

24　*Ibid.*, 216.

Chapter 4

1　*Ibid.*, 101.

2　*Ibid.*

3　*Ibid.*, 166.

4　Cornish, *The Sable Arm, Negro Troops in the Union Army, 1861-1865*, 173.

5　McPherson, *The Negro's Civil War: How American Blacks Felt and Acted During the Civil War*, 165-166.

6　Margaret Humphreys, *Intensely Human: The Health of the Black Soldiers in the American Civil War.* (Baltimore: Johns Hopkins University Press, 2008), 18.

7　*Ibid.*, 15.

8　*Ibid.*, 19.

9　Barrow, *Black Confederates*, 45.

10　*Ibid.*

11　Wilson, *The Black Phalanx African American Soldiers in the War of Independence, the War of 1812 and the Civil War*, 183.

12　Cornish, *The Sable Arm, Negro Troops in the Union Army, 1861-1865*, 229-230.

13　Rollins, *Black Southerners in Gray: Essays on Afro-Americans in Confederate Armies*, 62.

14　McPherson, *The Negro's Civil War: How American Blacks Felt and Acted During the Civil War*, 176.

15　Wilson, *The Black Phalanx African American Soldiers in the War of Independence, the War of 1812 and the Civil War*, 139-140.

16　Cornish, *The Sable Arm, Negro Troops in the Union Army, 1861-1865*, 159-160.

17 *Ibid.*, 160.

18 Wilson, *The Black Phalanx African American Soldiers in the War of Independence, the War of 1812 and the Civil War,* 95.

19 Cornish, *The Sable Arm, Negro Troops in the Union Army, 1861-1865,* 161.

20 *Ibid.*, 158.

21 *Ibid.*, 166-7.

22 *Ibid.*, 168.

23 Lardas, *African American Soldier in the Civil War USCT 1862-1866,* 44.

24 Cornish, *The Sable Arm, Negro Troops in the Union Army, 1861-1865,* 172.

25 *Ibid.*

Chapter 5

1 Barrow, *Black Confederates,* 49.

2 Rollins, *Black Southerners in Gray: Essays on Afro-Americans in Confederate Armies,* 9.

3 Barrow, *Black Confederates,* 70.

4 Rollins, *Black Southerners in Gray: Essays on Afro-Americans in Confederate Armies,* 15.

5 Daily (Columbus Georgia) Sun, 26 November 1861.

6 Barrow, *Black Confederates.* (Gretna: Pelican Publishing Company, 1995), 39.

7 Rollins, *Black Southerners in Gray: Essays on Afro-Americans in Confederate Armies.* (Murfreesboro: Southern Heritage Press, 1994), 10.

8 *Ibid.*, 120.

9 Hargrove, *Black Union Soldiers in the Civil War,* 4.

10 *Ibid.*

11 *Ibid.*

12 *Ibid.*

13 *Ibid.*

14 Rollins, *Black Southerners in Gray: Essays on Afro-Americans in Confederate Armies,* 61-62.

15 *Ibid.*, 63-64.

16 Rodriguez, *Black Confederates in the U. S. Civil War: A Compiled List of African-Americans Who Served the Confederacy,* 2-224.

17   McPherson, *The Negro's Civil War: How American Blacks Felt and Acted During the Civil War,* 149.

18   *Ibid.,* 45.

19   *Ibid.,* 147.

20   *Ibid.,* 149.

21   *Ibid.,* 198.

22   Lardas, *African American Soldier in the Civil War USCT 1862-1866,* 27.

23   Cornish, *The Sable Arm, Negro Troops in the Union Army, 1861-1865,* 240.

24   *Ibid.,* 246.

25   *Ibid.,* 241.

26   Lardas, *African American Soldier in the Civil War USCT 1862-1866,* 28.

27   *Ibid.,* 29.

28   The Lieber Code, General Order Number 100 allows ". . . summary execution of . . . guerilla forces if caught in the act of carrying out their missions."

29   Wilson, *The Black Phalanx African American Soldiers in the War of Independence, the War of 1812 and the Civil War,* 73.

30   Lardas, *African American Soldier in the Civil War USCT 1862-1866,* 30-31.

31   McPherson, *The Negro's Civil War: How American Blacks Felt and Acted During the Civil War,* 200.

32   Cornish, *The Sable Arm, Negro Troops in the Union Army, 1861-1865,* 187.

33   Gladstone, *United States Colored Troops 1863-1867,* 170.

34   Cornish, *The Sable Arm, Negro Troops in the Union Army, 1861-1865,* 188.

35   Wilson, *The Black Phalanx African American Soldiers in the War of Independence, the War of 1812 and the Civil War,* 78.

36   Gladstone, *United States Colored Troops 1863-1867,* 247.

37   *Ibid.*

38   McPherson, *The Negro's Civil War: How American Blacks Felt and Acted During the Civil War,* 204.

39   Cornish, *The Sable Arm, Negro Troops in the Union Army, 1861-1865,* 184.

40   Wilson, *The Black Phalanx African American Soldiers in the War of Independence, the War of 1812 and the Civil War,* 84.

Chapter 6

1   Sung to the tune of the *Yellow Rose of Texas.*

2   The name is disputed. Some say it is based upon a remark by Jefferson Davis that Hood had a lion's heart and a head of wood. Hood's troops called him "Old Pegleg" because he rode with a cork leg replacing the one that had been amputated.

3   Richard M. McMurry, *John Bell Hood and the War for Southern Independence.* (Lincoln: University of Nebraska Press, 1982), 167.

4   Hargrove, *Black Union Soldiers in the Civil War*, 177.

5   U. S. War Department. *The War of Rebellion: A Compilation of the Official Records of the Union and Confederate Armies.* (Washington D.C., 1880-1901), 38/3: 622-624

6   Steven E. Woodworth, *Decision in the Heartland The Civil War in the West.* (Westport: Praeger Publishers, 2008), 292.

7   Donald Stoker, *The Grand Design Strategy and the U. S. Civil War.* (New York: Oxford University Press, 2010), 378-383.

8   McMurry, *John Bell Hood and the War for Southern Independence*, 162-166.

9   John Allan Wyeth, *That Devil Forrest, The Life of General Nathan Bedford Forrest.* (Baton Rouge: Louisiana State University, 1989), 473.

10 McMurry, *John Bell Hood and the War for Southern Independence*, 177.

11 Logsdon, *Eyewitnesses at the Battle of Nashville*, 27.

12 Association of Graduates, United States Military Academy. *The Register of Graduates and Former Cadets of the United States Military, 2010*, 1053.

13 *Ibid.*, 1052.

14 James Lee McDonough, *Nashville. The Confederacy's Last Gamble.* (Knoxville: The University of Tennessee Press, 2004), 16.

15 *Ibid.*, 158.

16 *Ibid.*, 159.

17 *Ibid.*, 160.

18 *Ibid.*, 159.

19 *Ibid.*

20 Horn, *The Decisive Battle of Nashville.* (Knoxville, University of Tennessee Press, 1978), 172.

21 Hargrove, *Black Union Soldiers in the Civil War*, 193.

22 McDonough, *Nashville. The Confederacy's Last Gamble*, 163.

23 Logsdon, *Eyewitnesses at the Battle of Nashville*, viii.

24 Wyeth, *That Devil Forrest, The Life of General Nathan Bedford Forrest,* 482.

25 *Ibid.*

26 McMurry, *John Bell Hood and the War for Southern Independence,* 175.

27 Logsdon, *Eyewitnesses at the Battle of Nashville,* v.

28 It was Cleburne who had urged Jefferson Davis and Robert E. Lee to enlist Blacks in the Confederate army in return for their freedom. It would be only weeks before the collapse of the Confederacy that Cleburne's advice was heeded. By then, it was too late and Cleburne was dead.

29 Logsdon, *Eyewitnesses at the Battle of Nashville,* viii.

30 Ervin L. Jordan, Jr., *Black Confederates and Afro-Yankees in Civil War Virginia.* (Charlottesville: University Press of Virginia, 1995), 627-628.

31 McMurry, *John Bell Hood and the War for Southern Independence,* 176.

32 Logsdon, *Eyewitnesses at the Battle of Nashville,* v.

33 Horn, *The Decisive Battle of Nashville,* 167-174.

34 Logsdon, *Eyewitnesses at the Battle of Nashville,* 10.

35 *Ibid.,* 11.

36 Horn, *The Decisive Battle of Nashville,* 22-23.

37 Logsdon, *Eyewitnesses at the Battle of Nashville,* 2.

38 *Ibid.*

39 *Ibid.,* 4.

40 *Ibid.,* 5.

41 *Ibid.,* 17.

42 Jack Hurst, *Nathan Bedford Forrest, A Biography.* (New York: Vintage Books, 1994), 238.

43 *Ibid.,* 9.

44 *Ibid.,* 28.

45 *Ibid.,* 8.

46 *Ibid.,* 10.

47 *Ibid.,* 17.

48 *Ibid.,* 19.

49 *Ibid.,* 11.

50 *Ibid.,* 20.

51 *Ibid.,* 21.

52 *Ibid.*

53 *Ibid.*

54 *Ibid.,* 24.

55 Horn, *The Decisive Battle of Nashville,* 96.

56　Lincoln had actually test fired the Spencer early in the war and endorsed its use.

57　Benson Bobrick, *The Battle of Nashville.* (New York: Alfred A. Knopf, 2010), 95.

58　Logsdon, *Eyewitnesses at the Battle of Nashville,* 40.

59　*Ibid.*

60　*Ibid.,* 41.

61　Hunt, *Observations of T. J. Hunt in the Civil War: A Narrative of the Military Life of T. J. Hunt in the Sioux Indian and Civil Wars of 1862-1865,* 20.

62　Cornish, *The Sable Arm, Negro Troops in the Union Army, 1861-1865,* 284.

63　McDonough, *Nashville. The Confederacy's Last Gamble,* 164.

64　Logsdon, *Eyewitnesses at the Battle of Nashville,* 46.

65　McDonough, *Nashville. The Confederacy's Last Gamble,* 166.

66　*Ibid.,* 167.

67　U. S. War Department, *The War of Rebellion: A Compilation of the Official Records of the Union and Confederate Armies, Vol. XLV, Pt. 1.,* 132-133.

68　McDonough, *Nashville. The Confederacy's Last Gamble,* 167.

69　Logsdon, *Eyewitnesses at the Battle of Nashville,* 38.

70　Horn, *The Decisive Battle of Nashville,* 95-6.

71　*Ibid.,* 97.

72　U. S. War Department, *The War of Rebellion: A Compilation of the Official Records of the Union and Confederate Armies,* Vol. XLV, Pt. II, 194-5, 210.

73　*Ibid.,* 194-195.

74　*Ibid.,* 210.

75　Logsdon, *Eyewitnesses at the Battle of Nashville.* (Nashville: Kettle Mill Press, 2004), 47.

76　*Ibid.,* 48.

77　*Ibid.,* 57.

78　*Ibid.,* 63.

79　*Ibid.,* 64.

80　*Ibid.,* 67.

81　*Ibid.,* 65.

82　Bobrick, *The Battle of Nashville,* 99.

83　Logsdon, *Eyewitnesses at the Battle of Nashville,* 70.

84　*Ibid.,* 76.

85　*Ibid.*

[86]   Horn, *The Decisive Battle of Nashville*, 136-138.

[87]   *Ibid.*, 126.

[88]   *Ibid.*, 128-129.

[89]   Logsdon, *Eyewitnesses at the Battle of Nashville*, 87.

[90]   Hargrove, *Black Union Soldiers in the Civil War*, 193.

[91]   Logsdon, *Eyewitnesses at the Battle of Nashville*, 95.

[92]   *Ibid.*, 103.

[93]   Cornish, *The Sable Arm, Negro Troops in the Union Army, 1861-1865*, 284.

[94]   Bobrick, *The Battle of Nashville*, 100-101.

[95]   Horn, *The Decisive Battle of Nashville*, 163.

[96]   Logsdon, *Eyewitnesses at the Battle of Nashville*, 108

[97]   *Ibid.*, 110.

[98]   Horn, *The Decisive Battle of Nashville*, 163.

Epilogue

[1]   Ezra J. Warner, *Generals in Blue Lives of the Union Commanders*. (Baton Rouge: Louisiana State University Press, 1964), 17-18.

[2]   *Ibid.*, 60-61.

[3]   Association of Graduates, United States Military Academy. *The Register of Graduates and Former Cadets of the United States Military, 2010*, 540.

[4]   Warner, *Generals in Blue Lives of the Union Commanders*, 160-161.

[5]   *Ibid.*, 183-186.

[6]   Association of Graduates, United States Military Academy. *The Register of Graduates and Former Cadets of the United States Military, 2010*, 1630.

[7]   *Collections of the Minnesota Historical Society, Volume XIV, Minnesota Biographies, 1655-1912*, 356.

[8]   Warner, *Generals in Blue Lives of the Union Commanders*, 243-244.

[9]   Association of Graduates, United States Military Academy. *The Register of Graduates and Former Cadets of the United States Military, 2010*, 541.

[10]   Warner, *Generals in Blue Lives of the Union Commanders*, 288-289.

[11]   *Ibid.*, 368-369.

[12]   *Ibid.*, 420-421.

[13]   *Ibid.*, 425-426.

[14]   Hargrove, *Black Union Soldiers in the Civil War*, 17.

[15]   *Ibid.*, 441-444.

[16]   Ibid., 473-474.

[17]   Association of Graduates, United States Military Academy. *The Register of Graduates and Former Cadets of the United States Military, 2010*, 360.

[18]   United States Military Academy. *Sixth Annual Reunion of the Association of Graduates of the United States Military Academy at West Point, New York June 17, 1875*. (New York: A. S. Barnes & Company, 1875), 74-77.

[19]   Warner, *Generals in Blue Lives of the Union Commanders*, 517-518.

[20]   Association of Graduates, United States Military Academy. *The Register of Graduates and Former Cadets of the United States Military, 2010*, 1825.

Appendix A

[1]   National Park Service, *Civil War Soldiers & Sailors System*. http://www.civilwar.nps.gov/cwss/

[2]   Horn, *The Decisive Battle of Nashville*, 172.

[3]   Frederick H. Dyer, *A Compendium of the War of the Rebellion, Vol.1-3*. (New York: Thomas Yoseloff, 1959).

Appendix B

[1]   Inscribed on the Iwo Jima Memorial in Washington, D. C.

[2]   McPherson, *The Negro's Civil War: How American Blacks Felt and Acted During the Civil War*, 157-161.

[3]   *Harpers Weekly*. 14 June 1862, 372.

[4]   The government asked that the medals be returned; however, this occurred fifty years after the Civil War. Most veterans were dead by then and those still alive were not interested in returning the medals even if they understood the request.

[5]   U. S. Army. http://www.history.army.mil/moh.html

[6]   The issue started with claims that African Americans in World War II were denied the MOH due to racism. The result was that some of their awards were upgraded to the MOH after Pentagon review. Jackson's file was included in the review although many years after the Civil War: a long journey and an amazing story.

[7]   Hargrove, *Black Union Soldiers in the Civil War*, Appendix H.

Appendix C

1   Cornish, *The Sable Arm, Negro Troops in the Union Army, 1861-1865*, 142.

2   *Ibid.*, 143.

3   *Ibid.*, 145-146.

4   McPherson, *The Negro's Civil War: How American Blacks Felt and Acted During the Civil War*, 190.

5   *Ibid.*, 190-191.

6   Wilson, *The Black Phalanx African American Soldiers in the War of Independence, the War of 1812 and the Civil War.* 126.

7   E. B. Long, *The Civil War Day by Day, An Almanac 1861-1865.* (New York: Doubleday & Company, Inc., 1971), 387.

8   Cornish, *The Sable Arm, Negro Troops in the Union Army, 1861-1865*, 153-156.

9   Long, *The Civil War Day by Day, An Almanac 1861-1865*, 466.

10 Cornish, *The Sable Arm, Negro Troops in the Union Army, 1861-1865*, 173.

11 Lardas, *African American Soldier in the Civil War USCT 1862-1866*, 53.

12 *Ibid.*, 6.

13 *Ibid.*

14 Wilson, *The Black Phalanx African American Soldiers in the War of Independence, the War of 1812 and the Civil War,* 259.

15 Cornish, *The Sable Arm, Negro Troops in the Union Army, 1861-1865*, 274.

16 Ibid., 275.

17 Wilson, *The Black Phalanx African American Soldiers in the War of Independence, the War of 1812 and the Civil War,* 264.

18 McPherson, *The Negro's Civil War: How American Blacks Felt and Acted During the Civil War*, 229-231.

19 Claxton, *Uncommon Valor A Story of Race, Patriotism, and Glory in the Final Battles of the Civil War*, 2.

20 Long, *The Civil War Day by Day, An Almanac 1861-1865*, 670.

21 Robert E. Lee. *HQ Northern Virginia, General Order No. 9*, 10 April 1865, 1.

22 There would be other skirmishes, such as Palmetto Ranch in Texas and the surrender of other Confederate forces such as Kirby Smith's, but the war was over, at last. It had been a long journey to get there.

23   Stroker, *The Grand Design Strategy and the U. S. Civil War*, 389.

24   *Ibid.*, 398.

25   Hunt, *Observations of T. J. Hunt in the Civil War: A Narrative of the Military Life of T. J. Hunt in the Sioux Indian and Civil Wars of 1862-1865*, 11-13.

26   *Ibid.*

27   *Ibid.*

28   Long, *The Civil War Day by Day, An Almanac 1861-1865*, 688.

Appendix D

1   Adams, Doctors in Blue, *The Medical History of the Union Army in the Civil War*, 16.

2   Civil War Society, *Civil War Society's Encyclopedia of the Civil War: The Complete and Comprehensive Guide to the American Civil War*, 235.

3   *Ibid.*

4   *Ibid.*, 236.

5   Adams, *Doctors in Blue. The Medical History of the Union Army in the Civil War*, 5.

6   Cunningham, *Doctors in Gray. The Confederate Medical Service*, 3.

7   *Ibid.*

8   *Ibid.*, 5.

9   *Ibid.*

10   *Ibid.*

11   *Ibid.*, 7.

12   *Ibid,*. 11.

13   *Ibid.*

14   Cunningham, *Doctors in Gray. The Confederate Medical Service*, 225.

15   James M. Schmidt and Guy R. Hasegawa, *Years of Change and Suffering: Modern Perspectives on Civil War Medicine.* (St. Paul: Edinborough Press, 2009), 64-65.

16   *Ibid.*, 58.

17   Miller, *Lincoln's Abolitionist General: The Biography of David Hunter*, 235.

18   Cunningham, *Doctors in Gray. The Confederate Medical Service*, 220.

19   Adams, *Doctors in Blue. The Medical History of the Union Army in the Civil War*, 5.

20   Cunningham, *Doctors in Gray. The Confederate Medical Service*, 219.

21   *Ibid.*

22   *Ibid.*

23   Schmidt, *Years of Change and Suffering: Modern Perspectives on Civil War Medicine,* 58.

24   *Ibid.,* 90

25   Adams, *Doctors in Blue. The Medical History of the Union Army in the Civil War,* 113.

26   *Ibid.,* 115.

27   Cunningham, *Doctors in Gray. The Confederate Medical Service,* 218.

28   Civil War Society, *Civil War Society's Encyclopedia of the Civil War: The Complete and Comprehensive Guide to the American Civil War,* 235.

29   Lardas, *African American Soldier in the Civil War USCT 1862-1866,* 13.

30   *Ibid.*

31   Humphreys, *Intensely Human: The Health of the Black Soldiers in the American Civil War,* 7.

32   *Ibid.*

33   *Ibid.,* 12.

34   *Ibid.,* 9.

35   *Ibid.*

36   *Ibid.,* 43.

37   *Ibid.,* 44.

38   Adams, *Doctors in Blue, The Medical History of the Union Army in the Civil War,* 43.

39   *Ibid.,* 45.

40   Cunningham, *Doctors in Gray, The Confederate Medical Service,* 163.

41   *Ibid.,* 164.

42   Adams, *Doctors in Blue, The Medical History of the Union Army in the Civil War,* 206.

43   *Ibid.,* 207.

44   *Ibid.,* 208.

45   *Ibid.*

46   *Ibid.,* 211.

47   *Ibid.,* 213.

48   *Ibid.*

49   *Ibid.*

50   *Ibid.,* 176.

51   Cunningham, *Doctors in Gray. The Confederate Medical Service,* 178.

52   *Ibid.,* 179.

53   *Ibid.*

54   *Ibid.*, 180.

55   *Ibid.*, 21.

56   *Ibid.*, 22.

57   *Ibid.*

58   *Ibid.*, 27.

59   *Ibid.*, 28.

60   *Ibid.*, 26-27.

61   *Ibid.*, 21.

62   *Ibid.*, 107.

63   Adams, *Doctors in Blue. The Medical History of the Union Army in the Civil War*, 27.

64   *Ibid.*, 194.

65   *Ibid.*, 32.

66   *Ibid.*

67   *Ibid.*

68   *Ibid.*, 33.

69   *Ibid.*, 40.

70   Schmidt, *Years of Change and Suffering: Modern Perspectives on Civil War Medicine,* 69.

71   *Ibid.*, 70.

72   *Ibid.*

73   *Ibid.*, 72.

74   *Ibid.*, 78.

75   Adams, *Doctors in Blue. The Medical History of the Union Army in the Civil War*, 46.

76   Humphreys, *Intensely Human: The Health of the Black Soldiers in the American Civil War,* 63.

77   Gladstone, *United States Colored Troops 1863-1867,* 24.

78   Schmidt, *Years of Change and Suffering: Modern Perspectives on Civil War Medicine,* ix.

79   *Ibid.*, 25.

80   Cunningham, *Doctors in Gray. The Confederate Medical Service,* 37.

81   Adams, *Doctors in Blue. The Medical History of the Union Army in the Civil War*, 10.

82   Cunningham, *Doctors in Gray. The Confederate Medical Service,* 29.

83   *Ibid.*

84   *Ibid.*, 33.

85   *Ibid.*, 34.

86   Civil War Society, *Civil War Society's Encyclopedia of the Civil War: The Complete and Comprehensive Guide to the American Civil War,* 307-308.

87   Adams, *Doctors in Blue. The Medical History of the Union Army in the Civil War.* (New York: Henry Schulman, 1952), 5.

88   Newberry, *What The U.S. Sanitary Commission is Doing in the Valley of the Mississippi,* 2.

89   *Ibid.*, 4.

90   *Ibid.*, 4-5.

91   *Ibid.*, 11.

92   *Ibid.*, 13.

93   Adams, *Doctors in Blue. The Medical History of the Union Army in the Civil War,* 6-7.

94   *Ibid.*, 7.

95   *Ibid.*, 8.

96   *Ibid.*, 14.

97   *Ibid.*, 16.

98   *Ibid,* 20.

99   *Ibid.*

100 *Ibid.*, 21.

101 Cornish, *The Sable Arm, Negro Troops in the Union Army, 1861-1865,* 16.

102 *Ibid.*, 20.

103 Adams, *Doctors in Blue. The Medical History of the Union Army in the Civil War,* 21.

104 *Ibid.*, 22.

105 Cornish, *The Sable Arm, Negro Troops in the Union Army, 1861-1865,* 38.

106 Cunningham, *Doctors in Gray. The Confederate Medical Service,* 141.

107 *Ibid.*, 109.

108 *Ibid.*

109 *Ibid.*

110 *Ibid.*, 110.

111 *Ibid.*

112 *Ibid.*, 180.

113 *Ibid.*, 181.

114 Mary Gardner Holland, *Our Army Nurses, Stories from Women in the Civil War.* (St. Paul: Edinborough Press, 1998), iii.

115 *Ibid.*

116 *Ibid.*, v.

117 *Ibid.*, ii.

118 *Ibid,* v.

119 *Ibid.*, iv.

120 *Ibid.*

121 *Ibid.*

122 Adams, *Doctors in Blue. The Medical History of the Union Army in the Civil War,* 176.

123 *Ibid.*, 180.

124 *Ibid.*, 69.

125 Holland, *Our Army Nurses, Stories from Women in the Civil War,* iii.

126 *Ibid.*

127 *Ibid.*, 72.

128 *Ibid.*

129 *Ibid.*

130 Cunningham, *Doctors in Gray. The Confederate Medical Service,* 76-77.

131 *Ibid.*, 77.

132 Schmidt, *Years of Change and Suffering: Modern Perspectives on Civil War Medicine,* ix.

133 *Ibid.*, 39.

134 *Ibid.*, 40.

135 *Ibid.*

136 *Ibid.*, 41.

137 *Ibid.*, 42.

138 *Ibid.*

139 Cunningham, *Doctors in Gray. The Confederate Medical Service,* 13.

140 Adams, *Doctors in Blue. The Medical History of the Union Army in the Civil War,* 25.

141 *Ibid.*

142 *Ibid.*

143 *Ibid.*

144 *Ibid.*, 60.

145 *Ibid.*, 61.

146 *Ibid.*, 63.

147 *Ibid.*

148 *Ibid.*

149 *Ibid.*, 75.

150 *Ibid.,* 76.

151 *Ibid.,* 77.

152 *Ibid.,* 90.

153 *Ibid.,* 91.

154 *Ibid.*

155 *Ibid.,* 96.

156 *Ibid.,* 97.

157 Cunningham, *Doctors in Gray. The Confederate Medical Service,* 119.

158 *Ibid.*

159 *Ibid.*

160 *Ibid.,* 121.

161 *Ibid.,* 129.

162 *Ibid,* 114.

163 *Ibid.,* 115.

164 *Ibid.*

165 Humphreys, *Intensely Human: The Health of the Black Soldiers in the American Civil War,* 74.

166 *Ibid*

167 *Ibid.,* 76.

168 Adams, *Doctors in Blue. The Medical History of the Union Army in the Civil War,* 125.

169 *Ibid.,* 128.

170 Humphreys, *Intensely Human: The Health of the Black Soldiers in the American Civil War,* 82.

171 *Ibid.*

172 *Ibid.*

173 *Ibid.,* 86.

174 *Ibid.,* 89.

175 *Ibid,* 90.

176 *Ibid.*

177 Eggleston, *10th Minnesota Volunteers, A History of the Action in the Sioux Uprising and the Civil War with a Regmental Roster.*

178 Cunningham, *Doctors in Gray. The Confederate Medical Service,* 106.

179 *Ibid.,* 31-32.

180 *Ibid.,* 87.

181 *Ibid.,* 88.

182 *Ibid.,* 91.

183 H. H. Cunningham, *Doctors in Gray. The Confederate Medical Service.* (Baton Rouge: The Louisiana State University Press, 1958), 91.

184 *Ibid.*

185 Sally Jenkins and John Stauffer, *The State of Jones, The Small Southern County that Seceded from the Confederacy.* (New York: Anchor Books, 2010).

186 Cunningham, *Doctors in Gray. The Confederate Medical Service,* 45.

187 *Ibid.*

188 *Ibid.,* 46.

189 *Ibid.,* 50.

190 *Ibid.,* 72.

191 *Ibid.*

192 *Ibid.*

193 *Ibid.,* 73.

194 *Ibid.,* 38.

195 *Ibid.,* 40.

196 *Ibid.*

197 Adams, *Doctors in Blue. The Medical History of the Union Army in the Civil War,* 108.

198 *Ibid.*

199 *Ibid.,* 214.

200 Cunningham, *Doctors in Gray. The Confederate Medical Service,* 80-81.

201 *Ibid.,* 83.

202 *Ibid.,* 85.

203 *Ibid.*

204 Schmidt, *Years of Change and Suffering: Modern Perspectives on Civil War Medicine,* 197.

205 Cunningham, *Doctors in Gray. The Confederate Medical Service,* 135.

206 Schmidt, *Years of Change and Suffering: Modern Perspectives on Civil War Medicine,* 109.

207 *Ibid.,* 111.

208 *Ibid.*

209 *Ibid.,* 114.

210 *Ibid.,* 115.

211 *Ibid.,* 119.

212 Cunningham, *Doctors in Gray. The Confederate Medical Service,* 111.

213 Humphreys, *Intensely Human: The Health of the Black Soldiers in the American Civil War,* 67.

214 Cunningham, *Doctors in Gray. The Confederate Medical Service.*, 221.

215 Ibid., 220-221.

216 *Ibid.*, 221.

217 *Ibid.*, 222.

218 *Ibid.*, 224.

219 Schmidt, *Years of Change and Suffering: Modern Perspectives on Civil War Medicine,* 134.

220 *Ibid.*, 133.

221 *Ibid.*, 128.

222 *Ibid.*, 129.

223 Cunningham, *Doctors in Gray. The Confederate Medical Service*, 232.

224 *Ibid.*

225 *Ibid.*, 234.

226 *Ibid.*, 237.

227 *Ibid.*, 242.

228 *Ibid.*, 237.

229 Schmidt, *Years of Change and Suffering: Modern Perspectives on Civil War Medicine,* 143.

230 *Ibid.*, 145.

231 Cunningham, *Doctors in Gray. The Confederate Medical Service*, 182.

232 *Ibid.*

233 Civil War Society, *Civil War Society's Encyclopedia of the Civil War: The Complete and Comprehensive Guide to the American Civil War,* 237.

234 Adams, *Doctors in Blue. The Medical History of the Union Army in the Civil War,* 14.

235 Schmidt, *Years of Change and Suffering: Modern Perspectives on Civil War Medicine,* 57.

236 Civil War Society, *Civil War Society's Encyclopedia of the Civil War: The Complete and Comprehensive Guide to the American Civil War,* 238.

237 Cunningham, *Doctors in Gray. The Confederate Medical Service*, 163.

238 *Ibid.*

239 Adams, *Doctors in Blue. The Medical History of the Union Army in the Civil War,* 199.

240 Cunningham, *Doctors in Gray. The Confederate Medical Service*, 185.

241 *Ibid.*, 186.

242 *Ibid.*

243 *Ibid.*, 170.

244 *Ibid.*

[245] Humphreys, *Intensely Human: The Health of the Black Soldiers in the American Civil War,* 46.

[246] *Ibid.,* 11.

[247] *Ibid.,* 48.

[248] *Ibid.*

[249] *Ibid.,* 49.

[250] *Ibid.,* 190.

[251] *Ibid.,* 169.

[252] *Ibid.*

[253] *Ibid.,* 191.

[254] *Ibid.,* 20.

[255] *Ibid.,* 191.

[256] *Ibid.,* 202.

[257] *Ibid.,* 203.

[258] *Ibid.,* 204.

[259] *Ibid.,* 196.

[260] *Ibid.*

[261] *Ibid,* 198.

[262] *Ibid.,* 200.

[263] *Ibid.,* 206.

[264] *Ibid.,* 307.

[265] *Ibid.,* 208.

[266] *Ibid.,* 205.

[267] *Ibid.,* 188.

[268] *Ibid.,* 210.

[269] *Ibid.,* 211.

[270] *Ibid.*

[271] *Ibid.,* 212.

[272] *Ibid.*

[273] *Ibid.*

[274] *Ibid.*

[275] *Ibid,* 259.

[276] *Ibid.,* 210.

[277] *Ibid.,* 211.

[278] *Ibid.*

[279] U.S. Department of War. *General Order Number 105.*

[280] *Ibid.*

281 Eggleston, *10th Minnesota Volunteers, A History of the Action in the Sioux Uprising and the Civil War with a Regmental Roster.*

282 Cunningham, *Doctors in Gray. The Confederate Medical Service*, 42.

283 *Ibid.*, 43.

284 McPherson, *The Negro's Civil War: How American Blacks Felt and Acted During the Civil War*, 174.

285 Barrow, *Black Confederates*, 17.

286 Humphreys, *Intensely Human: The Health of the Black Soldiers in the American Civil War*, 6-7.

287 Wilson, *The Black Phalanx African American Soldiers in the War of Independence, the War of 1812 and the Civil War*, 80.

288 Humphreys, *Intensely Human: The Health of the Black Soldiers in the American Civil War*, 11.

289 *Ibid.*

290 *Ibid.*, 12.

291 *Ibid.*

292 *Ibid*

293 *Ibid.*, 57.

294 *Ibid.*

295 U. S. War Department. *Official Army Register of the Volunteer Force of the United States Army for the Years 1861, 1862, 1863, 1864; Volume 8.*

296 Humphreys, *Intensely Human: The Health of the Black Soldiers in the American Civil War*, 59.

297 *Ibid.*, 60.

298 *Ibid.*, 61.

299 *Ibid.*, 69.

300 *Ibid.*, 71.

301 *Ibid.*, 105.

302 *Ibid.*, 117.

303 *Ibid.*, 108.

304 *Ibid.*, 137.

305 *Ibid.*, 131.

306 *Ibid.*, 126.

307 *Ibid.*, 142.

308 *Ibid.*, 159

INDEX